Russian Politics and
Presidential Power

For Knox Eric Ogden

SAGE was founded in 1965 by Sara Miller McCune to support the dissemination of usable knowledge by publishing innovative and high-quality research and teaching content. Today, we publish over 900 journals, including those of more than 400 learned societies, more than 800 new books per year, and a growing range of library products including archives, data, case studies, reports, and video. SAGE remains majority-owned by our founder, and after Sara's lifetime will become owned by a charitable trust that secures our continued independence.

Los Angeles | London | New Delhi | Singapore | Washington DC | Melbourne

Russian Politics and Presidential Power

Transformational Leadership from Gorbachev to Putin

Donald R. Kelley

FOR INFORMATION:

CQ Press

An Imprint of SAGE Publications, Inc.

2455 Teller Road

Thousand Oaks, California 91320

E-mail: order@sagepub.com

SAGE Publications Ltd.

1 Oliver's Yard

55 City Road

London, EC1Y 1SP

United Kingdom

SAGE Publications India Pvt. Ltd.

B 1/I 1 Mohan Cooperative Industrial Area

Mathura Road, New Delhi 110 044

India

SAGE Publications Asia-Pacific Pte. Ltd.

3 Church Street

#10-04 Samsung Hub

Singapore 049483

Library of Congress Cataloging-in-Publication Data

Names: Kelley, Donald R., 1943- author.

Title: Russian politics and presidential power / Donald Kelley, University of Arkansas.

Description: First edition. | Los Angeles : CQ Press, 2016. | Includes bibliographical references and index.

Identifiers: LCCN 2016015135 | ISBN 9780872894044 (pbk. : alk. paper)

Subjects: LCSH: Executive power—Russia (Federation) | Executive power—Soviet Union. | Presidents— Russia (Federation) | Presidents—Soviet Union. | Russia (Federation)—Politics and government—1991- | Soviet Union—Politics and government—1985-1991.

Classification: LCC JN6696 .K45 2016 | DDC 947.086—dc23

LC record available at https://lccn.loc.gov/2016015135

This book is printed on acid-free paper.

Acquisitions Editor: Carrie Brandon

Editorial Assistant: Duncan Marchbank

Production Editor: Bennie Clark Allen

Copy Editor: Amy Marks

Typesetter: C&M Digitals (P) Ltd.

Proofreader: Wendy Jo Dymond

Indexer: Jean Casalegno

Cover Designer: Gail Buschman

Marketing Manager: Amy Whitaker

16 17 18 19 20 10 9 8 7 6 5 4 3 2 1

Contents

Preface

When Mikhail Gorbachev became general secretary of the Communist Party, all of us who studied the Soviet Union knew that change was coming. The Brezhnev + 2 era was over; it had lasted for twenty-one years, and it had its good points and bad. But now change would come, because that's what new leaders do. But our conventional wisdom told us that it would be gradual and probably not fundamentally change the course of the nation. We were wrong. Change came, slowly at first and then with increasing speed. Reforms become revolutions, and eventually revolutions play out and somebody picks up the pieces.

Trying to understand that trajectory in the broader context of Russian history is the point of this book. Revolutions and reconstructions do not occur in isolation. Both play out in the context of a nation's history. You cannot escape that past; it shapes revolutions and the new order that emerges. But you also cannot escape your notion of the future, especially if much of your history has been about willing a new and better future into existence.

That's where authoritarian modernizers come in. They are transformational leaders who set out to build that future, always rejecting at least some portion of the past and sometimes reinterpreting the works of past modernizers whose ideas had misdirected the nation. The premise of this book is that this perspective is helpful in understanding both the disintegration of the Soviet Union and the nature and modus operandi of the Russian Federation that rose in its place. It doesn't explain everything, of course; culture, formal institutions, and the serendipitous interplay of a hundred other variables of time and place and circumstance all play a role. But it is a place to begin, one that provides a link between the past and the future and that helps in understanding the present.

There is remarkably little theoretical literature about the phenomenon of authoritarian modernizers in the conventional literature in history, political science, economics, and psychology. Modernization theory—itself an internally conflicted body of thought about the causes and consequences of the phenomenon—also offers little specific discussion of authoritarian modernizers per se other than to note that they rarely, if at all, foster the emergence of open and liberal democracies. Much of what is valuable comes not from the scant body of theory but rather from the historical studies of modernization in Turkey, Iran, Japan, Germany, Russia, China, and the newly independent nations emerging from colonial rule after World War II, some of which are cited in Chapter 1. Much of the conceptual model set forth in the first chapter is my own synthesis, cobbled together out of the theoretical literature and the more comprehensive country-specific studies. It is not offered as an implicit value judgment. Authoritarian modernizers are not inherently either good or bad, at least in the conventional sense in which we judge those who lead us. Nor are they inherently right or wrong, although the notions of modernity they pursue may be out of touch with reality. The concept is offered as what Max Weber would have called an "ideal type," a paradigm meant to inspire and direct our thought rather than as a final and definitive statement of what constitutes an authoritarian modernizer in all cases and for all time. Some will fit the paradigm better than others; some will succeed in the role, and others will fail; and some will be lauded as the founding fathers of a modern state, while others will be condemned as manipulative authoritarians who cloaked their dictatorial ways with the promise of a better future.

In the Russian case, there is a little bit of all of the above.

Acknowledgments

I wish to thank the reviewers who provided insightful commentary and feedback that helped improve the manuscript, particularly Barbara Chotiner (University of Alabama), Richard Farkas (Depaul University), Gerry Hudson (The Ohio State University), and Irina Vakulenko (The University of Texas at Dallas). Additionally I would like to thank the editorial and production staff at CQ Press for their efforts, including Charisse Kiino, Nancy Loh, Elise Frasier, Sarah Calabi, Matthew Byrnie, Zachary Hoskins, Michael Kerns, Carrie Brandon, Duncan Marchbank, Bennie Clark Allen, and Amy Marks.

SAGE Publishing also wishes to thank the following reviewers for their kind assistance:

Barbara Chotiner, *University of Alabama*
Richard Farkas, *DePaul University*
Gerry Hudson, *The Ohio State University*
Irina Vakulenko, *University of Texas at Dallas*

About the Author

Donald R. Kelley is professor of political science at the University of Arkansas, Fayetteville, where he has taught since 1980.

His publications on Russia include *The Economic Superpowers and the Environment: The United States, the Soviet Union, and Japan,* co-author, 1976; *Soviet Politics in the Brezhnev Era,* editor, 1980; *The Solzhenitsyn–Sakharov Dialogue: Politics, Society, and the Future,* 1982; *The Politics of Developed Socialism,* 1986; *Soviet Politics from Brezhnev to Gorbachev,* editor, 1987; *Old Myths and New Realities in United States–Soviet Relations,* co-editor, 1990; *Perestroika Era Politics: The New Soviet Legislature and Gorbachev's Political Reforms,* co-editor, 1991; *The Sons of Sergei: Khrushchev and Gorbachev as Reformers,* co-editor, 1992; *Politics in Russia and the Successor States,* 1999; and *After Communism: Perspectives on Democracy,* editor, 2003.

Other books include *The Clinton Riddle,* co-editor, 2004; *Divided Power: The Presidency, Congress, and the Formation of American Foreign Policy,* co-editor, 2005; and *Taking the Measure: The Presidency of George W. Bush,* co-editor, 2013.

He is currently writing *Looking Ahead: Alternative Futures for the International System.*

1

Executive Power in Russian Politics

The office of the Russian presidency is a relatively new creation. In constitutional terms, it has existed in its present form only since 1993, when Russia's current constitution was written amid the turmoil of the early Yeltsin years. The office itself has had only three incumbents, Boris Yeltsin, Vladimir Putin, and Dmitry Medvedev. Even during its brief existence, the Russian presidency has undergone considerable evolution marked both by the personalities and strategies of the incumbents and by the broader transformation of the Russian state, within which it is unquestionably the single most important institution. For the foreseeable future, Russian political life will be defined by the continuing transformation of the presidency, and although it seems at times as if Russia's presidents have been making up the rules as they deal with the day-to-day issues confronting them, the broader perspective reveals a remarkable continuity linking Russia's past with its present and likely future.

The most important thing to realize about the Russian presidency is that it cannot be understood without a broader examination of the place of executive authority throughout the history of the nation. The office, and the men who have held it, do not stand outside the sweep of Russian history. They and the system they govern are influenced by its tsarist and communist past as much as they are by the notion of what constitutes democratic rule in the twenty-first century.

Throughout Russian history there is well-established precedent of turning to what social scientists call "authoritarian modernizers" in a time of troubles.[1] During the twentieth century, many nations—Turkey, Japan, and China are the best examples—created similar political systems to navigate a disruptive but arguably necessary period of industrialization and social transformation.[2] What seems to set Russia apart is the frequency with which such leaders have taken the reins of power to modernize the nation. From Peter the Great to Putin, Russia time and time again has been led by men who sought to transform the nation. Such leaders have set out to drag Russia, sometimes kicking and screaming, into whatever constituted their vision of a better future, one in which a newly "modernized" nation would stand as an equal with the most powerful states of the day.

Virtually all of Russia's authoritarian modernizers have, to some degree, copied their reforms from other presumably more advanced nations. The willful rush to catch up with more powerful and advanced nations usually was animated by a national inferiority complex and a fear that Russia's future and perhaps its very existence were in danger. Sometimes the fear had solid justification. Peter the Great and Alexander II were shocked out of their complacency by embarrassing military defeats, and Joseph Stalin's headlong rush to industrialize Russia was motivated, at least in part, by the growing fear of Germany and "capitalist encirclement."

But despite their willingness to copy from other nations, Russia's authoritarian modernizers also have sought to impose a certain "Russianness" on their reforms. Sometimes they tried to limit the impact of borrowed Western technology, attempting to insulate political and social life from the influence of Western ideas of constitutional monarchy and democracy. At other times they have created a distinctly Russian variation of Western philosophies. V. I. Lenin and Stalin fundamentally rewrote traditional Marxism to serve the needs of the moment. Mikhail Gorbachev tried and failed to create Russian versions of democratic and market socialism, and his successors initially offered a hybrid theory of "sovereign democracy."

Although the motivation to produce such hybrid forms is certainly understandable, it nonetheless leaves observers with the task of sorting out what is distinctly Russian, what has been borrowed, and how each component has affected the other. We should admit from the beginning that any effort to answer this question risks distortion in two directions. On one hand, we could set the bar for accepting Russia as a democracy so high that we preclude its admission to the club of democratic nations. Even the most widely accepted democracies fall short of perfection; the playing field is never completely level, the institutional structures never completely representative, and the leaders never completely devoid of human failings. But on the other hand, we could set the bar so low that any failure to approximate democratic rule could be explained away as just another consequence of Russian history or culture.

What Does Executive Leadership Mean in the Russian Context?

If asked what *executive leadership* means in the Russian context, any sophomore political science major could give the generic answer accepted in most successful democracies. The executive official of government is that person who has been chosen to manage the executive functions of the state. That definition is not as circular at it might seem, at least in the sense that every government must have someone whose job it is to run the day-to-day activities of the state. To paraphrase former U.S. president Harry Truman, that executive official sits where the buck stops.

But then things get more complicated. De facto executive power may lie completely outside the state or at a lower level within the official hierarchy. In most of the communist states, real power resided in the highest party office, usually called the general or first secretary, leading to the common description that the party *ruled* while the state *governed*. Or in more unique cases, the de facto leader may hold a lesser office within the state hierarchy; Deng Xiaoping led China from the post of deputy premier, although there was no doubt about who was really in charge.

The most important lesson from our perspective is that we should not fixate on a single institutional form if we want to understand the role of executive leadership in the Russian system. Students of American politics are lucky; there is a *presidency* that stands independently of the identity of individual presidents. Historically, Russia is not yet at a point at which that distinction is meaningful.

Authoritarian Modernizers: The Prototype

The concept of authoritarian modernizers is hardly new. It has been applied to many leaders and revolutions for well over a century. It originally described the revolutionary transformation of a nation from a pre-industrial, largely traditional, and relatively weak position into a modern, socially transformed, and powerful player in the international community. It had many different iterations: from peasant nation to industrial power;

from colonized or externally controlled nation to an independent state; from one belief system usually rooted in religion, traditional society, and preindustrial social and political norms to a secular messianic ideology promising the transformation of social, political, and economic life, often with a vision of worldwide relevance; or in its most recent form as communism has fallen or been transformed, from an inefficient and collapsing economic and political system isolated from economic and cultural globalization to an emerging market-oriented postindustrial economy and internationalized culture able to take its place in an increasingly interconnected and interdependent world.

Whatever else such modernizing revolutions are, they are quintessentially about power. Power shifts from the old leadership to new leaders who promise to transform the nation. It empowers some to transform others, often through violent and draconian social revolutions from above. In most of the authoritarian modernizations of the late nineteenth and twentieth centuries, these transformations reached deeply into the social structure and psyche of the nation. New class identities emerged, as did "class enemies" and "enemies of the people." Economic transformations changed the social profile of the nation. National and ethnic identities were transformed, as Russians, Ukrainians, and others became soviet citizens, later to reverse the process as the Soviet Union and soviet identity collapsed. More invasively, authoritarian modernizers got into the heads of their soon-to-be transformed citizens, promising to create the "new _____ man," the blank space to be filled in by the nature of the future society they would inhabit.

Revolutions led by authoritarian modernizers also embody a conscious and self-serving *political formula*. By political formula, we refer to a combination of programmatic and tactical elements that set forth the agenda of authoritarian modernization and offer a rationalization of the new political and economic pecking order. Like most revolutionaries, authoritarian modernizers set out to do something—to overthrow the old and presumably regressive regime, to create a new political and social order, to move the nation forward toward their vision of the future, to end foreign occupation or influence, and to salve the nation's embarrassment over its "backwardness." They also articulate a strategy for revolution, usually combining a destructive stage in which they take control and then a transformational stage in which they implement their program. Taken together, these two elements comprise a political formula that offers direction, strategy, and self-justification. The two must operate in tandem for the revolution and transformation to succeed. Utopian vision without organization and strategy leads nowhere; organization and strategy without direction transform nothing.

The concept of authoritarian modernizer may be vested with different meanings at different points in time. Although the notion first emerged in connection with the rapid industrialization and social transformation of allegedly backward nations in the late nineteenth and early twentieth centuries, the central idea has gone through a series of iterations with the passage of time. In the Russian context, Peter the Great and Alexander II were both authoritarian modernizers working within their own specific historical contexts. Lenin and Stalin followed in their footsteps, albeit pursuing radically different goals implemented and rationalized by very different ideological and social agendas. A central theme of this examination of executive leadership in the Russian and soviet contexts is that the basic concept of authoritarian modernizer continues to be relevant in the late soviet and post-soviet eras. Gorbachev, Yeltsin, Putin, and Medvedev all fall within an updated version of being an authoritarian modernizer in the late twentieth and early twenty-first centuries. For our purposes, it is irrelevant that their actions disassembled most of the political, economic, ideological, and social features of the old order, substituting an incomplete and flawed democracy operating within the context of a mixed economy. The important point is that Russia and its contemporary leaders are pursuing and ultimately modifying a version of modernity that is widely accepted in today's world, one that in their view would not have emerged without strong leadership from above.

Richard Sakwa acknowledges the post-communist iteration of modernity in his most recent book on the Putin presidency: "In the post-communist transition period, the 'dictatorship of the proletariat' envisioned by Marx as the period of extra-legal class dominance of the makers of the socialist revolution, in the 1990s gave way to the dictatorship of the executive designed to push through a modernization process that would ultimately render that dictatorship, as it would for Marx, redundant. . . . It was Putin's achievement not only to reconstitute the state, but also to endow it with renewed legitimacy drawn from its developmental agenda."[3]

What does modernization mean in this context? The truthful if initially unhelpful answer is many things. But three important characteristics must be present. First, the model must be flexible and eclectic enough to include all of the aspects of modernization that are relevant within the context and timeframe in which it is applied; in some cases political or economic transformations will be the key, while in others broader social and cultural changes may be equally important. It also must establish a tactical link between the goals and mechanisms of the authoritarian transformation, what we termed a *political formula* earlier in this chapter.

Second, it must be flexible enough to permit both tactical and substantive reinterpretation of what "modern" means. Leaders who begin to transform their nation often alter course along the way, sometimes forced to do so by circumstances beyond their control, sometimes because their initial understanding of modernity was flawed or unreasonably utopian, and sometimes because they must include elements of the premodern culture to preserve the nation's unique identity and win broad public support.

Third, the model must provide a clear distinction between the role of authoritarian modernizer and that of conventional authoritarian rulers. The distinction is important for both intellectual and political reasons. If we argue that the concept of authoritarian modernizer is an important explanatory tool in understanding political and social changes in Russia and many other nations, then it must be possible for us to see the distinctions between these transformational leaders and the rule of status quo autocrats and dictators. Alexander II clearly fits the transformational model, but Alexander III does not; Lenin and Stalin must be included, and perhaps some of Nikita Khrushchev's actions. But Leonid Brezhnev should not, except for the feckless rhetoric about "developed socialism." Gorbachev, Yeltsin, Putin, and Medvedev also must be regarded as authoritarian modernizers, despite the myriad differences in policy and style that separate them.

Having a clear understanding of what being an authoritarian modernizer means is also important politically. For better or worse, the term almost always conveys a positive mantle of decisive and progressive leadership. Such leaders change their nations and the world around them, allegedly for the better, despite the collateral costs. Although history may offer a more balanced judgment, their contemporaries often either deify them, creating leadership cults and accepting their authoritarian ways as a necessary cost of the modernization, or demonize them, calling them false prophets of a flawed future. It is therefore not surprising that even the most conventional of petty dictators and presidents-for-life seek to cloak themselves in the mantle of modernizing autocrats. Conversely, it is not surprising that even the most well-meaning of the critics of genuine modernizers seek to deny them such a lofty pedestal. It is easy to understand that Putin's critics vehemently attack the notion that he should be thought of as such a modernizer. To grant him membership in that exclusive club is to offer some degree of legitimacy despite the collateral costs of his actions.[4]

An even more refined distinction has emerged in the post-communist world between "competitive" or "electoral authoritarianism" and traditional authoritarian rule. In "competitive" or "electoral authoritarian" nations "core democratic institutions" and electoral processes "exist and are meaningful, but . . . are systematically violated in favor of . . . the incumbent." Elections still matter and the voters could, under the right circumstances, use them to vote out incumbents. The important question is "what are these circumstances?" There is an elusive tipping point beyond which competitive authoritarianism crosses the line into full-blown traditional authoritarianism, just as there is a potential tipping point beyond which opponents may recapture control through the ballot box or spill into the streets to reject leaders who have won blatantly rigged elections.[5]

Characteristics of Authoritarian Modernizers

Any discussion of the phenomenon of authoritarian modernizers entails three elements: (1) the motivations that lead them to undertake the transformation of their nation; (2) the model of modernity they wish to create, which will vary from country to country and time to time; and (3) the specific mechanisms and organizational forms through which modernization will be accomplished.

Motivation. Authoritarian modernizers often act in response to a sense of inferiority. Whatever the specific circumstances, they view their nation as backward, especially in comparison with the major powers of the day, which may have defeated them militarily, forced them to open their societies to foreign economic and cultural penetration, or simply outpaced them in their efforts at building a better future. Foreign control and penetration were important in the minds of Japanese and Chinese modernizers in the late nineteenth and early twentieth centuries. Emergence from colonial rule and exploitation also figured prominently in the minds of third-world modernizers from Gamal Abdel Nasser in Egypt to Sukarno in Indonesia. Undeniable decline, capped by defeat and the loss of empire at the end of World War I, led to the emergence of Kemal Atatürk and the transformation of Turkey. Embarrassing military defeats in the Crimea, the Russo-Japanese

War, and World War I shaped the thinking of a succession of authoritarian modernizers in tsarist and soviet Russia. Half a century later Gorbachev, Yeltsin, and Putin would follow a more contemporary version of a similar path, rejecting a failed authoritarian model and a languishing economy for a new version that would pull Russia forward into a democratic political order with a modernized, postindustrial, market-driven economy.

In many cases, authoritarian modernizers' views of the West's economic and military preeminence produced a love–hate response. Although they wished to copy many of the techniques and cultural modalities of more advanced nations, they also usually insisted on applying them in distinctly idiosyncratic ways.

Model of the Future. Authoritarian modernizers are future oriented. Their rejection of the nation's backwardness inevitably carries with it an image of the future they wish to create, sometimes embodied in a complex chiliastic ideology with broader global implications, and sometimes expressed more modestly in terms of economic, social, and political changes for their nation alone. Whatever its initial scope, that belief system carries with it both immediate and long-term implications.

In practical terms, this vision of the future expresses an immediate agenda rooted in the revolutionaries' diagnosis of the nation's ills. It may be relatively explicit and action oriented, setting forth specific policy choices, or it may be far more general, offering generic solutions such as a shift from a capitalist to a socialist economy (or, in its late-twentieth-century incarnation, precisely the opposite). Whatever its rationale, it addresses pressing and immediate needs, justifies the overthrow of the old regime and the suppression of whatever remaining social elements that might seek to restore it, legitimates the sweeping economic and social changes and collateral damage that accompany revolution, and rationalizes the institutionalization of an authoritarian regime capable of imposing the new order.

These visions of the future usually boil down to simplistic action programs, at least at first. Lenin spoke of the dictatorship of the proletariat and then the New Economic Policy (NEP) as the initial practical manifestations of the socialist revolution, and Stalin substituted the creation of socialism in one country and the five-year plans as the day-to-day marching orders toward the future. Subsequent leaders would offer a "new course" (Georgi Malenkov, who briefly challenged Khrushchev in the mid-1950s), the "full flowering of socialism" (Khrushchev's overly optimistic promise of a better life), and "developed socialism" (Brezhnev's high-tech version of economic and social management, always long on theory and short on accomplishments). Gorbachev's notions of *perestroika* and *glasnost* completed the agenda for the soviet era. The uncharacteristic theoretical silence of the Yeltsin years was eventually replaced by Putin's concept of the "power vertical" and "sovereign democracy."

Modernizing the Post-Socialist Economy: Reversing the Earlier Model. In many ways, the transformation of the Soviet Union into post-communist Russia is an example of a new generation of authoritarian modernizers reversing or merely amending the work of previous authoritarian modernizers. To be sure, the meaning of "modern" is radically different. The model of post-socialist modernization is a reversal of the earlier Leninist and Stalinist models of economic growth and modernity. While it maintains many, if not all, of the features of authoritarian leadership cast within a framework of formally democratic institutions, it disassembles most, if not all of the institutional and behavioral modalities that had characterized the state-controlled, centrally planned economy of the socialist era.

In the real world of post-communist Russia, the economic transition was far more complex and disruptive. Everything crashed at the same time, or so it seemed. Therefore, everything had to be rebuilt. Central planning was discarded, publicly owned property was privatized, and the de facto social contract that promised a safety net of subsidies and social services was shredded. As in any revolutionary transition, some people came out of the transformation better off than others, and not surprisingly, the winners quickly found ways to convert their economic assets into political influence.

The new economic model was about more than just the distribution of wealth and influence. It also articulated a view of what a modern economy would be in the twenty-first century. Not unlike its Western counterparts, which had already gone through or were in the middle of the so-called second industrial revolution, the future Russian economy was initially portrayed in terms of emphasis on high technology, especially in the areas of intellectual technology, automation, space, medicine, and cutting-edge sectors such as nanotechnology. In many ways, it reflected both an analysis of the advanced economies and the wishful thinking of the late soviet era, which had promised advances optimistically labeled as "developed socialism," a "scientific and technological revolution," and the "scientific management of society"—promises that were never fulfilled.

How the Modernizing State Is Ruled. The title of this section is an unapologetic homage to two of the most influential works written about the way the Soviet Union really worked: Merle Fainsod's *How Russia Is Ruled,* first published in 1953, and Jerry Hough's expanded and revised version of the Fainsod text, *How the Soviet Union Is Governed,* published in 1979, both by Harvard University Press. They were the seminal works of their day. Both told us in practical terms what happened the day after the revolution was over and the new leadership had to answer the more prosaic questions of how to run the country and how to implement the lofty goals that until the day before had been no more than platitudes and dreams.

All authoritarian modernizers who make it into power eventually have to answer those questions. Not surprisingly, each finds a different response that combines elements of their unique road to power, the characteristics of their nation, their definition of "modern," and the institutional and human tools at their disposal. But typically there are some common elements, including (1) a new mechanism of rule, usually vested in some version of a single-party directed by a revolutionary and modernizing cadre that may go through several iterations and generations as modernization progresses; (2) the presence of a charismatic leader at the center of a leadership cult, both of which may be renewed in modified form as leadership changes; (3) the dominance of an executive "branch," although real leadership may be vested in another post; (4) an extensive bureaucratization of the state and single-party structure, often with deep intertwining of both hierarchies and mutual interdependence in terms of day-to-day rule; and (5) a model for rapid economic development and modernization, sometimes directly linked to state control or implemented through a mixed public–private economy with an important leadership role reserved for state-owned and directed industries.

Central to virtually all authoritarian modernizing regimes is the existence of a dominant and sometimes exclusive single party. It may be institutionalized through the so-called Leninist model, built around a revolutionary or modernizing cadre that continues to justify its leadership by its alleged role in leading the transformation, or it may be more loosely organized through the dominance of a mass-based party that effectively controls the government. Such models were typical of the Soviet Union and East European communist regimes and of China under Sun Yat-sen, Chiang Kai-shek, and communist leaders from Mao Zedong onward, or in less authoritarian form in dominant parties such as Japan's Liberal Democratic Party or Mexico's Institutional Revolutionary Party (PRI).

That difference, of course, is critically important in one sense; the mechanisms through which the Communist Party of the Soviet Union and its counterparts controlled society were both qualitatively and quantitatively different from the ways in which the Liberal Democrats or the PRI held on to power.

A unique feature of such modernizing parties is the extent to which they penetrate and control society. Although the party's own extensive bureaucratization and penetration of society are important elements of that dominance, they also legitimate their role by mobilizing popular support and symbolic mass involvement, by mediating disputes among and/or co-opting the leadership of disparate and newly emerging segments of the society, and by creating a bandwagon effect that draws into their ranks ambitious and upwardly mobile supporters. Sometimes that dominance comes through the forceful exclusion of potential rivals. In the Soviet Union and other systems that had copied the Leninist model, control was built in to the very institutional fabric of the political system; the Communist Party supervised the appointment of all policy-making officials throughout the society through the *nomenklatura* system, and it had the final word on the selection of candidates for "election" to public office. With one name on the ballot—until Gorbachev introduced multicandidate elections in the late 1980s—the outcome was virtually certain; soviet voters never had to wait up on election night to see what color the map would turn. It always was red.

Another common feature is the presence of strong, charismatic leaders at critical points in the creation and transformation of the modernizing regime. The leader becomes the focal point of the regime, simultaneously the image of both progress and stability, and the larger-than-life personification of the present and the future. To be sure, the persona often is a gross exaggeration or an outright invention, but it is a useful invention, one that offers identification, adulation, and an element of simplicity and stability in an otherwise rapidly changing world.

Extensive bureaucratization also is a hallmark of authoritarian modernizing regimes. Such regimes are quintessentially statist, often intertwining the governmental bureaucracy with a similar bureaucratization of a revolutionary party that must now transform itself into an effective government. The agenda before the party/state is enormous; not only must the revolution be consolidated but also the regime must reach into the society to transform it at all levels. Bureaucracy becomes the tool of both political survival and programmatic implementation.

A nation may go through different and even conflicting developmental models yet remain within the general parameters of an authoritarian modernizing state. This is particularly true of the Soviet Union, which scrapped the model of a centrally planned and government-managed economy for a mixed market–public sector economy functioning with an essentially authoritarian state.

What Can We Learn From Past "Executives"?

If we accept the notion that the specific institutional form of leadership may be less important than the function of leadership itself, what insights do we gain? It is the premise of this study that the roles of tsar, general secretary, or president are interchangeable, at least for our immediate purposes. Whatever their title, they fit a common mold in terms of their sense of what constituted and legitimated effective transformational leadership.

If this premise is correct, then we should begin our study of the post-communist Russian presidency with a quick survey of earlier leaders who served at critical transformational moments.

Earlier Authoritarian Modernizers

Peter the Great (1672–1725): The (Semi-) Europeanization of Traditional Russia. Peter the Great is generally regarded as the first in a series of authoritarian modernizers who sought to transform Russia. He was motivated by his genuine curiosity about the West and also by his well-justified fear of the modern military technology of his neighbors. Like many leaders who would follow, he quickly realized that the modernization of Russia's military required a more thorough transformation of the nation.[6]

In 1697 Peter personally launched his "Great Embassy" to the West, a journey to the European powers of the day both to seek diplomatic support and to study Western technology and society. Upon his return to Russia, Peter initiated a series of reforms. Western craftsmen he brought with him laid the foundation for modern armaments industries, including shipbuilding. Peter imposed a cultural revolution on the nation; Western clothing and social mores were demanded of his nobles, and, most offensively, beards were forbidden.

The crowning achievement of Peter's modernization effort was the creation of a new European-style city on the Gulf of Finland that bore his name: St. Petersburg. As Russia's "window on the West," it was to provide commercial and diplomatic access to the continent and to lead the further Westernization of Russia through institutions such as St. Petersburg State University and the Academy of Sciences.

Peter also transformed the nature of the Russian state. Traditional power centers such as the *streltsi*—conservative hereditary home-guard military forces who bitterly opposed reforms—were destroyed, their leaders frequently executed. In their place emerged a loyal praetorian guard and the Secret Chancellery, the precursor to a future host of secret police organizations.

Deeply involved in all aspects of these changes, Peter created a cult of the personality that guaranteed his preeminence. He obtained, but never used, the right to designate his own successor. Physically as well as politically towering over his retinue, he dominated political life. He centralized top-level decision making into a council that he personally dominated; accurately but privately termed the "Most Drunken Council" for its decision-making style, it ran the nation as an extension of Peter's will.

Most of the nation initially embraced Peter's reforms more out of fear than heart-felt support, and after his death there were modestly successful attempts to roll back some of his changes. But for the most part, the spirit if not the details of the reforms survived, as did the style of their implementation. The lesson of the era of Peter the Great was clear—change came from above.

Alexander II (1818–1881): Progressive Reform in the Nineteenth Century. If Peter the Great sought to force his nation to embrace dramatic reforms, Alexander II attempted to lead it through a less traumatic transformation to modernize it in the 1860s. Much of the initial motivation came from military defeat. Russian forces had fared poorly in the Crimean War (1853–1856), and in the face of these difficulties, the nation engaged in a period of soul-searching to discover the causes of such weakness and to bring Russia up to the best standards of the day.[7]

That critical self-examination led to the conclusion that much of the nation's weakness could be traced to its antiquated economy, especially agriculture, where the ancient institution of serfdom still existed. Alexander II issued a decree in 1861 that ended the serfs' status as the property of the landowners. Individual peasant families eventually were to become owners of land obtained through the breakup of large estates, reimbursing the nobles for the land through "redemption payments," a sort of long-term mortgage. Had it worked the way Alexander II intended, this reform would have transformed the nation. Peasants would cease to be a potentially revolutionary force because they now owned the land, excess rural population would now be free to move to the newly created industries, profitable family-owned farms would invest a portion of their earnings into modernizing agriculture itself, and newly enriched nobles would wisely invest the money they received from the peasants into infrastructure and industrialization.

It didn't work out that way, of course. But the wave of optimism stoked by emancipation of the serfs emboldened the tsar to launch other reforms. Commitments were made to improve the nation's infrastructure, especially in transportation and communication; to reform the judiciary; to improve and expand the educational system, broadening access to secondary and even higher education to elements of the society once excluded; to modernize the military; and to recruit civil servants from a broader strata of society. At the political level, modest reforms were attempted or considered. Local councils called *zemstva* were created to assist in municipal and regional government. Although their membership was composed mostly of local nobles, they were intended to provide a bridge between the formal institutions of the state and a nascent civil society. Shortly before his assassination in 1881, the tsar considered the formation of indirectly elected advisory bodies, a thought that died with him.

V. I. Lenin (1870–1924): Making Revolution in Russia. Credited as the founder of socialism in Russia and the guiding spirit of the seizure of power from the provisional government in October 1917, Lenin began the transformation of Russia from its tsarist past into the new age of socialism. Unquestionably he left his mark on the nation, as well as on the leaders who would follow, from Stalin to Putin. But many of Lenin's notions about what should follow the seizure of power were wrong. Incapacitated by his first stroke in 1922, and dead two years later in 1924, he left his followers a much clearer picture of how to make a revolution and cling to power than of what to do with that power once they consolidated rule.[8]

Lenin's greatest contributions lay in his reinterpretation of Marxism to justify a socialist revolution in a marginally industrialized nation and in his operationalization of the doctrine from abstract economic theory into a cookbook for revolution.[9] Russian Marxists had a seemingly unsolvable problem in the late nineteenth century: If they took their doctrine literally, the Russian revolution lay years, perhaps decades, in the future. Spontaneous workers' uprisings would occur first in the most industrialized nations, starting probably in Germany. Revolution in Russia made sense only if it could somehow trigger revolution elsewhere. For Lenin, the solution was bold and simple: a dedicated revolutionary party—a *vanguard*, as he termed it—would seize power on behalf of an as yet small and immature proletariat. Once in power, it would use the mechanism of the state to further industrialize the nation, thereby creating the working class in whose name it had seized power.

The authoritarian dimension of the new dictatorship of the proletariat emerged quickly at the end of the civil war in 1921. Facing a rebellion within his own party, Lenin imposed strict discipline and banned "factionalism," effectively suppressing any debate over the future course of events. His Bolsheviks also quickly consolidated their control over the soviets, the legislative bodies that had sprung up during the revolution. To extend the party's control over the rest of the society, Lenin authorized the creation of a party bureaucracy that would penetrate all elements of governmental, social, and economic life. It quickly became the de facto power center working within the formal institutions of government. Although he would later have second thoughts just before his death, he did not block the appointment of Joseph Stalin—regarded by most within the party leadership as a capable, if not too bright, bureaucrat—to the all-important role of party general secretary, which controlled the bureaucracy.

While Lenin tightened his control over the party and the party's control over government, he paradoxically backed away from launching a rapid economic transformation of the nation. Consistent with his own inclinations as an authoritarian modernizer and the implications of the dictatorship of the proletariat, he initially had committed the new regime to the rapid creation of the industrial proletariat in whose name the Bolsheviks had seized power. But by 1921 the nation was in no condition to launch such a bold initiative. The economy had been destroyed by World War I and the civil war, and the rebellion by a once pro-Bolshevik naval garrison at the Kronstadt base in the Gulf of Finland convinced Lenin that concessions were necessary. They took the form of the New Economic Policy, or NEP, which restored a limited market economy. Described as a temporary expedient—a "breathing space," Lenin called it—the NEP was to restore the economy and win back public support for the still-insecure regime. Eventually, but no one said exactly when, the NEP would end and the march toward the future would begin again.

The NEP caused considerable debate within Bolshevik circles. Especially after Lenin's death in 1924, the party divided bitterly over how long to maintain the economic and political concessions that it implied. All of the major candidates for Lenin's mantle took a position, only to be outmaneuvered by Stalin's ability to play one off against another and by the growing strength of the party bureaucracy that he controlled.

Joseph Stalin (1879–1953): Transforming Russia into the New Soviet Union. If Lenin is to be credited with overthrowing the old order and forging a disciplined party, Stalin must be acknowledged as the leader who transformed a vague notion of a communist future into a workable plan of action and perfected the mechanisms of single-party rule.

At the time of Lenin's death, the regime faced a critical dilemma. If the NEP were adopted as a long-term policy, the new Bolshevik regime seemingly abandoned its role in transforming the economy and society. To the extent that the party backed away from that commitment, it lost the sense of mission that had emboldened it to revolution and the ability to rationalize its repressive rule in terms of the party's role as an authoritarian modernizer.[10] But the other option—rapid industrialization—also was fraught with dangers. The success of the NEP had brought a tenuous calm between the regime and society that would be destroyed by industrialization. Especially in the countryside, where a new class of relatively well-off peasants called the *kulaks* had grown strong, any attempt to nationalize the land would risk civil war.

While much of the success of Stalin's machinations can be explained by the growing power of the party bureaucracy, which he led as general secretary, it is also important to acknowledge the significance of the ideological reinvigoration of the party and its mission that Stalin provided. It is what a recent U.S. president, George H. W. Bush, once called "the vision thing." By the mid-1920s, much of the "vision thing" had gone out of the Russian revolution. Lenin was dead, and the party squabbled over the choice of his successor; the world revolution was postponed and, to some, abandoned; the brave march forward to the future as an industrialized nation was marking time; and the sense that a dedicated band of revolutionaries could will the future into existence had weakened.

Stalin changed all of that with his notion of "socialism in one country," which lay at the core of his policies to industrialize and transform the nation. Offering himself as a realist who could adapt Marxism to the needs of post-revolutionary Russia, Stalin argued that the nation must turn inward and concentrate on the development of socialism in a single country, the newly created Union of Soviet Socialist Republics (USSR). That required full-scale industrialization and central control over the economy through five-year plans that set forth ambitious goals and mobilized national resources. It also meant the collectivization of agriculture, both to control the rural population and to destroy the *kulaks.*

As a part of this disciplined and single-minded march toward a redefined future, Stalin also paved the way for a cultural revolution. The emergence of the "new soviet man" would accompany the creation of a mighty socialist state. A new cultural genre—socialist realism—defined new enemies and heroes, and the media drummed the new images and role models into the people at every turn.

Stalin further consolidated his rule over the party, and the party's control of society. He used the patronage powers of the general secretaryship to create a loyal cadre of supporters, the so-called *nomenklatura.* They constituted a new administrative and political elite, and held virtually all important decision-making positions in soviet society. Ultimately indebted to "the leader," or *vozhd,* as he was known in Russian, they rose to complete control as the purges from 1935 to 1939 destroyed the old Bolshevik elite.[11]

Stalin the man also became Stalin the symbol. A massive personality cult was created that portrayed the *vozhd* as a benevolent authoritarian figure, simultaneously capable of ruthless discipline and boundless empathy with the common people. "Stalin," a name that he took years earlier to confuse the tsar's secret police, meant "man of steel." He was at once the defender of the nation against foreign and domestic enemies, the architect of the future, the friend of the diverse peoples of the Soviet Union, and a role model for young and old.

On the positive side, Stalin's domestically focused socialism in one country also gave the people a sense of stability and an optimistic vision of the future. The revolutions of 1917, the civil war, and the political instability that followed Lenin's death and Stalin's purges had destroyed the fabric of Russian society. Stalin offered stability, order, and the promise that the people and their nation would prosper.

Nikita Khrushchev (1894–1971): The First Attempt at Reform. In some ways, it is inappropriate to list Nikita Khrushchev in the company of other Russian and soviet leaders whom we have termed authoritarian modernizers. Although he eventually inherited a title similar to that of Stalin (he became party *first* secretary rather than general secretary, a not-too-subtle reminder of his diminished powers), he never consolidated his leadership as fully as Stalin. Indeed, he was the only leader of the Soviet Union to be removed from power by a de facto vote of no confidence by top-level party officials in October 1964, having narrowly survived a similar coup attempt in 1957.[12]

But in other ways, including Khrushchev among those leaders who sought to transform post-Stalinist Russia is entirely justified, especially if we consider the fundamental changes in the nature of soviet leadership that emerged with his rise to power. All future leaders from Khrushchev to Gorbachev had to accept two new realities. First, none would ever be permitted to accumulate the power that Stalin enjoyed. All would work within a new context labeled "collective leadership," a setting in which a first-among-equals might emerge but one also within which that leader would be carefully limited by others within the Politburo and the Central Committee.

The second reality was equally compelling: The Stalinist system was increasingly antiquated and demanded reform. Another round of "modernization" would be necessary to update the earlier modernizations of the Stalin era, and it would have to be forced on now-entrenched power centers in the party and government. The problem was that these two imperatives—political stability and reform—were irreconcilable. Too much stability prevented serious reform, and too much reform upset the stability of the regime and, in larger context, the entire nation.

Khrushchev's role as the first leader who had to cope with this contradiction was not an easy one.[13] By the mid-1950s, it was apparent that Khrushchev was consolidating his position as first-among-equals, but certainly not as an undisputed leader. Policy shortfalls and the growing concerns among other senior party leaders that he was attempting to escape the boundaries of collective leadership soon produced opposition to his reforms. Seeking a way to sweep aside this opposition, Khrushchev launched a bold initiative: In February 1956, at the Twentieth Party Congress, he delivered the famous "de-Stalinization" speech. It selectively denounced Stalin's "crimes" in ways that inculpated many of Khrushchev's current opponents. The meaning was clear: Khrushchev was launching an assault against other top party officials, hoping to clear the deck for his own reform agenda. Economic failure and events in Eastern Europe soon forced Khrushchev to retreat, but he would return to the de-Stalinization ploy again and again over the remainder of his career.

Khrushchev's reforms were a hodgepodge of efforts to modernize the economy and nudge the party toward a managerial role. They included (1) an erratic foreign policy that eased cold war tensions but also provoked the Cuban missile crisis that nearly brought nuclear war; (2) poorly planned economic reforms that included greater emphasis on consumer goods, decentralization of control, and loosening of central planning; and (3) reforms within the communist party that would have begun to push aside the Stalinist old guard and modernize its style of leadership.

In June 1957, Khrushchev's opponents struck back, winning a de facto vote of no confidence within the party Politburo, which they assumed would be the death knell of Khrushchev's power. Khrushchev outwitted them, demanding that the full session of the Central Committee be convened. The larger body, to which Khrushchev had appointed many supporters, rejected the dismissal.

Khrushchev forgot the lesson, but future opponents did not. In October 1964, after several more partially successful attempts to impose further reforms, and after several additional efforts to use de-Stalinization as a political weapon, Khrushchev once again found himself before a hostile Politburo, a majority of whom demanded his resignation. But the outcome was different; that Politburo majority had already selectively convened its own majority within the Central Committee, which con-firmed the dismissal. The Khrushchev era was over.

Throughout some of the headiest years of the Khrushchev era, a young man from a backwater village just outside of Stavropol clearly kept tabs on what was happening. Inspired by the reforms, and anxious to experiment back home even during the least imaginative years of the Brezhnev admin-istration, he would subsequently refer to himself as "a child of the Twentieth Party Congress."[14] He would eventually get most, if not all of it right. His name was Mikhail Gorbachev.

The Brezhnev Era: The Long Calm before the Storm

In most ways, Leonid Brezhnev (1906–1982) was not an authoritarian modernizer who set out to transform the Soviet Union. He more clearly fit into the model of Alexander III or Stalin in the postwar years as a leader who sought to use his powers to consolidate stability at home and win recognition of the USSR as a global superpower.[15] But in other ways, he did have a "vision," at least in theory, which would modernize the economy and the society while leaving single-party rule intact. That vision was expressed in the newest Marxist buzzword, "developed socialism." It combined technological modernization of the economy with Western ideas of a conflict-free postindustrial society and a managerial revolution. It would bring the increasingly stagnant Soviet Union into the modern world, if only the leadership would accept its imperatives and rise to the occasion.[16]

When the dust cleared after the unprecedented coup that removed Khrushchev from office, two things were apparent. First, collective leadership was still very much in vogue. Khrushchev had overplayed his hand by repeatedly returning to the de-Stalinization issue to attack his opponents. Although the failure of many of his policies had contributed to his downfall, his real offense lay in his efforts to remake the party as an agent of reform and to marginalize the senior elite that resisted such changes. The vulnerability of any future leader was now a proven reality.

This new reality was demonstrated quickly by the new lineup of top leaders. Whereas Khrushchev had held the top posts in the party (first secretary) and the government (chair of the Council of Ministers), responsibility was now divided. Brezhnev emerged as party first, and later general secretary, and Alexei Kosygin, viewed as an efficient manager with long experience in the economy, became chair of the Council of Ministers. Although Brezhnev eventually emerged as a clear first-among-equals, other senior leaders such as Mikhail Suslov (in charge of ideology), Andrei Gromyko (foreign minister), Yuri Andropov (head of the Committee for State Security, or KGB), and a host of central party and government officials and regional party secretaries were accorded continuing visibility and power.

The second thing that was apparent was the new leadership's willingness to assure the Communist Party as a whole that its dominant position would not be challenged. Two interwoven messages went out: First, the *nomenklatura*, that is, party members who held virtually all decision-making offices in every aspect of soviet society, were guaranteed job security. Like tenure in colleges and universities, that assurance gave them jobs for life, with no pressure to retire and the promise of reassignment to another important position if they failed in their present post. Second, the party also would not be pressured to change its style of leadership; there would be no need for old dogs to learn new tricks to maintain their relevance, as Khrushchev had demanded.

By the early 1970s, an informal power-sharing arrangement emerged. Much like Western notions of corporatism, in which institutionalized economic and social interests are directly represented in government, this arrangement saw the party Politburo and Central Committee emerge as microcosms of the powers-that-be of the soviet establishment. At the Politburo level, important interests such as heavy industry, agriculture, the military, the foreign ministry, and the KGB held full (voting) membership; also present were the party secretaries of important union republics such as Ukraine, Belarus, and others. The pattern was repeated for the candidate (nonvoting) members as well, including the representatives of less important party bodies and government ministries or sectors of the economy and less important regions. The party Central Committee, a larger body that usually met only twice a year, was cast from the same mold.[17]

The result produced a decision-making style that refused to make hard decisions. Consensus was to be valued above problem solving. Showdown votes were avoided at all cost, and action was deferred unless virtually unanimous agreement emerged. In a telling admission, Brezhnev once revealed that when the Politburo could not reach agreement, a committee would be appointed to study the matter. Since any major reform proposals inevitably stepped on the toes of one or more of the vested interests or regions represented on that body, little was done, leading to a deepening "stagnation" of soviet society.

The Brezhnev era ended on November 10, 1982. An already ill leader who had been the subject of a domestic and international death watch for years ignored the advice of his doctors and stood atop Lenin's tomb for the November 7 parade honoring the revolution. It was the last straw, and he died three days later. With his passing, the party now had the opportunity to choose new leaders who would deal with the nation's growing problems. For three years, it failed in the task.

The Uncertain Interregnum: Andropov and Chernenko

From November 1982 to March 1985, the soviet leadership and the nation itself were adrift. Two interim leaders took the stage, both too ill to govern effectively and too devoid of innovative ideas to address the nation's problems. The first was Yuri Andropov (1914–1984), whose most notable achievements were to have turned the KGB into an effective intelligence agency and to suppress the growing dissident community. To his credit, he was viewed as the least corrupted member of the old generation; he had run the KGB as a tight ship, a hopeful sign to those in the leadership who wanted to see a new sense of order and discipline. He was also touted as a closet reformer, with detailed knowledge of all aspects of soviet society and an interest in the modest but successful economic reforms in Eastern Europe, where he had served earlier in his career. During his brief tenure in office, he initiated modest reforms and sought to impose a greater sense of discipline, both with little lasting impact. His most significant achievement came through his promotion of the Politburo's youngest member, Mikhail Gorbachev, to the status of seeming heir apparent. Gorbachev, whose had been responsible primarily for agriculture, was given broad responsibilities for the economy as a whole, internal party affairs, and foreign policy.

When Andropov died on February 9, 1984, the Politburo refused to follow his lead and name Gorbachev as his successor. After several days of wrangling, it elected another member of the old guard, Konstantin Chernenko (1911–1985), as the new general secretary. Chernenko had been extremely close to Brezhnev, acting as his alter ego in his last few years. His selection indicated that the Politburo was unwilling to pass leadership on to a younger generation. Chernenko lasted for thirteen months, a period in which de facto leadership increasingly was delegated to his staff. He died on March 10, 1985, and for a while the Politburo debated whether to turn once again to another "safe" candidate or to shift power to a new generation.[18]

This time, it would act more wisely.

Notes

1. Cyril E. Black, *The Dynamics of Modernization*, Harper, 1968.

2. Andrew Mango, *Atatürk: A Biography of the Founder of Modern Turkey*, Overlook, 2002; M. Surku Hanioglu, *Atatürk: An Intellectual Biography*, Princeton University Press, 2011; Peter R. Moody, *Tradition and Modernization in China and Japan*, Wadsworth, 1995; Marius B. Janson, *The Making of Modern Japan*, Belknap, 2002; Marie-Claire Bergere and Janet Lloyd, *Sun Yat-sen*, Stanford University Press, 2000; Jay Taylor, *The Generalissimo: Chaing Kai-shek and the Struggle for Modern China*, Belknap, 2011; Whitney Steward, *Mao Zedong*, Twentieth Century Books, 2006; Maurice Meisner, *Mao Zedong: A Political and Intellectual Portrait*, Polity, 2007; and Ezra F. Vogel, *Deng Xiaoping and the Modernization of China*, Belknap, 2011.

3. Richard Sakwa, *Putin Redux: Power and Contradiction in Contemporary Russia*, Routledge, 2014, 21.

4. Bobo Lo and Lilia Shevtsova, "A 21st Century Myth: Authoritarian Modernization in Russia and China," Moscow Carnegie Center, 2012.

5. William Zimmerman, *Ruling Russia: Authoritarianism from the Revolution to Putin*, Princeton University Press, 2014, 221; Steven Levitsky and Lucan A. Way, *Competitive Authoritarianism: Hybrid Regimes after the Cold War*, Cambridge University Press, 2010; and Andreas Schedler, ed., *Electoral Authoritarianism: The Dynamics of Unfree Competition*, Lynne Rienner, 2006.

6. Robert K. Massie, *Peter the Great: His Life and Times*, Random House, 1981; and Lindsey Hughes, *Peter the Great: A Biography*, Yale University Press, 2004.

7. Werner Eugen Mosse, *Alexander II and the Modernization of Russia*, I. B. Tauris, 1992.

8. Margaret J. Goldstein, *V.I. Lenin*, Twentieth Century Books, 2007; Dmitri Volkoganov, *Lenin: Life and Legacy*, Harper Collins, 1994; and Robert Service, *Lenin: A Political Life*, Belknap, 2000.

9. Alfred G. Meyer, *Leninism*, Westview, 1986; and R. N. Carew-Hunt, *The Theory and Practice of Communism*, Penguin, 1963.

10. Robert Service, *Stalin: A Biography*, Belknap, 2006; and Edvard Radzinsky, *Stalin*, Anchor, 1997.

11. Abdurakhman Avtorkhanov, *The Communist Party Apparatus*, Meridan/World, 1968; and Jerry F. Hough and Merle Fainsod, *How the Soviet Union Is Governed*, Harvard University Press, 1979, 409–449.

12. William Taubman, *Khrushchev: The Man and His Era*, Norton, 2004; Edward Crankshaw, *Khrushchev: A Biography*, Sphere, 1968; Roy Medvedev, *Khrushchev: A Biography*, Anchor Books/Doubleday, 1983; and Sergei Khrushchev and William Taubman, *Khrushchev on Khrushchev: An Inside Account of the Man and His Era*, Little Brown, 1990.

13. Martin McCauley, *The Khrushchev Era: 1953–1964*, Longman, 1995, 17–51; and George Breslauer, *Khrushchev and Brezhnev as Leaders: Building Authority in Soviet Politics*, Unwin Hyman, 1982, 4–136.

14. Donald R. Kelley, *Politics in Russia and the Successor States*, Harcourt Brace, 1999, 151.

15. Breslauer, *Khrushchev and Brezhnev*, 137–293; William Thompson, ed., *The Soviet Union under Brezhnev*, Longman, 2003; Donald R. Kelley, ed., *Soviet Politics in the Brezhnev Era*, Praeger, 1980; and Edwin Baker and M. A. Sandle, eds., *Brezhnev Reconsidered*, Palgrave Macmillan, 2003.

16. Donald R. Kelley, *The Politics of Developed Socialism: The Soviet Union as a Post-industrial State*, Greenwood, 1986.

17. Valerie Bunce and John Echols III, "Soviet Politics in the Brezhnev Era: Pluralism or Corporatism," in Kelley, ed., *Soviet Politics in the Brezhnev Era*, 1–26.

18. Zhores Medvedev, *Andropov*, Penguin, 1984; Ilya Zemtsov, *Chernenko: The Last Bolshevik: The Soviet Union on the Eve of Perestroika*, Transaction, 1988; and Donald R. Kelley, *Soviet Politics from Brezhnev to Gorbachev*, Praeger, 1987.

2

The Gorbachev Presidency

After the uncertainty and drift of the Andropov and Chernenko interregnum, Mikhail Gorbachev now held the most powerful office in the Soviet Union. But in many ways, it was a mixed blessing. The old guard of Leonid Brezhnev's era still dominated the Politburo, the Central Committee, and most of the other command centers in the party and government. They finally had been forced to accept a new and more dynamic leader, but they had not forgotten the lesson inherent in Nikita Khrushchev's fall. General secretaries served at the pleasure of the higher echelons of the party. Before Gorbachev still lay the life-or-death tasks of consolidating his position and finding an agenda that dealt with the nation's problems.

The Gorbachev era began with little seemingly changed in terms of the institutional arrangements. Gorbachev was elevated to the post of general secretary of the Communist Party of the Soviet Union, the single most important position and the true location of political power since Khrushchev had restored the party to its dominant role in the 1950s. As general secretary, Gorbachev controlled, at least on paper, the all-powerful party bureaucracy, itself a virtual shadow government. He also was regarded as first-among-equals in the Politburo, the party's top policy-making body. Until the creation of a presidency for the Soviet Union in 1990, he held no important post in the government.

Slightly complicating the institutional arrangements, since the adoption of the 1977 "Brezhnev constitution" there existed a newly created position of head of state that most commentators simply called the "presidency." Officially titled the chairman of the Presidium of the Supreme Soviet, it was created to give Brezhnev an official niche in the state structure that permitted him legally to speak for the nation and to sign treaties. Its role was separate from the head-of-party post of general secretary and the government-based chairman of the Council of Ministers. It was a legal convenience, but not a separate power base. During the Gorbachev era, it dropped off the radar that tracked politically significant people and events.[1]

By the end of the Gorbachev era, the institutional arrangements would be completely different. Gorbachev himself would create an alternative power base in the presidency of the Union of Soviet Socialist Republics and resign as party general secretary after the August 1991 coup attempt. Most of the fifteen union republics that made up the Soviet Union would create copycat presidencies of their own, and local communist leaders would use them to try to cling to power as the nation disintegrated. In the Russian Federation, Boris Yeltsin would use the Russian presidency to return from political oblivion, to which he had been sent in disgrace for suggesting that Gorbachev move even faster with reforms. At the end, it was this war of the presidencies that ended just over seventy-four years of communist rule.

The Starting Point: What Gorbachev Intended

This chapter addresses the details of the new institutions and the battles fought in their name, but it is important from the outset to understand the political realities that led to their creation. For Gorbachev, the new presidency was both a weapon and a safe haven. As opposition to his reforms grew, he found that many of his efforts could be turned against him. Perestroika (restructuring), which Gorbachev hoped would inspire confidence in economic reforms, remained a poorly defined promise that raised expectations but brought little immediate benefit. Glasnost (openness) initiated a free discussion of new ideas and of the failure of the leadership itself, with Gorbachev hoping to use it as a weapon against his opponents but eventually falling victim to its use against him. Democratization and the end of monopoly power for the Communist Party, which Gorbachev hoped to use to exert pressure on his opponents, eventually enabled the regime's critics to gain power in local, republic-level, and national legislative bodies. Within the Communist Party as well, Gorbachev met with increasing opposition as he demanded that the party learn to function within a competitive democratic system and to earn its power through the ballot box.

It is within this context that Gorbachev sought leverage by creating a new legislature in 1988, the Congress of People's Deputies. Its lower house, the Congress itself, was enormous; with 2,250 deputies, only one third directly elected by the population as a whole, it was to meet twice a year as a sounding board of public opinion. Its function was to debate public issues and suggest formal legislation to the upper house, the Supreme Soviet. That body, which contained 542 members elected by the lower house from among its own members, would meet frequently enough to act as a real legislative body.

The political motivation behind the creation of the Congress was simple and confrontational. Gorbachev's real intention was that the Congress would give him a new public forum in which to press his case for reform and to attack conservative opponents. The 2,250-member Congress was big enough to represent the newly articulate diversity of soviet society. In addition to the 750 members chosen by direct ballot in single-member districts, it contained another bloc of 750 chosen in ethnic constituencies, and a third bloc of 750 chosen to represent various organized interests in the society (100 delegates from the Communist Party itself, other groups of delegates such as the 25 from the Academy of Sciences, down to single delegates from small organizations such as the Society of Stamp Collectors). In many ways, it was intended to be a forum dominated by grassroots activists rather than by party officials and professional politicians.

The Supreme Soviet was a very different political animal. At that level, where real legislation would be written, the *apparatchiki* and professional politicians clearly had the upper hand, as Gorbachev had intended. If the larger Congress were to function as an expanded town hall meeting, with Gorbachev the visible master of ceremonies, the smaller body was reserved for the "serious" people whose knowledge of how to govern would keep the ship on an even keel.[2]

Gorbachev's institutional reforms also established a new office—the presidency of the USSR. For Gorbachev, the new office was both an opportunity and a trap. As a self-proclaimed "child of the Twentieth Party Congress" during the Khrushchev era, he could not forget the final lesson of that period: Party secretaries who get seriously out of step with the top echelons of the party itself, represented in the Politburo and the Central Committee, can easily be voted out of office. For the sake of security and in the face of rising criticism from within the party (and elsewhere), Gorbachev needed something more secure.

If worse came to worst, the presidency could provide that security. Elected by the members of the Congress of People's Deputies, the president stood outside the party chain of command. Although Gorbachev had been nominated by the party bloc of 100 within the third category of delegates, he had been elected by the Congress as a whole, officially independently of his party post. Reality, of course, was exactly the opposite, but the legal fiction might prove a lifeline if he were dismissed from the general secretary position by a vote of the Politburo and the Central Committee.

The new presidency also was a bully pulpit from which to build public support. The formal powers of the office—considered in detail later in this chapter—weren't its real value. The real value lay in its visibility and its sense of newness. The power of the office, as Richard Neustadt once observed about the American presidency, was the power to persuade.[3] And Gorbachev was—or thought he was—very good at that.

But there also was a considerable downside to the new presidency. As Thomas M. Nichols observes, it unmistakably put its first and only occupant in the crosshairs of full responsibility for failure as well as success. With greater clarity than ever before, everybody knew where the buck stopped.[4]

Gorbachev's Rise to Power

Gorbachev began the journey toward his fate as the last leader of the USSR on March 2, 1931, born in the small village of Privolnoye, near Stravropol in one of the nation's most important agricultural regions. He worked on a collective farm during World War II and in 1950 found himself on the road to Moscow to study law at one of the nation's elite universities, Moscow State University. Selection to that university inevitably opened the door to possible future advancement, but the choice to study law was less auspicious. Gorbachev compensated by being active in the university's Komsomol, the party's youth organization and a frequent starting point for upward mobility. Full membership in the Communist Party came while he was still at the university. Gorbachev graduated in 1955 and, with his law degree and party card in hand, returned to Stavropol.[5]

MIKHAIL GORBACHEV

- Born March 2, 1931, in Privolnoye, North Caucasus, near Stavropol.
- Graduated from Moscow State University in 1955 with a degree in law; received a correspondence degree in agriculture in 1967 from the Stavropol Institute of Agriculture.
- Joined the Communist Party while at Moscow State University.
- Became active in the Communist Party at Moscow State and continued to rise in its professional bureaucracy as an *apparatchik* upon his return to Stavropol.
- In 1970, appointed first secretary of the Stavropol Communist Party organization, the most politically important post at the regional level.

- Began to experiment with reforms of the collective farms in Stavropol, bringing him to the favorable attention of higher party officials.
- Made a member of the Communist Party Central Committee in 1971.
- Promoted to head the Communist Party Secretariat's Agricultural Department in 1978, bringing him back to Moscow.
- Made a candidate (nonvoting) member of the Politburo in 1979; promoted to full (voting) member in 1980, making him the youngest member of the country's de facto ruling body.
- Groomed by General Secretary Yuri Andropov as a successor in 1982–1983 but passed over in favor of Konstantin Chernenko upon Andropov's death in 1984.
- Chosen as general secretary of the Communist Party upon Chernenko's death in March 1985.
- Began initially cautious economic reforms, culminating in 1986 with the introduction of perestroika.
- Introduced proposals for multicandidate elections and the appointment of nonparty members to government positions in January 1987, followed by more radical proposals for economic reform.
- Introduced glasnost in 1988, calling for more openness and transparency in public life.
- Proposed the creation of a new legislature, the Congress of People's Deputies, along with a vaguely defined presidency in June 1988; multicandidate elections for the new body were held in March and April 1989; Gorbachev became the chairman of the Supreme Soviet, or de facto head of state in May 1989.
- In March 1990, elected by the Congress of People's Deputies to the newly created presidency.
- On foreign policy, continued reforms begun in 1985 with the suspension of the deployment of SS-20 missiles in Eastern Europe; met with U.S. president Ronald Reagan in Reykjavik, Iceland, in October 1986; in 1987 both sides agreed to remove intermediate-range missiles from Europe; in February 1988, Gorbachev began to withdraw soviet forces from Afghanistan; in that same year Gorbachev abandoned the Brezhnev Doctrine that justified control over Eastern Europe.
- By 1990, pressure was rising for a revision of the Union Treaty that created the USSR in 1922; non-Russian republics sought greater freedom within or outright succession from the Soviet Union; by August 1991 a tenuous compromise emerged that produced a new version of the Union Treaty to be signed in Moscow on August 20, 1991.
- Opponents to the new treaty attempted a coup on August 19–21, the failure of which led to the eventual breakup of the Soviet Union and Gorbachev's resignation as general secretary of the Communist Party.
- On December 25, 1991, Gorbachev resigned from the presidency, transferring power to the heads of the fifteen nations to emerge from the USSR.

A new wife also went along. While at the university, Gorbachev met, and by his own account, was swept off his feet by Raisa Titorenko. By soviet standards, she was a product of the new upper middle class; bright, ambitious, well educated and cultured in ways initially beyond the experience of the lad from Privolnoye, she would soon be a partner in Gorbachev's rise to power, a rarity at a time when wives remained in the background.

Gorbachev also took back to Stavropol the aspirations for reform and change that began with Joseph Stalin's death. The hope for reform was in the air. Now back in Stavropol, Gorbachev watched with great interest. It is certain that a low-level party official far from Moscow knew little of the political battles within the Kremlin itself. But he did sense that change was possible and that a new leader had emerged who was willing to take chances. He watched from a distance, at first optimistically after the Twentieth Party Congress raised hopes that more reform was possible and then cautiously as Khrushchev's removal from power confirmed that there were limits to such change. He would bide his time, tend to his job, broaden his network of supporters and mentors, and do what he could in Stavropol.

His initial job in Stavropol was in the Komsomol, an appropriate posting for someone who had been active in its branch at Moscow State University. In 1962, he transferred to full-time party work in agriculture, which he had studied since his return. That made him an *apparatchik,* a member of the *nomenklatura,* and took him over the threshold into being a professional politician, soviet style. Except agriculture wasn't the best specialization for upward mobility; it was the poor stepchild in terms of national priorities, and the system of collective and state farms created by Stalin left it mired in mismanagement and failure. But it was Stavropol's most important economic asset, and Gorbachev's success and sense of innovation quickly brought him to the attention of higher party officials in Moscow.

In 1970, Gorbachev was made first secretary of the Stavropol region. Although the post was technically within the Communist Party and not the government, it was the most important job in town. Regional party secretaries were virtual princes within their own fiefdoms; they were responsible to Moscow (the "center," as they called it) for everything in the region. Success as a regional party secretary was one of the rites of passage on the way to better things.[6]

Gorbachev prospered, in part because he had schooled himself in the problems of soviet-era agriculture and continued to experiment with highly visible reforms that seemed to offer some hope for improvement without abandoning the collective and state farms. He was able to secure backing from important patrons in Moscow such as Fyodor Kulakov, the party secretary in charge of agriculture, and Mikhail Suslov, the gray eminence in charge of ideology. When Kulakov died in 1978, Gorbachev was transferred to Moscow to take up his post in the national party leadership. A year later he was named a candidate member of the Politburo, and full voting membership came in 1980. He was the youngest member of that body by almost a decade, positioned—perhaps—to be the first leader of the next generation of general secretaries.

It didn't quite work out that way, at least for a while. After Brezhnev's death in 1982, the top post went to Yuri Andropov, a former KGB chief who groomed Gorbachev as his successor. But when Andropov died, the still-cautious Politburo named Konstantin Chernenko to the top post. He lasted only thirteen months. While there was still some resistance to Gorbachev's appointment, changes in the Politburo itself and the strong endorsement of Andrei Gromyko, the long-serving foreign minister, finally brought the ambitious young man from Privolnoye to his nation's top leadership position. He was now the general secretary of the Communist Party of the Soviet Union, the post from which virtually everyone since the Stalin era had tried to shape Russia's future.[7]

From General Secretary to President

When Gorbachev took up the office of general secretary, no one, least of all Gorbachev himself, could have predicted the outcome. He was very much a product of the system—a dedicated communist committed to the construction of socialism in the Soviet Union, and simultaneously a member of the next generation of leaders who had bided their time during Brezhnev's long tenure. He started out as a cautious reformer, eager to confront the dual tasks of consolidating his own power and pursuing a reform agenda that improved but did not destroy the institutions and the nation he served. In some ways, he personally was never able to resolve these conflicting goals. Now in retirement, with his Nobel Peace Prize in hand, he dabbles occasionally in Russian politics by collaborating in the creation of short-lived and hopelessly outgunned reform parties, and comments on the present state of affairs. In his last bid for public office—a run for the presidency of the Russian Federation in 1996—he received 0.5 percent of the vote. He is, as one of his earlier biographers put it, "the man who changed the world," but not in the way he intended.[8]

What he intended to do at the beginning was fairly simple, at least in theory. He wanted to be a gradualist who adapted the Communist Party and the government to the long-ignored issues that had left Russia with growing internal problems and declining international power. Under Brezhnev, the Soviet Union had "stagnated," as the official interpretation of the recent past puts it. Gorbachev's first moves to consolidate power within the party were fairly traditional. Within months, he had removed from the Politburo most of those who had questioned his selection. He also began to retire many of the Brezhnev-era regional party secretaries, a task he began while Andropov was in office. As general secretary, he controlled the appointment of new party officials and used his patronage power to bring new, and it was hoped loyal, leaders to the fore. He would frequently reach beyond the Garden Ring, Moscow's equivalent to the Capital Beltway, to bring promising regional party secretaries to the center, including a hard-driving leader from Sverdlovsk named Boris Yeltsin.

More broadly, and more threateningly, Gorbachev sought to weaken the role of the *nomenklatura*, whose support could make or break party general secretaries. At first there was no frontal assault; instead, the party's role was simply gradually reduced. The justification was seductively Marxist and, therefore, beyond reproach: Soviet society had matured to a point at which detailed party supervision and guidance were no longer needed.

The Reform Agenda: Politics and Policy

Like any skilled politician, Gorbachev sought to fashion a reform agenda that did two things: consolidate his own personal hold on power and simultaneously deal with the nation's problems. It was a difficult balancing act. Reform meant challenging the Brezhnev-era establishment, and that brought increasing personal risk. To his credit, Gorbachev took great risks as he pushed an ever-more-radicalized reform agenda, hoping at each step to forge new alliances and to secure a new power base to preserve a dynamic balance between the needs for reform and stability. But it was also true that at critical moments, especially near the end, Gorbachev backtracked and hesitated to carry reforms through to their logical conclusion.

Glasnost

Gorbachev embraced *glasnost* as an important element of his reform agenda. The term means openness, candor, and truth, and the contemporary Western buzzword that best carries both its content and political implications is *transparency*. At its simplest, it was about changing the nation's information policy. If economic reform were to succeed, especially in the realm of innovation, censorship had to be ended. Once the government began to retreat, there was no stopping the pressures to extend glasnost to all issues and all media.[9]

Glasnost also had a more focused political goal. For generations, virtually all soviet citizens knew that the government lied to them, misinformed them, and forbade public discussion of politically sensitive issues. That manipulation was especially resented by the intelligentsia and the growing professional and middle classes. Any government—and any individual leader—willing to break that silence potentially stood to win the gratitude and support of a vast audience that simply yearned to be told how things really were. Gorbachev gambled on being that leader, and at first the bet paid off.

Glasnost also was used as a blatant political weapon. Skillfully targeted investigative journalism could be a useful tool to discredit Gorbachev's opponents, whose number was increasing as reforms challenged vested interests in the party and government. Gorbachev threatened to fill in the "blank spots" of party history, suggesting that he would use glasnost as Khrushchev had used de-Stalinization to reveal the misdeeds of what was left of the Brezhnev generation. Gorbachev had unwittingly opened a Pandora's box that quickly escaped his control. Glasnost for reform soon spawned glasnost against reform and then against Gorbachev himself.

The Economy: Perestroika

Perestroika simply means rebuilding or reconstruction, and when applied in a social context, it conveys the notion of structural reform. It became the generic buzzword for Gorbachev's attempts to change both the economy and the nation's political life. It was always ambiguous, as it was meant to be. It meant different things to different audiences. To the rapidly growing number of political activists, it was about the details of economic and political change and about the balance sheet of who would gain or lose power and wealth. To the broader population, it was more about hope that things somehow would get better. It engendered a revolution of rising expectations that inevitably could not be satisfied.

As it applied to the economy, *perestroika* at first meant little more than an attempt to improve the central planning system. Gorbachev promised a "speeding up" of economic activity to deal with widespread problems left over from the Brezhnev era and greater reliance on the "human factor" of production, a nod in the direction of Western notions of the importance of human relations management. At first, little was heard of possible structural reforms.[10]

Without doubt, the economic problems Gorbachev inherited were daunting. In 1985, the annual growth rate was about 1.5 percent and dropping, continuing a decline that had begun in the mid-1970s. Technologically, soviet industry was a generation or more behind its Western counterparts, and the gap was widening. State subsidies sustained inefficient and overstaffed factories, and entrepreneurship was discouraged by the complex bureaucracy of the state planning system. Shortages were increasingly common, and rationing was introduced in some areas, such as consumer goods. The much-touted "food program" of the late Brezhnev years, which was designed to provide a more diverse and better diet to the average citizen, had failed, and soviet agriculture was hamstrung by the system of state and collective farms. Prices were set by the state, concealing the real value of raw materials and manufactured goods. A concealed deficit rose rapidly. The Soviet Union remained cut off from the growing global economy, and the ruble remained unconvertible. The so-called "black" and "gray" economies flourished, in some ways compensating for the failures of the formal structures, but at a price. Corruption was widespread and dispiriting.

Gorbachev's first effort at meaningful structural reform came in July 1987, two years after his assumption of power. Factories were now permitted some latitude to cultivate a market beyond the formal production goals set by the government. Soon factories began to reorient their production toward the expanding private market. Additional reforms were offered in May 1988. Privately owned cooperatives could now be formed independently of the state planning system. Reminiscent of V. I. Lenin's New Economic Policy of the 1920s, private entrepreneurs were encouraged to strike out on their own in the area of consumer goods manufacturing and services, especially in those areas in which state enterprises proved least successful.

The once-powerful Ministry of Foreign Trade lost its stranglehold over economic ties with other nations. Now individual factories and ministries could negotiate on their own to reach whatever agreements proved mutually beneficial. Joint ventures were also encouraged, and the initial requirement that the soviet partner exercise majority control was soon eased.

Despite these efforts, things got worse. Although the cooperatives improved access to consumer goods and services in the cities, they initially had little impact elsewhere. State-subsidized industries—the old dinosaurs of the Stalin years—continued to lose money, and reducing their costly and unproductive workforce was politically impossible. The all-important question of privatization was discussed gingerly among economists, but political leaders danced carefully around the issue. Some denounced it on ideological or social grounds, whereas others positioned themselves to become the first generation of post-communist oligarchs.

Judicial Reform

At first Gorbachev largely ignored the question of legal reform. In truth, the judicial branch was simply considered to be one of many mechanisms through which the regime implemented and enforced its policies. Like many institutions in the early soviet period, it played its assigned role in the class struggle to advance the interests of the proletariat over its real and imagined "class enemies," later shifting to a more neutral posture after the advent of a "classless society" in the Stalin era. It always was an instrument of Communist Party rule, however, and certainly not the first that needed serious reform after Gorbachev came to power.

The pre-Gorbachev judicial system was an effective tool for single-party rule. The legalities aside, two realities defined its role. First, the Communist Party controlled the choice of key personnel at all levels of the judicial system. Perhaps more revealing was the long-standing process of "telephone justice," the term used to describe the reality that party officials frequently called prosecutors and judges to dictate how a case should be handled and what decision the judges should hand down. They didn't always call, of course, but the judges knew they could, and acted accordingly.

If detailed reform of the judicial system remained a low priority for Gorbachev, he demonstrated that theoretically his heart was in the right place. Trained as a lawyer at Moscow State University, he spoke out in favor of the creation of a "law-governed state" in which both the rulers and the ruled would operate within the law. It was more than just a platitude. Rather it was an important part of a much broader assault on the dominant role of the Communist Party, which had never felt itself bound by such restrictions.

Foreign Policy

Gorbachev's reform agenda was tied inextricably to the nation's foreign policy. Although the Soviet Union had reached parity with the West in terms of the arms race late in the Brezhnev era, the standoff was a tenuous balance that could be easily upset. The soviet deployment of intermediate-range ballistic missiles in Eastern Europe had led the Americans to match with the positioning of Pershing and cruise missiles in Western Europe. Such intermediate-range weapons introduced a new and potentially destabilizing element into the balance of forces between the two sides, threatening both with the need to add a new and costly weapons system into the mix of strategic and conventional forces.

For its part, the new Ronald Reagan administration seemed more than willing to up the ante. During Reagan's first term, presidential rhetoric returned to the confrontational tone of the early cold war. The Soviet Union was labeled an "evil empire," and Washington seemed more than willing to develop new high-tech weaponry, where it clearly had the advantage, and to engage what it viewed as soviet-inspired revolutionary movements in the third world. Most threatening from Moscow's perspective was the Reagan administration's endorsement of the Strategic Defensive Initiative (SDI, or "Star Wars"), which averred that an umbrella-like defense system could be built to shield the United States from any soviet missile attack.

Economic reform of any sort also required a reassessment of foreign policy. Any attempt to deal with the nation's growing economic problems imposed certain limitations on foreign policy choices. A commitment to rise to the challenge of the deployment of intermediate-range missiles and pursue a soviet version of SDI would require considerable investment at a time when the standard of living for the average Russian had begun to decline. Improving the lot of the consumer meant either shifting investment from the defense sector or opening the country to cheap imports. Acquiring Western technology also required opening the door to contacts with the more advanced capitalist nations, both to encourage foreign investment and to find a market for soviet exports to pay for modernization. Any way that you looked at it, a hardline foreign policy reduced reform options at home. The choice between guns and butter could not be avoided.

To his credit, Gorbachev quickly came to the conclusion that a fundamental reassessment of the ideological basis of soviet foreign policy was in order. Although in the real world the Soviet Union had acted like any other nation in the conduct of its foreign affairs, there remained a distinctly Marxist theory of how the world worked. It posited that the USSR's foreign policy was "class based" and therefore fundamentally different from the policies of other non-socialist nations. In 1987, Gorbachev rejected this basic premise and set forth the theoretical basis for the end of the cold war. In *Perestroika: New Thinking for Our Country and the World*, published simultaneously in Russian and English, he turned the Marxist argument on its ear: Universal human interests take precedence over class interests, tacitly undercutting the last vestiges of commitment to soviet-inspired revolutions. According to "new thinking," the world was now increasingly interdependent; security could only be mutual among all major powers, based more on political and diplomatic efforts than on military strength alone; and there would be no victors in a future nuclear war. Gorbachev increasingly spoke of the importance of global human values and of "our common European home," linking the fate of the Soviet Union to Western Europe.[11]

With the theoretical compass now reset, Gorbachev got down to the serious business of changing the world. He had already made some headway in improving relations with the West even before becoming general secretary. Under Andropov, he had become a sort of roving ambassador, showing a new face of soviet power to the West and convincing once-skeptical conservative leaders such as British prime minister Margaret Thatcher that "we can do business together." Once in power, he moved quickly to change the tone of soviet foreign policy. In April 1985, he suspended the soviet deployment of intermediate-range nuclear missiles in Eastern Europe, salving one of the sore points that had roiled the North Atlantic Treaty Organization (NATO) and the Warsaw Treaty nations. In September of that year, he proposed that both the United States and the USSR cut their nuclear arsenals in half. In November, he had his first meeting with Reagan at a summit in Geneva, Switzerland. Although there were no concrete agreements, both men were positively impressed with each other. In January 1986, Gorbachev upped the ante, proposing the elimination of all intermediate nuclear forces (INFs) in Europe and the destruction of all nuclear weapons by 2000.

In October 1986, Gorbachev and Reagan met again in Reykjavik, Iceland, to discuss INFs in Europe. Although the meeting ended in a continuing stalemate, the changing tone set the stage for an important breakthrough. Soon after, both nations agreed to remove all such weapons from Europe and to limit INF warheads and delivery systems to 100 for each side outside of Europe. They also agreed in principle to eliminate all nuclear weapons by 1996, four years ahead of Gorbachev's earlier proposal, although issues of verification and the development of SDI scotched the implementation of the agreement. But the most important deal had been struck—INFs were off the table, with the formal agreement signed in 1987—and the stage was set for further cooperation.

Early in 1988, Gorbachev began the withdrawal of soviet military forces from Afghanistan. Initially begun as what Moscow thought would be a quick and low-cost intervention in an Afghan civil war, the conflict had dragged on inconclusively since 1979. Nearly 28,000 soviet soldiers had been killed, and the continuing intervention had become a litmus test of Moscow's true willingness to change its foreign policy.

Gorbachev also sought to improve relations with China. Chinese leaders were deeply suspicious of the soviet leader's reforms at home, and continuing tensions associated with the increasing militarization of the disputed Russian–Chinese border stoked a long-standing dispute. Gorbachev's efforts to resolve these issues brought about a summit meeting in Beijing in May 1989, the first high-level exchange since the split between the two nations.

Far more important in the long run was Moscow's continued involvement in Eastern Europe. Its strategic importance as a buffer zone had diminished over the years, and the occasional efforts of countries like Poland, Hungary, and Czechoslovakia to break free or at the least to reduce Moscow's control had always resulted in a crisis in which Moscow had to dramatically reassert its control, usually also producing a distinct chill in relations with the West. Since the soviet invasion of Czechoslovakia in 1968, Moscow defined its role in the region in terms of the Brezhnev Doctrine. Stripped of its rhetoric about the solidarity of socialist nations, this doctrine said that Moscow reserved the right to intervene in the domestic affairs of any Eastern bloc country that attempted unacceptable internal reforms (that usually meant ending the dominant role of the local Communist Party) or threatened to leave the Warsaw Treaty organization.

The problem was that Gorbachev's own reforms at home now sounded very much like those that the doctrine denied to Eastern Europeans. In 1988, Gorbachev made it clear that the Brezhnev Doctrine no longer applied, and in July 1989, speaking before the Council of Europe, he confirmed that each of the satellite nations would be permitted to choose its own course of reforms. That opened the floodgates to the end of communism in Eastern Europe as each nation sought its own path to democratic reforms and disengagement from the Warsaw Treaty. The Berlin Wall came down, setting the stage for the eventual reunification of Germany, which Gorbachev openly supported.[12]

Only weeks after the fall of the Berlin Wall, Gorbachev met with the new U.S. president, George H. W. Bush, in a hastily arranged summit in Malta. The meeting produced an informal declaration by both sides that the cold war was over, although none of the other countries that had been a part of the opposing alliance systems took part. Malta was chosen because it was the site of a February 1945 meeting between U.S. president Franklin Roosevelt and British prime minister Winston Churchill, both on their way to the Yalta Conference at which the outlines of the coming cold war became increasingly apparent. Forty-four years later, Malta, long neutral in the cold war, was to host the end of the confrontation.

Over the next two years, both the Council of Mutual Economic Assistance, the soviet-led economic bloc, and the Warsaw Treaty Organization, the Eastern counterpart to NATO, were formally dissolved. Soviet troops were withdrawn from the Warsaw Treaty area as quickly as they could be resettled at home. In November 1990, both the United States and the USSR signed the Treaty on Conventional Forces in Europe, which sought to reduce and to place future limits on nonnuclear armaments, although considerable dispute would later arise over implementation and compliance. Later that year, the USSR joined Western nations in condemning the Iraqi invasion of Kuwait, setting the stage for United Nations–sanctioned military action. In the summer of 1991, Gorbachev and Bush signed the Strategic Arms Reduction Treaty (START), which provided for the first time for a drawdown of both sides' nuclear arsenals and the destruction of delivery systems.[13]

In 1990, Gorbachev received the Nobel Peace Prize. Only one other Russian had ever received this most coveted accolade: the scientist-turned-dissident Andrei Sakharov, held under house arrest for much of the Brezhnev era and freed by Gorbachev to join in the reform movement. Gorbachev also was named *Time* magazine's Man of the Decade, having already been honored as Man of the Year. The world was clearly changing, and much of it was more than willing to recognize Gorbachev's role. But at home it was a different story.

Political Reform: Democratization

Perestroika also included a transformation of the nation's political institutions. Subsumed under the general buzzword *democratization,* these changes were both an end and a means. As a goal, they were consistent with Gorbachev's desire to modernize soviet society; as a theoretically correct Marxist, he accepted the reality that the modernization of society, long ignored during the Brezhnev period of "stagnation," required that the nation's political institutions also be transformed. Both the Communist Party and the government at all levels must be made more responsive and accountable to the public. In Gorbachev's way of thinking, this would further strengthen the public's commitment to building a socialist society. As he saw it, a transformed and democratic Communist Party would still lead the nation, now earning its power through the ballot box. There was a danger, of course: The party might reject the new role, in which case it would lose both its relevance and its commanding position in a new democratic order. But Gorbachev assumed, at least at first, that the party, under his leadership, would rise to the challenge.

But then again, it might not. That led Gorbachev to hedge his bets. The newly democratized institutions could provide an alternative power base for a general secretary who came under fire from the party hierarchy. Gorbachev could not ignore the lesson of Khrushchev's dismissal. Party leaders can be voted out of power whenever the Politburo and the Central Committee choose. The creation of a new national legislature, the Congress of People's Deputies, would require the simultaneous creation of a new top-level executive position, whether envisioned as the de jure head of state as the chairman of the Presidium of the Supreme Soviet (the Brezhnev-era title) or as a newly created presidency (the position that eventually emerged). That post could provide Gorbachev with a safe haven in the coming storm.[14]

Democratization was also a means to an end. Like glasnost, Gorbachev envisioned it as a way to win public support for reform. Initially the gamble seemed to pay off. The first (and only) election to the new national legislature, the Congress of People's Deputies, brought a significant number of nonparty and reform-oriented delegates into office, although the soviet era "establishment" retained majority control, especially in the smaller but more important Supreme Soviet. Elections to local soviets produced even more striking results; in many instances, the establishment was completely swept from power. Reformers took control in Moscow and Leningrad, and in the latter, Anatoly Sobchak, a professor in the law school at St. Petersburg State University who had emerged as the leader of reform forces in city, began to advance the career of a former KGB operative turned reformer named Vladimir Putin.

But like glasnost, democratization also could be turned against its creator. Despite the initial rush of excitement and hope that greeted the first wave of democratic reforms, things began to sour. Gorbachev soon found himself under attack from two directions. On one hand, a growing number of opponents argued that the process of reform should be accelerated, and public resentment of the lagging pace of economic reforms soon found its voice through the ballot box. On the other hand, fear that reforms had gone too far, deeply rooted in the more conservative elements of the Communist Party, also found voice through the de facto communist dominance of the Supreme Soviet.

Far more dangerous to Gorbachev's hopes for reform were the emerging nationalist movements at the union republic level.[15] Following Gorbachev's lead, most union republic leaders created, usually in simplified form, a republic-level Congress of People's Deputies. In the subsequent elections, two trends emerged. First, the representatives of legitimate nationalist movements, long suppressed by soviet authorities, became important players in the political process. Second, seeing the handwriting on the wall, many high-level communist leaders downplayed their Communist Party connections and their past cooperation with Moscow and "discovered" their true national identity. In both cases, the ascendance of local nationalist issues soon changed politics at the republic level and complicated the relationship with central authorities, setting the stage for the eventual breakup of the Soviet Union.

Democratization of the Communist Party

Getting control of the party itself and convincing it to accept internal democratization were the first steps. Gorbachev proceeded cautiously at first. At the Twenty-Seventh Party Congress, convened exactly thirty years after the congress at which Khrushchev had denounced Stalin, Gorbachev increased pressure for internal reforms, calling on the party to acknowledge its recent shortcomings and fill in the "blank spots" in its history. A year later, he ratcheted up the pressure, calling on the party to redefine its relationship with the government. In the past, the party had provided policy leadership and also reserved the right to meddle in the day-to-day affairs of government. Now Gorbachev called for it to take a step back, retaining its role as the directing force of soviet society but permitting the government to deal with implementing its program. Resistance continued from within the party bureaucracy, leading Gorbachev to call for a party conference (not the same as a congress) in the near future to consider even more radical changes.[16]

The squabbling over calling a party conference soon revealed a further polarization within the party. Two roughly defined factions existed. One, led by Yegor Ligachev, a conservative member of the Politburo, resisted further changes and defended the traditional role of the party. The second, led by Boris Yeltsin, who had grown increasingly radical in his new post as de facto mayor of Moscow, called for speeding up and deepening of reforms. Gorbachev occupied the middle ground, hoping that he could play one element against the other.

The party conference was finally convened in June 1988. It was a turning point in Gorbachev's efforts to change the institutional features of the Stalinist system. Despite misgivings on the part of conservatives, the conference endorsed Gorbachev's proposal to scrap the old legislature and create a new Congress of People's Deputies. Partially to be chosen through truly competitive elections, it would establish a more direct line of communication between the people and the regime. Not incidentally, it would provide a new post for Gorbachev himself, first as speaker of the legislature and then, after some further adjustment to the constitution, as president of the nation as a whole.

At first the new arrangement seemed perfect for Gorbachev. He masterfully orchestrated the first publicly televised session of the Congress, demanding the implementation of his reform agenda and prodding the delegates to embolden their actions. It was great political theater, drawing a virtual gavel-to-gavel audience of ordinary citizens who had never seen the like. The Congress chose Gorbachev to the highest executive position that then existed, the equivalent of a speaker of the house, although the role still seemed largely ceremonial and was different from the post of prime minister, which still supervised the ministries. Gorbachev quickly began to transfer the base of his operations from the Central Committee headquarters on Old Square to the Kremlin, where the legislature was located. Although the physical distance between the two locations can be walked in ten minutes, the political distance can be measured only in light years. Like Stalin and Khrushchev before him, he had moved the center of the political universe in a direction that he hoped benefitted him.[17]

The Gorbachev Presidency

The creation of a new legislature and the appointment of Gorbachev to its most important executive post—but not yet a *presidency*—was an important victory, yet real and potential problems still existed. Gorbachev remained the target of growing criticism from within the conservative party bureaucracy. If the 1989 elections had indeed been the wake-up call that Gorbachev intended, not everybody got the same message. Some read it the way Gorbachev hoped—reform efforts had real public support, and it was politically expedient to get on the bandwagon. But others took away the opposite message—reform, and Gorbachev as its leader, were dangerous and should be vigorously opposed. The debate within the party intensified, especially as the question of greater autonomy or outright independence for the non-Russian republics raised the stakes to the survival of the Soviet Union itself.

The second problem lay in the insidious nature of democratization itself. If you get a little, you'll probably want more. The balance that had been institutionalized in the Congress of People's Deputies was what Gorbachev had wanted. The Congress would more broadly represent the people as a whole and probably be a more radical body in criticizing the government and pressing for more reform. The smaller and more experienced Supreme Soviet would be a check on the zeal of the lower body, and it would be the real power center in terms of legislative and administrative decision making.

Further complicating the equation was the reality that growing rivalry emerged between the executive "branch" and the legislature. Technically, of course, the speaker of the legislature was chosen from among its own members, but Gorbachev soon sought to ignore that distinction. Motivated by the need to create an alternative power base separate from the party, and now at least partially set apart from the Congress itself, Gorbachev called for the creation of a strong executive office. The idea had been discussed earlier and rejected as too radical a change. Planning to define the new post began in earnest shortly after the election of the Congress of People's Deputies and provoked a serious battle within the party, which clearly understood its implications. The Politburo debated the question in mid-January 1990. Ligachev, the de facto second secretary and leader of the conservative faction, opposed creation of the new office, arguing that it would accelerate the shift of power from the party to the government. In the end, the Politburo dutifully approved Gorbachev's request. Early in January 1991, the proposal went to the Supreme Soviet, which approved it on February 7. Several weeks of meetings followed to hammer out the details of the office and to win support from the union republics and the legislature. On March 6, the Congress of People's Deputies approved the changes needed to the constitution, and almost anticlimactically ten days later, Gorbachev was elected by an overwhelming vote of 1,817 to 113 to become the first—and only—president of the USSR.[18]

Gorbachev got his presidency, but what sort of presidency was it? At first glance, it seemed powerful, at least on paper. The president would nominate the prime minister, subject to confirmation by the legislature; had a veto over legislation; could dismiss the government; could issue presidential decrees that had the force of law; could ask the Congress of People's Deputies to dissolve the Supreme Soviet and choose a new one from among its own ranks; could institute direct presidential rule and invoke states of emergency, although subsequent legislative approval would be necessary; could act as commander-in-chief of the armed forces; and could set forth "the main directions of the USSR's foreign and domestic policy." As the situation deteriorated, the president was granted special authority to deal with economic problems and nationality issues.

From the start, there were limitations and liabilities. Gorbachev had been chosen by the Congress of People's Deputies, not the people themselves; thus, his "democratic" legitimacy could easily be challenged, especially as the new crop of "presidents" who emerged in the union republics won their spurs in popular (but frequently manipulated) elections. Second, the central government in Moscow was rapidly losing power and authority to the union republic governments, further compromising the power of the national presidency. While he retained the post of general secretary of the Communist Party and would even be reelected in the last party congress, Gorbachev had clearly cast his lot with the government and the new presidency, making it easier for those who remained in the Politburo eventually to plot a coup against their former comrade.

Piecing together the presidential staff proved difficult. It was cobbled together by drawing from Gorbachev's own circle of advisors and from the Central Committee staff on Old Square. The old Central Committee work style was difficult to change, which hardly inspired a deepening of reforms. The Presidential Council was said to function just like the old Politburo; same room, participants in the same seats, same refreshments.[19] The more things change. . . .

The Presidency of the Russian Federation

Before giving a more detailed accounting of the creation of the office of the Russian presidency, it is necessary to tell the beginning of the story before the disintegration of the Soviet Union. The last year of the Soviet Union was marked by growing struggle between the central government in Moscow (Gorbachev's stronghold, although his power was slipping) and the republic governments. Copying Moscow's lead, as they always did, the republics created their own versions of the Congress of People's Deputies and a presidency. In some republics, especially in the Baltics, free elections brought independent nationalists to power. In other areas, especially Central Asia and the Ukraine, former communist leaders quickly discovered their national roots and retained power under a new flag, frequently through manipulated elections. In others, the new arrangement produced a mixture of the old and the new.

The Russian Federation was the most important of those mixed cases. Always the most important of the fifteen republics that made up the Soviet Union, its grievances against the center were different from most of the other republics. To be sure, soviet authorities had always suppressed purely Russian nationalism, preferring instead the officially sanctioned version of "soviet" identity. To the extent that some Russian nationalists resented this fiction, they welcomed the creation of a purely Russian-level government as a means to an end. Russians also resented the fact that Moscow poured investment into non-Russian areas, especially the least developed or where such largess was intended by buy local support.

But the real importance of the creation of a new legislature and presidency for the Russian Federation lay in its role in setting the stage for a battle between the two men who most shaped the history of their nation—Mikhail Gorbachev and Boris Yeltsin. For our immediate purposes, suffice it to say that the Russian presidency was different from the soviet presidency in one important way—it was popularly elected, giving the incumbent real legitimacy. Each man would use the newly created legislatures and presidencies for his own political purposes, Gorbachev to bring new life to his reform agenda and reduce the threat of the party bureaucracy, and Yeltsin to stage a political comeback and take revenge on Gorbachev, who had tried to destroy him.

The Battle of the Presidents

Both Gorbachev and Yeltsin began their careers in remarkably similar fashion—as up-and-coming regional party secretaries whose performance and connections brought them to important posts in Moscow. Gorbachev had made the leap during the Brezhnev years; Yeltsin followed later in the Gorbachev era, initially with Gorbachev himself as his patron. Yeltsin's initial experiences in the capital radicalized him. He now became what Gorbachev derisively called an "ultra-perestroikist," someone who wanted to speed dangerously ahead with reforms. The two fought openly in 1987, much to Yeltsin's disadvantage. Broken and demoted to a mid-level job in the vast bureaucracy, Yeltsin would be no more than a very small footnote in a very big history of the era.

Gorbachev's insistence on creating a new legislature, and the extension of that idea to the republics, gave Yeltsin the mechanism to make a comeback. In March 1989, Yeltsin was elected to the Congress of People's Deputies of the Soviet Union; a year later he won a seat in the Russian Republic's Congress and was soon elevated to the post of speaker. In June 1991, he was popularly elected to the presidency, setting the stage for a war of presidents.

The rivalry between the two men was about more than just institutional roles and disagreement about the pace of reforms. It was deeply personal. At its root lay fundamentally different styles of leadership. Gorbachev was cerebral, calculating, and self-assured, almost to the end. He knew how to fix the country and how to win popular support, but he probably never fully understood those who opposed his reforms. He lectured, explained, and hectored, often speaking over the heads of the general public. It was your job to understand him, not his job to understand you. The definitive moment of his career—his zenith—came at the first session of the national Congress of People's Deputies, where he played ringmaster to the new circus of soviet democracy. Yeltsin, by contrast, had the common touch. Far from cerebral and polished, he spoke his mind and shot from the hip. He had his faults, but that just made him human. And he connected, at least at first. Whereas Gorbachev could analyze the causes and cures for the nation's worsening problems, Yeltsin could feel your pain, and he knew how to turn it to political purpose. His defining moment came not on the floor of the new Congress but precariously on the top of a tank, where he stood to defend democracy against counter-revolution during the August 1991 coup attempt.

The deepening conflict between Gorbachev and Yeltsin centered on two issues—economic reform and the relationship between the central government in Moscow and the increasingly bold republic-level govern-ments. Gorbachev's always-vague plans for perestroika had never spelled out concrete guidance; now the economy was in shambles, and a clear course of action was needed. Two different responses were possible. The first envisioned a gradual transition, with privatization and subsidies and price supports, especially for basics such as food and rent, withdrawn slowly so as to diminish the social and political ramifications. The other course was a cold-turkey transition that saw a quick shift to a market econ-omy. Leading economists drew up a 500-day transition timetable, sort of halfway between the two extremes. Now no longer certain that he could control events, Gorbachev equivocated. Yeltsin strongly endorsed the pro-posal, in part because it accelerated the reform process and probably in part because his bold action underscored Gorbachev's uncertainty.[20]

The second issue was the nationalities question, and particularly whether some or perhaps all of the republics could break away. The USSR had been created by the Union Treaty in 1922, and the fiction had always been maintained that the "sovereign" republics could exercise their right of secession. In reality, three things had held the union together: the sheer power of the central government's military forces, now in decline and pos-sibly unreliable; the presence of the Communist Party, now in shambles at the center and virtually destroyed in many of the republics; and the mutu-ally profitable economic ties that linked all republics, now compromised by the economic problems at all levels and the growing propensity for regional officials to withhold taxes from the center.

Attempting to forestall the total disintegration of the Soviet Union, Gorbachev tentatively began to discuss the possibility of "revisions" to the Union Treaty. Initially details were scarce, but the talks held out the possibility that perhaps the Baltic republics could leave altogether, while a looser union could be created for the others, possibly with different levels of membership from weak to strong association. As the republics acquired increasing latitude, interest in a tightly knit union diminished. A "war of laws" began, with the laws of the central government applicable in the republics only if the republics themselves seconded them.[21]

For his part, Yeltsin turned up the heat from his vantage point as president of the Russian Republic. In June 1991, the Russian legislature proclaimed sovereignty, as many of the other republics had or soon would do as well. The republics began to talk directly to one another about the nature of a new Union Treaty. Yeltsin's increasingly visible role as the leader of the most important republic and the primary thorn in Gorbachev's side gave him additional influence and perhaps inspired others to stand up to the center.

Increasingly uncertain of the future, Gorbachev began to hedge his bets at the Twenty-Eighth Party Congress in July 1990. He was reelected to the office of general secretary, now far less important than the presidency. Over the summer, he continued to walk a tightrope between the party's reformist and conservative factions. Late in the year he seemed to shift to a more conservative stance, replacing a number of proreform cabinet members with new appointees overwhelmingly drawn from the military or security apparatus. He backed away from further economic reform, undoubtedly because difficult decisions were now required, and took a harder line on loosening Moscow's control over the republics. These moves cost him support from liberal forces and brought the resignation of Eduard Shevarnadze, the foreign minister and future head of an independent Georgia.

Stung by these events, Gorbachev shifted to the center once again, reviving the idea of creating a new Union Treaty. A March referendum had produced mixed signals. Although 76 percent of those who voted supported the continued existence of the Soviet Union in one form or another, six of the fifteen republics refused to participate, indicating their interest in breaking away. Late in April, the leaders of the nine republics that took part pledged to speed up the drafting of a new treaty and implicitly acknowledged that the others could leave the union. The agreement also promised the drafting of a new constitution and elections six months after the treaty was signed.

The new treaty was to be signed in Moscow on August 20, 1991. The day didn't quite go as planned. On August 19 a long-considered coup attempt was launched. Its leaders constituted themselves as the State Committee on the State of Emergency; in fact, many had been promoted during Gorbachev's brief shift to the right months earlier. They constituted the usual suspects for such events: the minister of defense, the minister of the interior (who controlled the national police), the head of the KGB, and an assortment of real and token leaders of the conservative bloc. Their stated goals seemed modest—the restoration of public order, a "reconsideration" of the draft Union Treaty, and promises to continue other reforms. But their intent was clear.

Gorbachev was out of town—literally. He was at his dacha at Foros, in the Ukraine. He had been informed of the pending coup the day before and asked to sign a decree establishing a state of emergency, seemingly legitimizing the event. He refused, at least according to his own account, and was held in isolation for the next several days as events unfolded in Moscow. In time-honored soviet tradition, his captors explained that he was "ill" and needed rest.

On the morning of August 19, Moscovites awakened to an announcement that the State Committee had taken control of the government. Presumably loyal troops moved into the city, and a few top-level reformers were taken into custody. But not Boris Yeltsin. He rushed to his office at the so-called "White House"—the seat of the Russian Republic government, far from the Kremlin—to take control of an emerging resistance movement. From the beginning, military units began to express support for the Yeltsin government, include key tank units sent to the White House. In one of the most dramatic moments of the transformation of Russia, Yeltsin climbed onto a tank to rally the crowd and the nation—and, inexplicably, state-controlled television carried it verbatim on the evening news. Around the country, similar resistance movements emerged in the major cities; but other areas cautiously bided their time to let events unfold.

The next day was a standoff. Pro-Yeltsin crowds at the White House grew in size and self-confidence, while the leaders of the State Committee planned for an assault on the White House. The assault was labeled "operation *grom*"—thunder—and was to begin at two the next morning. One hour before the scheduled attack, an incident at a makeshift barricade near the White House caused the death of three civilians, and the crowd responded by burning an armored personnel carrier. In the face of civilian resistance and growing dissention within the military forces designated to dislodge Yeltsin's government, the leaders of the coup lost their nerve and ordered the withdrawal of all military forces from Moscow. Seeking to find a political solution to the crisis they had created, they sent a delegation to Foros to negotiate with the still-imprisoned Gorbachev. He refused to meet with them. With communications restored to his dacha, Gorbachev voided all of the plotters' proclamations and returned to Moscow to reclaim the leadership of his nation.[22]

Except it wasn't his anymore. He was not welcomed back as a hero, but as a bumbling leader whose own actions in appointing many of the plotters to positions of authority had nearly destroyed the hope for democratic reform. Yeltsin was the man of the hour, and he rose to the role with single-minded resolve. The Russian Republic's legislature at the White House was now clearly in charge, not the national government in the Kremlin. Called to account for his unwitting contributions to the failed coup attempt, Gorbachev tried to adjust to the new reality. On August 24, he resigned his post as general secretary of the Communist Party and called upon the Central Committee to disband. But he refused to condemn the party per se, hoping that its more progressive elements might still play a role in public life. Yeltsin went further, banning the party in the Russian Republic and seizing its assets.

While Gorbachev and a few of the republic leaders tried to revive consideration of a new and even looser Union Treaty after the coup attempt, there was little hope of success. A new draft offered in November opted for the creation of a limited and poorly defined coordinating role for a new central government; it was initially backed by Yeltsin, who correctly saw that Russia would emerge as a senior partner in any new arrangement, and by some of the Central Asian republics, which hoped to continue economic ties with the center. Opposition was strongest from the Ukraine, which delayed its decision until after a December 1 referendum on independence. Not surprisingly, the Ukraine voted heavily for a complete break from Moscow, killing any chance that a central government could be formed.

On December 7, the leaders of Russia, the Ukraine, and Belarus signed the Belavezha Accords, which formally proclaimed the dissolution of the Soviet Union and the creation of a looser association called the Commonwealth of Independent States. On December 24, under pressure from some of the other republics that wished to be a part of the new commonwealth, the leaders of all of the former republics except Latvia, Lithuania, Estonia, and Georgia signed the Alma-Ata Accords, which broadened the new association's membership but did little to make its role any clearer.

The next day, December 25, Gorbachev resigned from the presidency. Formal power soon passed from the Kremlin to the republic governments, which were now independent states. Gorbachev's revolution was over, and the immediate future of Russia lay in the hands of his worst enemy, Boris Yeltsin. The crimson hammer-and-sickle flag of the Soviet Union was lowered in the Kremlin, and the Russian tri-color was raised, signifying the end of an era. Lenin's experiment had lasted seventy-four years, one month, and twenty-eight days, including all the extra days for leap years.

Gorbachev as an Authoritarian Modernizer

Assessing Gorbachev as an authoritarian modernizer is a complex task. We would prefer not to think of him in these terms; modernizer yes, but authoritarian? There is little doubt that by the end of his tenure in office, his vision of the future included a modernized post-single-party democratic political system that he hoped would be ruled by a popularly elected Communist Party and dominated, at least at first, by a president elected by the Congress of People's Deputies. Had the Soviet Union survived, it is highly likely that future presidential elections would have handed over to the electorate the choice of the top office. Precisely that transformation had occurred in the French Fifth Republic, after which the Russian office had been modeled. Once stability had returned in the early 1960s, Charles de Gaulle amended the French constitution to create a popularly elected presidency to replace the originally indirectly elected office. Gorbachev also accepted the need for a market-based economy, although he was uncertain of the path forward to its creation and largely unconcerned with the collateral costs and the redistribution of wealth into private hands. He reluctantly came to accept substantial changes in the nature of soviet federalism and the revision of the Union Treaty. In some cases he himself had initiated a process of change only to lose control as more radical leaders came forward. In other cases, like the growing demand for greater regional autonomy and eventual secession, he had to cope with issues that others put on the table. There is little argument that, in his own way, Gorbachev was willing to prod both the Communist Party and the nation as a whole into the new future he envisioned for them.

To Gorbachev's credit, his goals were bold and grew more revolutionary with time. He began his rule with a general but progressive notion of what "modern" could mean in the Soviet Union of the late twentieth century, one that grew more radical with time. In Gorbachev's hands, the reforms accepted Western notions of an open society, a mature industrial economy, and democratic rule, albeit with strong executive leadership.

They promised a sweeping transformation of the society from top to bottom, including a rejection of the earlier Leninist-Stalinist authoritarian model of transformational rule, but not the premise that political leaders could and should reshape society; a deemphasis and rebooting of the roles of both the Communist Party and the state; the creation of a new business model for the economy in many ways parallel to the mixed market-/state-regulated and state-manipulated economies of the West, coupled with technological and managerial modernization, entrepreneurialism, and globalization; and a profound shift in the nation's foreign and defense policies and a rejection of the ideological premises that had provided the rationalization of Moscow's foreign policy since the revolution. To be sure, the list was often long on rhetoric and hope and short on detail and road maps, but that was consistent with the actions of other authoritarian modernizers whose programs had been put forth in bits and pieces.

There also was a distinctly authoritarian side to Gorbachev's role as a modernizer. Clearly he was no Lenin or Stalin, and he never tried to be. But he knew that he needed to consolidate his own personal power if he were to survive and find whatever combinations of sticks and carrots would be needed to lead the Soviet Union through a process of disruptive reforms. That led him to shift power from one institutional base (the Communist Party) to another (the government, especially a newly created and not democratically elected presidency). At first, Gorbachev thought he could use the visibility and unique nature of the presidency to lead an unruly Congress of People's Deputies and more malleable Supreme Soviet and to win public support. But Gorbachev was never elected to anything in an open and democratic election. The presidency never developed as the power base and bully pulpit that Gorbachev had intended, and he never possessed the legitimacy and popular support needed to press forward with further reforms. Weakened by continuing divisions within the Congress and the Supreme Soviet and Gorbachev's equivocation, and outflanked by the rise of powerful elected presidents at the republic level, the presidency never became the institutional weapon that Gorbachev had hoped.

Therein lies a subtle but important distinction between the authoritarian modernizers of the late nineteenth and early twentieth centuries and their counterparts in today's world. In one important sense, the nature of the playing field has changed in terms of the legitimation and formal institutionalization of those who aspire to be the authoritarian modernizers of today's world. The almost global spread of democracy described by Samuel Huntington in *The Third Wave*, the fall of communism in the

Soviet Union and Eastern Europe, and the Arab Spring now place far greater importance on the formal institutionalization of democratic rule.[23] On this issue, Gorbachev's presidency was fatally flawed in part because it could not lay claim to a direct popular mandate. At the time he probably thought that the distinction made little difference, at least in the short term; his personal popularity would bridge the gap. But as other republic-level leaders like Yeltsin won office by popular vote and Gorbachev's popularity waned, it increasingly eroded his legitimacy in office. This is not to say, of course, that elections alone are the key to legitimacy. But authoritarian modernizers go to increasing lengths to make it appear that they have legitimately won popular support and to risk the consequences of popular rejection. As noted in Chapter 1, contemporary authoritarian modernizers frequently create what analysts now term "electoral authoritarianism," in which elections are "broadly inclusive" but "minimally pluralistic . . . competitive . . . [and] open," but which under certain circumstances can topple even the most authoritarian government.[24] Elections still remain important both as sources of legitimacy and as points of vulnerability; they still count in ways far more significantly than the staged single-party elections of the soviet era. As we will see, Yeltsin wisely resisted the recommendation from some of his staff to "postpone" the 1996 presidential election, although there was a real chance that he could lose. And Putin refused to see the constitution of the Russian Federation amended to permit him to run for a third consecutive term. Both chose to risk the possibility of defeat to preserve the electoral process as a critical component of democratic legitimacy.

Notes

1. Jerry F. Hough and Merle Fainsod, *How the Soviet Union Is Governed*, Harvard University Press, 370–375.

2. Robert T. Huber and Donald R. Kelley, eds., *Perestroika Era Politics: The New Soviet Legislature and Gorbachev's Political Reforms*, M. E. Sharpe, 1991; and Donald R. Kelley, *Politics in Russia and the Successor States*, Harcourt Brace, 1999, 276–281.

3. Richard E. Neustadt, *Presidential Power: The Politics of Leadership*, Wiley, 1960.

4. Thomas M. Nichols, *The Russian Presidency: Society and Politics in the Second Russian Republic*, St. Martin's, 1999, 42–43.

5. Mikhail S. Gorbachev, *Memoirs*, Doubleday, 1996; Zhores A. Medvedev, *Gorbachev*, Norton, 1986; George W. Breslauer, *Gorbachev and Yeltsin as Leaders*, Cambridge University Press, 2002; and Gail Sheehy, *The Man Who Changed the World: The Lives of Mikhail S. Gorbachev*, Harper Collins, 1990.

6. Jerry F. Hough, *The Soviet Prefects*, Harvard University Press, 1969.

7. Donald R. Kelley, *Soviet Politics from Brezhnev to Gorbachev*, Praeger, 1987.

8. Sheehy, *The Man Who Changed the World*.

9. Gorbachev, *Memoirs*, 201–214, 258–259; Joseph Gibbs, *Gorbachev's Glasnost: Soviet Media in the First Phase of Perestroika*, Texas A&M University Press, 1999; and Walter Laqueur, *The Long Road to Freedom: Russia and Glasnost*, Collier, 1990.

10. Gorbachev, *Memoirs*, 215–236; Mikhail Gorbachev, *Perestroika*, Harper and Row, 1987; Archie Brown, *Seven Years that Changed the World: Perestroika in Perspective*, Oxford University Press, 2009; Anders Aslund, *Gorbachev's Struggle for Economic Reform*, Cornell University Press, 1989; Anders Aslund, *Russia's Capitalist Revolution: Why Market Reforms Succeeded and Democracy Failed*, Peterson Institute, 2007; Jerry F. Hough, *Democratization and Revolution in the USSR, 1985–1991*, Brookings, 1997, 103–139, 341–373; Marshall Goldman, *Piratization of Russia: Russian Economic Reforms Goes Awry*, Routledge, 2003; Marshall Goldman, *What Went Wrong with Perestroika*, Norton, 1991; and Peter Reddaway and Dmitri Glinski, *The Tragedy of Russia's Reforms*, U.S. Institute of Peace, 2001, 231–308.

11. Mikhail Gorbachev, *Perestroika: New Thinking for Our Country and the World*, Harper Collins, 1987.

12. Glenn R. Chafetz, ed., *Gorbachev, Reform, and the Brezhnev Doctrine: Soviet Policy toward Eastern Europe, 1985–1990*, Praeger, 1993.

13. Jack Matlock, *Reagan and Gorbachev: How the Cold War Ended*, Random House, 2005; Coit R. Blacker, *Hostage to Revolution: Gorbachev and Soviet Security Policy, 1985–1991*, Council on Foreign Relations, 1993; John Lewis Gaddis, *The Cold War: A New History*, Penguin, 2006; and Raymond Garthoff, *The Great Transformation: American-Soviet Relations and the End of the Cold War*, Brookings, 1994.

14. Gorbachev, *Memoirs*, 278–325; Michael McFaul, Nikolai Petrov, and Andrei Ryabov, *Between Dictatorship and Democracy: Russia's Post-communist Political Reform*, Carnegie Endowment, 2004; and Michael McFaul, *Russia's Unfinished Revolution*, Cornell University Press, 2002.

15. Gorbachev, *Memoirs*, 326–347; and Hough, *Democratization and Revolution*, 214–248.

16. Gorbachev, *Memoirs*, 348-371; and Hough, *Democratization and Revolution*, 249–277.

17. Eugene Huskey, *Presidential Power in Russia*, M. E. Sharpe, 1999, 13–14.

18. Huskey, *Presidential*, 15–16.

19. Huskey, *Presidential*, 23–24.

20. Gorbachev, *Memoirs*, 378–397; and Aslund, *Gorbachev's Struggle for Economic Reform*.

21. Gorbachev, *Memoirs*, 389–396, 614–669; and Hough, *Democratization and Revolution*, 373–404.

22. Gorbachev, *Memoirs*, 626–672; Hough, *Democratization and Revolution*, 404-448; and Colton, *Yeltsin*, 263–292.

23. Samuel Huntington, *The Third Wave: Democratization in the Late Twentieth Century*, University of Oklahoma Press, 1991.

24. Andreas Schedler, ed., *Electoral Authoritarianism: The Dynamics of Unfree Competition*, Lynne Reinner, 2006.

3

The Yeltsin Presidency, 1991–1993

W hen the Russian tri-color was raised over the Kremlin, everything had changed, and nothing had changed, at least for the time being. Gone were the Soviet Union and its last leader, Mikhail Gorbachev. Gone too were the formal trappings of the soviet era. The Russian Federation had a new flag, a new coat of arms, and—briefly, until nostalgia took over—a new national anthem. The center of the political universe, the Communist Party, was deposed from its commanding position, disorganized and dispirited, and briefly banned until the courts overturned Boris Yeltsin's efforts to administer the death blow.

But some things had not changed. Almost all of the actors in the new game of democratic politics had been in government or party positions during the communist era, most in high-level posts. Although the formal institutions were different—the Congress of People's Deputies and the Supreme Soviet, as well as the presidency itself had existed only briefly before the fall of the Soviet Union—the people were the same, playing out new roles they did not fully understand and making it up as they went along. The constitution under which they ruled had been drafted in 1978, following the adoption of a new document for the Union of Soviet Socialist Republics itself, and subsequently amended nearly 200 times, especially after the beginning of Gorbachev's reforms.

Yeltsin's Path to Moscow

In many ways, Yeltsin was typical of the new leaders who emerged in the final years of the USSR. Thoroughly a creature of the old order, he and his cohorts saw both the failures of the system and the opportunities for personal advancement in learning to play the new game of democratic and ethnic politics. He had a foot in both worlds, but unlike Gorbachev, he managed to keep his balance as the ground shifted.

BORIS YELTSIN

- Born February 1, 1931, in Butka, Sverdlovsk Province; died April 23, 2007.
- Graduated in 1955 from the Ural State Technical University and began his career in the construction industry.
- Joined the Communist Party in 1961 and became a full-time *apparatchik* with his promotion to head of the party's construction administration in 1968.
- Promoted to Communist Party first secretary in Sverdlovsk in 1976, where he remained until Gorbachev transferred him to Moscow in 1985.
- Became a member of the Central Committee of the Communist Party of the Soviet Union in 1981.
- In April 1985, transferred to Moscow, soon advancing to the secretariat to oversee the construction industry.
- In December 1985, appointed the de facto mayor of Moscow; named a candidate (nonvoting) member of the Politburo two months later.
- In September 1987, concerned with the slow pace of reforms and corruption, Yeltsin attempted to resign from his Moscow post, relenting at Gorbachev's request; a month later, he publicly confronted Gorbachev at a Central Committee plenum over the pace of reforms and the cult of the personality arising around Gorbachev.
- Early in November 1987, Yeltsin was voted out as de facto mayor and demoted to a minor post in the construction ministry in Moscow; expulsion from the Politburo quickly followed.
- Using the new democratic reforms introduced by Gorbachev, Yeltsin won election to the USSR Congress of People's Deputies in March 1989, beginning his political comeback.
- In March 1990, he was elected to the Congress of People's Deputies of the Russian Federation and two months later was elected chairman of its presidium; in June 1991, he was popularly elected president in the nation's first democratic presidential balloting.
- In 1990–1991, Yeltsin became the leader of efforts to draft a new Union Treaty, successfully leading the opposition to the attempted coup in August 1991; in the following months, he was instrumental in efforts to negotiate an agreement for the breakup of the Soviet Union.
- In 1992 and early 1993, Yeltsin was increasingly at odds with an opposition-dominated legislature, producing gridlock; in September

1993, he disbanded the legislature, promising a new constitution and elections; near civil war resulted, with the military eventually siding with Yeltsin; elections in December 1993 produced another opposition-dominated legislature.
- Low in the polls and in poor health, Yeltsin faced sure defeat in the 1996 presidential election; he nonetheless rallied his supporters to win, warning that a loss would result in the return of communist rule.
- During his second term, poor health and depression compromised his ability to control events; he appointed and then dismissed a number of prime ministers, the last of whom was the relatively unknown Vladimir Putin.
- On December 31, 1999, Yeltsin resigned as president less than a year before the next scheduled election; he endorsed Putin as his successor.

Born on February 1, 1931, in the village of Butka near Sverdlovsk, now restored to the prerevolutionary name of Ekaterinburg, he took naturally to the construction business in which his father worked. He got a degree in construction from the Ural State Technical University in 1955. Although the school was a cut below Gorbachev's alma mater, Moscow State University, specialization in construction was a far more important and prestigious undertaking than law. He returned to Sverdlovsk and worked at increasingly important construction posts, building a reputation as a hard-driving administrator who could cut through the cumbersome bureaucracy and get things done, an especially valuable skill that brought him to the attention of his superiors.[1]

Yeltsin joined the Communist Party in 1961, and seven years later made the all-important shift to the party's *apparat*, or bureaucracy, where he continued to supervise construction. In 1976, he was named party secretary for the Sverdlovsk region, making him the most powerful leader there. The region prospered under his tutelage, and he gained a reputation for honesty and forthrightness in dealing with his superiors and the general public.

When Gorbachev became general secretary in 1985, he began to bring new blood to Moscow. In June of that year, Yeltsin was shifted to Moscow to head the party's construction department, which had a well-deserved reputation for corruption and malfeasance. Six months later, Gorbachev promoted him to the post of secretary of the Moscow city party committee, making him the de facto mayor of the city.

The new job provided both enlightenment and opportunity. Though no stranger to the reality that the party *nomenklatura* enjoyed privileges far beyond those of the average soviet citizen, Yeltsin was nonetheless astounded by the advantages reaped by the Moscow elite. He knew that Gorbachev had placed him in charge of the city to shake things up; that meant confrontation and the mobilization of public support for the assault on the entrenched power of the local elite. Yeltsin was more than equal to the task, at least at first. His highly visible assaults on local corruption and malfeasance caught the public eye, as did his criticism of the excessive lifestyle of the elite.[2]

It did not take long for opposition to emerge. His Moscow critics soon found receptive ears within the top national leadership, who by extension were guilty of the same excesses. Most important among his critics was Yegor Ligachev, who served as second secretary in charge of appointments to high-level posts. Their increasingly rancorous battle over the pace of Yeltsin's (and implicitly Gorbachev's) reforms provided rallying points for an ever more divided party. For his part, Gorbachev tried to walk the tightrope between them, a balancing act that was doomed to failure.

Early in September 1987, Yeltsin privately wrote to Gorbachev asking to be relieved from the Moscow post and from candidate membership in the Politburo, to which he had been elevated in February 1986. Whether the request was motivated by his growing frustration with opposition to his actions in Moscow—he had complained to friends about his increasing isolation—or by his hope to force Gorbachev to make a commitment to intensify reforms is uncertain. In either case, Gorbachev refused to take action, deciding instead to study the matter in greater detail. His inaction prompted Yeltsin to make a difficult choice: either to take even bolder action to force the pace of change or to accept the stalemate that now existed between reformers and conservatives.

Yeltsin chose the former course of action, and it nearly cost him his career and possibly his life. On October 21, 1987, at a full meeting of the party's Central Committee convened to discuss the approaching November 7 holiday, Yeltsin requested the floor at the end of the proceedings. His message was blunt. In spite of many achievements, reforms had also experienced "great difficulties." Perestroika and glasnost had raised unrealistically high expectations that could not be satisfied unless reforms came more rapidly and more fundamentally altered the system. Ligachev was singled out for direct criticism, and Gorbachev was portrayed as the subject of excessive glorification, reminiscent of earlier personality cults that surrounded soviet leaders. Most stunningly, Yeltsin asked to resign from his Politburo post, adding that his role as the mayor of Moscow should be left up to the city party committee. After some initial confusion about how to respond, Gorbachev and other top leaders made it clear to the delegates that Yeltsin had crossed the line. The decision about Yeltsin's tenure as Moscow's mayor was delayed until the city party committee's meeting three weeks later.

During the three-week interim, Yeltsin fell seriously, and potentially fatally, ill. Forced from his hospital bed, apparently under heavy sedation, Yeltsin came before the city party committee to accept his fate. While Gorbachev's opening comments remained civil, most of the other speakers savaged him. At the end, Yeltsin offered a ritual mea culpa, as had the victims of Stalin's purges. The outcome always had been certain: Yeltsin was dismissed from his post and, adding insult to injury, was assigned to a middle management position in the construction industry. As the meeting broke up, Yeltsin apparently slumped on the table before him, unable to rise. No one approached, and eventually Gorbachev himself helped him stand and walk from the room. Gorbachev probably thought it was an act of kindness and compassion for a defeated enemy, someone he probably would never see again. He was wrong.[3]

From Outcast to President

Gorbachev was wrong because Yeltsin's brief tenure in Moscow taught him an important lesson. Yeltsin had been correct in arguing that perestroika had set loose a revolution of rising expectations that could not be satisfied. To his credit, Gorbachev himself would soon recognize this problem and take bold steps to resolve it through democratic reforms. In reality, Gorbachev quickly lost touch with public sentiment and could not manipulate it as easily as he had hoped. Democratization became a Pandora's box, setting free an uncontrollable surge of public involvement through newly created democratic institutions and permitting the now-empowered voters to raise issues that had never been on Gorbachev's agenda.[4]

But democratization was only half the battle. Yeltsin also needed a new issue that would redefine the playing field to his advantage. To be sure, more conventional issues like the pace of reforms or the transformation of the economy were still important, but they were not "his" issues. Like many regional communist party leaders, Yeltsin found that new issue to be national identity—*Russian* nationalism, to be specific, not the patina of *soviet* nationalism that passed for the official identity of the "new soviet man."

Not far below the surface of these new soviet citizens lay some trace of what they had been before—Russians, or Ukrainians, or Lithuanians, and the like. Local leaders, now faced with truly democratic elections, saw an opportunity to exploit real and imagined grievances again the central government and to redefine themselves as champions of local interests instead of Moscow's overseers "parachuted" in to impose the center's will. Good "communists" quickly became good "nationalists," shifting label and loyalties out of concern for their own survival.[5]

For the non-Russian areas within the Soviet Union, the transition was fairly easy. Even those areas that had benefited economically from Moscow's policies, such as the Central Asian republics, soon sought to distance themselves from the center, and others, such as the Baltic republics, which had been forcefully incorporated into the USSR at the end of World War II, had real grievances that soon became the key issues of local elections. For the Russian Republic, the situation was more complex. On the one hand, Russians had always been the "big brothers" of the soviet family, acknowledged as the initial founders of socialism and the examples to be emulated by the "lesser" peoples. But on the other hand, Russians had always resented the implied burden that this imposed on them.

Yeltsin's attempt to return to the political arena was cautious at first, beginning with his participation in the Nineteenth Party Conference in June 1988. The conference, which was different from the normally scheduled party congresses, had been called by Gorbachev to deal with growing resistance to his reforms. Gorbachev had concluded that some way had to be found to put pressure on conservative elements within the party. His strategy was to call for further democratization of the party itself and the creation of a new legislature, the Congress of People's Deputies. Taking the floor as an ordinary delegate, Yeltsin demanded his own rehabilitation "within his lifetime" and the direct election of all public officials.

Yeltsin had found his new persona: an increasingly confrontational leader of a small but growing opposition movement. The underlying strategy, acknowledged by Yeltsin himself, is summarized in the Russian phrase "*klin klinom vyshibayut*," which is best expressed in the dictum that the best defense is a good offense. Confrontational by nature, Yeltsin rose to the challenge of speaking for a growing opposition. Most important, he found a voice that reached the people. His brief experience as a maverick leader in Moscow who challenged the privileges of the soviet elite had not gone unnoticed, and his ability to connect with ordinary people showed he had a common touch that most other leaders, including Gorbachev, never achieved.

Less than a year later, in March 1989, Yeltsin was overwhelmingly elected to Moscow's at-large seat in the newly constituted Congress of People's Deputies of the Soviet Union, winning 92 percent of the vote. The campaign itself had been nothing less than a grassroots revolution, an enormous outpouring of public support and activism not seen since 1917. Local party officials at first blocked his selection to the smaller and more important Supreme Soviet, only to be foiled by the willingness of an elected delegate to stand down and give his seat to Yeltsin, a move that Gorbachev grudgingly accepted. In the spring of the following year, Yeltsin easily won a seat in the Russian Republic's new legislature with 72 percent of the vote. Despite continuing opposition from the body's strong Communist Party contingent, he subsequently was elected speaker of the legislature, the de jure head-of-state post generally referred to as the "presidency." The outcast was now a "president," of a sort.[6]

The President Becomes a President

Yeltsin's post as the speaker of the Russian legislature wasn't a real presidency. A leftover from the soviet era, it was merely a formal head-of-state sinecure, lacking both real legitimacy and power. Facing stiff opposition from the Communist Party nominee, Yeltsin had been chosen by the legislature on the third ballot.

Yeltsin quickly came to realize that he needed three things to move ahead: a more fully articulated political program—a platform, if you will—that offered a simple, easily understood, and widely popular agenda around which to build a broader political movement; an organization within the legislature itself to unite reformers, linked to a broader political party to mobilize public support; and a new popularly elected presidency that would trump Gorbachev's claim to legitimacy.

The Yeltsin platform emerged slowly at first, developing and then radicalizing ideas about democratization and economic reform and adding a growing demand for Russian independence. Throughout the evolution of this agenda, Yeltsin found himself in constant competition with Gorbachev, who until early 1991 was trying to adapt his initial ideas of perestroika to deal with the revolution of rising political, economic, and social expectations. But whereas Gorbachev moved cautiously, Yeltsin advanced more rapidly. As Gorbachev pressed more boldly to force the Communist Party to democratize itself in the hope that it could legitimately win political power in free, multiparty elections, Yeltsin abandoned the party all together, demanding that all power be shifted to elected bodies and that the party's stranglehold over the bureaucracy be broken. A similar pattern emerged concerning economic reform. Yeltsin promised radical action, the so-called 500-day program that would quickly transform the economy, despite the inevitable disruption of such rapid change.[7]

The question of Russia's place within the Soviet Union became the most dramatic and disruptive issue in Yeltsin's agenda. He quickly realized the growing power of a simple idea: Russia, as well as the fourteen other republics, should be granted greater latitude and perhaps outright independence. In truth, Yeltsin followed the example of other republics in moving against the power of the central government in Moscow. Yeltsin was a latecomer to the issue of regional autonomy and independence, but his advocacy strengthened his hand considerably. He was at the helm of an issue that cut across all others and created strong bonds with the reform elements in all other republics. Now all had a common enemy—the "center," which was reluctantly trying to cope with pressures for reform. With Russia and its dynamic new leader, Boris Yeltsin, on board, the question of the fate of the Soviet Union itself emerged as the most important issue on the reform agenda.

With a reasonably coherent and constantly radicalizing reform agenda in place, Yeltsin could turn to the practical question of organizing an effective resistance movement. Yeltsin moved first at the national level, joining an already existing bloc of progressive and reform-minded deputies called the Inter-Regional Group of Deputies within the USSR Congress of People's Deputies.[8] Numbering 388 individuals—just over one sixth of the Congress's 2,250 deputies—it initially played an important role in bringing together the diverse and headstrong body of reformers. Yeltsin soon became the de facto leader of the bloc, but other prominent individuals such as Andrei Sakharov, the dissident physicist who had been held under house arrest during the later Brezhnev era, lent much to its legitimacy and international visibility. Like most such loose coalitions, it quickly fell into internal disputes over policy and leadership and about Yeltsin's efforts to build a larger coalition that reached out to the nation as a whole.

That broader effort took the form of several new organizations all built around the term "Democratic Russia." In fact there were several Democratic Russias, each built from different constituencies. The first to form was the Democratic Russia Caucus within the new Russian legislature. Composed of sixty or so hardcore delegates, it drew support from

other reformist factions and had great influence over uncommitted delegates. It played an instrumental role in Yeltsin's election as speaker of the
legislature and the eventual declaration of Russian sovereignty (but not yet
independence) in June 1990. In one form or another, it dominated the
legislature until early 1992.[9]

The Democratic Russia Movement, linked to but technically separate
from the Caucus, was one of the first attempts to organize a mass-based
political party. It reached out to anyone who supported a proreform and
anticommunist agenda. Not surprisingly, a number of factions soon
divided the movement, although all eventually backed Yeltsin during the
August 1991 attempted coup. Yeltsin was the key beneficiary of Democratic
Russia's activities, including its ability to mobilize votes in the legislature
and in general elections and its skill in turning out mass rallies at key
moments.

The creation of a popularly elected presidency in the Russian Republic
was a high priority for Yeltsin, especially as his personal battle with
Gorbachev intensified in 1990 and 1991. His speaker-of-the-legislature
"presidency," while important, did not establish parity with Gorbachev's
newly created national office. Like all such "presidencies" of the soviet era,
it was a weak post, largely ceremonial in nature. It provided Yeltsin with a
bully pulpit from which to argue his case, but it had little influence over the
actions of the legislature or the government.

Creating a directly elected presidency was not an easy task. The
Russian legislature quickly deadlocked in its efforts to amend the constitution. In frustration, it submitted two different drafts in November 1990,
one designed to create a strong, directly elected executive office largely
modeled after Gorbachev's presidency (itself copied from the Gaullist
presidency on the French Fifth Republic) and the other couched in less
forceful terms that greatly limited the powers of a popularly elected president. In a referendum held on March 17, 1991, the public overwhelmingly
supported the creation of a popularly elected president, but the wording
was neutral on the relative strength or weakness of the office.[10]

Under pressure from the referendum, the legislature voted to accept
the creation of a relatively strong, popularly elected presidency and scheduled the vote for June 12, 1991. Yeltsin was the odds-on favorite, but he did
not run unopposed. Against him was a virtual microcosm of the growing
cacophony of Russian political life: Vladimir Zhirinovsky, an ultranationalist whose Liberal Democratic Party and flamboyant style had earned him
considerable visibility, if not respect; General Albert Makashov, a military

Table 3.1   1991 Russian Presidential Election

Candidate	Party	Votes	Percentage
Boris Yeltsin	Independent	45,552,041	58.6
Nikolai Ryzhkov	Communist Party of the Soviet Union	13,395,335	17.2
Vladimir Zhirinovsky	Liberal Democratic Party	6,211,007	8.0
Aman Tuleev	Communist Party of the Soviet Union	5,417,464	7.0
Albert Makashov	Communist Party of the Soviet Union	2,969,511	3.8
Vadim Bakatin	Communist Party of the Soviet Union	2,719,757	3.5

SOURCE: D. Nohlen and P. Stover. (2010). *Elections in Europe: A Data Handbook.* Baden-Baden, Germany: Nomos.

figure who would side with the August 1991 coup attempt against Gorbachev; Nikolai Ryzhkov, a former soviet prime minister; Aman Tuleev, governor of the Kemerovo province; and Vadim Bakatin, a pro-Gorbachev moderate reformer. Yeltsin chose as his running mate the centrist Alexander Rutskoi, an Afghan war hero and reform-oriented communist, hoping to draw support from among other reformers and the military. The campaign lasted just over three weeks.

On June 12, for the first time in Russia's history, its people went to the polls to elect a national leader. Yeltsin won handily, with 58.6 percent of the popular vote. Ryzhkov got just over 17 percent, and Zhirinovsky 8 percent. The others came in with even lower percentages. On July 10, Yeltsin was sworn into office. He resigned from the speaker-cum-presidency post, handing it over to a presumably safe ally, Ruslan Khasbulatov.[11]

A Real President Gets a Real Nation

When Yeltsin took the oath of office in July, no one would have dared to predict how soon the president of a "sovereign republic" within the Soviet Union would become the chief executive of a sovereign and independent nation. To be sure, most of the trends that ultimately would bring about the end of both the Soviet Union and the communist experiment had been under way for some time. Four sharpening conflicts drove the process: the personal rivalries between the two leaders themselves; the collapse of the economy and the need to make a choice about the nature and pace of economic reforms, the fate of the party-state and ultimately the survival of the Communist Party itself, and the relations between central authorities in Moscow and republic-level leaders, couched in a quasi-legal discussion of the abrogation or revision of the Union Treaty, which formally created the USSR.

Personal Rivalries

The personal animosity between Gorbachev and Yeltsin was palpable. Gorbachev viewed Yeltsin as an opportunist who had betrayed and distorted his economic and political reforms. Gorbachev had been Yeltsin's patron, bringing him to Moscow and high office, only to see him denounce Gorbachev and the pace of his reforms.[12] For his part, Yeltsin viewed Gorbachev as a flawed and irresolute reformer. Like many who led the first battles of a revolution, Gorbachev grew cautious as his reforms created a revolution of rising expectations that far exceeded his own desires and expectations. For Yeltsin, boldness and resolution were needed to make hard decisions about the nation's future, and in Gorbachev he saw a growing lack of self-confidence and an increasing propensity to compromise.

Each showed little respect for the other's reforms. Gorbachev spoke dismissively of Yeltsin's return from political oblivion in 1990, and regarded his more ambitious reform agenda as opportunistic and destructive. While Yeltsin continued to argue for the preservation of some kind of union with an emasculated central presidency until after the August coup attempt, it was obvious that his real agenda was no less than a full-scale assault on Gorbachev. For his part, Yeltsin openly broke with Gorbachev early in 1991, confessing that it had been a "personal mistake to have been excessively trustful of the President" and calling for his "immediate resignation."[13]

The animosity grew petty and vindictive at times. It took Gorbachev over a week to pen the obligatory congratulations to Yeltsin after his popular election to the presidency of the Russian Republic in June 1991. Six months later, it was Yeltsin's turn. With the breakup of the Soviet Union, the Russian government moved quickly to occupy the Kremlin, formerly the seat of the USSR government and the location of Gorbachev's presidential suite. Yeltsin ordered that the presidential office be transferred to him on

December 26, the day after Gorbachev's resignation. The former president's personal belongings were boxed for his eventual removal; Gorbachev was not even permitted to clean out his own desk.[14]

Economic Reforms as a Political Issue

The fate of the Russian economy weighed heavily on both Gorbachev and Yeltsin, and their different approaches contributed to the growing conflict between them. Perestroika always had been a vague term, to be spun into different policies according to the philosophical bent or the personal advantage of the speaker.[15] By 1990, it was apparent that something had to be done; production had come to a standstill, the shops were bare, and the winter was long and cold. For Gorbachev, economic reform had always been a cerebral undertaking, a grand experiment that would transform but not uproot the national economy. In a perfect world, his transformed economy would be more efficient, more rationally managed, and more responsive to consumer demands at all levels. But there would still be a relatively large state sector regulated but not planned item-by-item by the government.

Reform also meant other things to other people. For the average and long-suffering consumers, it meant—they hoped—more and better everything: apartments, food, appliances, clothing, cars, all the material metrics of a modern successful industrial economy. But they also knew that any reform that could accomplish such an extensive transformation brought risks: factory closings and unemployment as state subsidies were withdrawn; inflated prices as subsidies no longer supported basic commodities like bread or rent; the disappearance of a minimal safety net of social, health, and educational services; and, perhaps most frightening, the very real prospect that they would fail while their neighbors enriched themselves.

There were also other ways to spin economic reform. For regional leaders, it could mean greater control over local resources. An important element in the growing demands for local sovereignty and possible secession came from the desire to control local resources. But although some regional leaders wanted to get Moscow's hand out of their pocket, others— like the Central Asian republics that had benefited from the center's investments—wanted to preserve a coherent national economy.

For the soviet managerial class, reform offered both problems and opportunities. Because of the centrally planned nature of the economy, the captains of industry were in fact government employees, many heavily dependent on state orders and even subsidies to keep their factories in production. Any shift to a market and demand-driven economy could mean trouble, especially to the degree that real competition emerged. But for others in the managerial class, economic reform could bring opportunity, especially after it became apparent that a substantial part of the state-owned economy would be privatized. A whole new class of entrepreneurs emerged, the "*nomenklatura* capitalists," who became the first elements of an expanding number of robber-barons and oligarchs who exercised great political influence.

For Yeltsin, the question of economic reform was a matter of substance and strategy. In substantive terms, he sought a solution that would quickly address the nation's economic problems. Yeltsin argued that the solution lay at the republic level. This argument was strengthened by the increasing propensity to look to regional rather and national solutions to a host of problems. What was needed, and what Yeltsin intended to offer, was a clear blueprint for quick and effective changes rather than a vague and grandiose scheme. Yeltsin made economic reform the most important issue in his bid for the elected presidency in 1991. Speedy reform toward a marketized economy became the watchword, with few of the details spelled out beyond election-year promises. But it worked, at least as a campaign strategy, producing a high level of support among voters concerned with bread-and-butter issues.

An irresolute Gorbachev virtually handed Yeltsin the issue. To Gorbachev's credit, the soviet president had instructed his numerous (and frequently divided) economic advisors to devise a rational plan to marketize the economy. An ambitious "500-day plan" eventually emerged in summer of 1990. On paper, it was a striking document. It recommended the creation of a competitive market economy, extensive privatization of state-owned resources, the deregulation of prices on all goods, integration into the world economy, and the transfer of power from the central to republic-level governments. At first Gorbachev appeared to endorse the 500-day plan.[16] Yeltsin quickly embraced the program, promising its rapid implementation in Russia, and the legislature quickly voted to accept it. A more cautious reform proposal was prepared by economists and managers closer to Gosplan, the state planning agency, and the ministries that would have been implemented over at least a decade and maybe longer.

Now faced with two competing versions of reform, Gorbachev equivocated. He asked his advisors to combine the two programs. When this did not produce an acceptable compromise, Gorbachev forwarded both of the original reform plans to the USSR Supreme Soviet, asking them to render the decision. They demurred and returned the drafts to him for resolution. Several weeks later, he submitted his own version of a compromise plan. Far more cautious in terms of the scope of reforms, his draft removed the commitment to rapid change.

Some context is helpful to understand this indecision. Increasingly doubtful that he could control the revolution he had started, Gorbachev grew more cautious in the fall of 1990. Although he eventually would embrace ambitious reforms later in the spring of 1991, his conservative shift to the right had far-reaching consequences. It considerably strengthened the opponents of reform and brought to power, through Gorbachev's own appointments, a number of those who led the coup attempt in August 1991. It also undercut support among the original cadre of reformers who now abandoned Gorbachev as a flawed and compromised leader. Most important, it emboldened regional leaders, including Yeltsin himself, to press even harder for greater latitude for their republics.[17]

Yeltsin's Economic Reforms: Phase I (1991–1993)

Yeltsin's economic reforms began even before the dismemberment of the Soviet Union and involved two major and interrelated initiatives: (1) structural changes at both the macro- and microeconomic levels that affected prices, the creation of a market, and the role of the government in the economy and (2) the privatization program, which shifted resources from public to private ownership.

In October 1991, shortly after the failure of the August coup attempt and before the formal demise of the Soviet Union, Yeltsin introduced significant economic reforms. They included sharp reductions in government spending aimed at public investment projects, the defense industries, and the subsidies for producers (usually inefficient factories with bloated workforces) and consumer goods (these established below-market prices for basic foodstuffs, housing, and a host of social services). Price controls were lifted on 90 percent of consumer goods and 80 percent of most other commodities. The goal was to reduce the heretofore concealed deficit, which had reached 20 percent of the national gross domestic product in the late soviet period. New taxes were imposed, and a largely unsuccessful effort was made to improve tax collection. The role of the government was to be significantly scaled down, and factories were expected to produce primarily for the growing public market as government orders were reduced. The ruble was gradually to be made convertible, and remaining restrictions on international trade and joint ventures were removed. There also was a clear downside to the reforms. Factory directors now faced an uncertain public market as government orders declined or ended; workers saw cuts in wages and possible dismissal; prices soared for everybody; and inflation rose to a stunning 2,000 percent in 1992. All these hardships produced a political backlash. Yeltsin and, especially, Yegor Gaidar, who spearheaded the reforms, were blamed for the economy's ills; late in 1992, Yeltsin attempted to deflect some of the blame to Gaidar, dismissing him as prime minister and appointing the more conservative Viktor Chernomyrdin to the post.

The second element of Yeltsin's economic reforms involved privatization of state-owned resources. The privatization of factories and other resources occurred in two waves: the voucher program, which began in October 1992, and the direct sale of stock in state enterprises, which was implemented by presidential decree in July 1994. The voucher program is covered in this chapter; the other program is covered in Chapter 4, which begins with the new 1993 constitution.

The voucher program started with the distribution of certificates to over 140 million Russians. Each held a nominal value of 10,000 rubles (63 U.S. dollars), which could be used to purchase shares in the large and medium-sized factories that the government had designated for privatization in this manner. Investors could directly purchase shares in these enterprises, or sell the vouchers to brokers at a discounted value. Within two years, the voucher program transferred 70 percent of the large and medium-sized industries and 90 percent of small enterprises into private hands, accounting for nearly two thirds of the industrial workforce. Despite its success, the program had not included the real giants of soviet industry, many of which would end up in the hands of the new super-rich oligarchs who acquired them during the second phase of privatization through rigged auctions and other sweetheart deals.[18]

The Reform of the Party-State

The fate of the party-state also became an important flashpoint. A unique feature of all Leninist systems, it merged two usually distinct power centers: the government and the dominant (or, in this case, only) political party. The hierarchies were intertwined; party membership was a requirement for all high-level posts in society, and government officials looked to the party for guidance.

With Gorbachev's reforms, the party's privileged position was now open to question. Gorbachev intended that a reformed Communist Party would remain an important and influential actor, but would now win its preeminence through competitive elections. With the removal of Article 6 of the 1977 soviet constitution, which provided that it would be the only legal party, the Communist Party was now cast into a broader competitive field. But other questions still remained: Could it still function as a political party and an informal network within government agencies and other social organizations? Should it be permitted to maintain its considerable infrastructure and financial advantages in a new era of competitive politics? Predictably, Gorbachev and Yeltsin differed on these issues.

At the Twenty-Eighth Party Congress held in July 1990, the party was dealt a further blow.[19] This was its last formal meeting, although no one knew it at the time. A vigorous debate took place among its three main factions: the conservative faction that increasingly opposed and even wanted to roll back Gorbachev's earlier reforms; the Gorbachev faction, now more cautious but still hoping for the internal democratization of the party itself; and the Yeltsin faction, which demanded even more rapid reforms within the party and the removal of party cells from within all organizations. Failing on all demands, Yeltsin dramatically resigned from the party, taking a small number of delegates with him. The Congress reelected Gorbachev as its general secretary despite mounting misgivings about his leadership.

The attempted coup in August 1991 dealt the death blow to the party, at least for a while. Upon his return to Moscow, Gorbachev resigned as general secretary, the post that had really ruled the nation from Stalin's day onward. He also called upon the Central Committee to resign in the hope that such a thorough housecleaning might set the stage for reform elements to assert themselves. Yeltsin went further, seizing all the party's assets and real estate (the old Central Committee building on Old Square soon became the executive office of the Russian president) and banning it from political activity, although the courts eventually voided the prohibition. The party-state, at least as it had been known, was now a thing of the past.

National Identity and the Union Treaty

Of all the issues that had been released from Pandora's box, unquestionably the most important was national self-identity, which quickly morphed into

demands for local autonomy, sovereignty, and independence. The first stir-
rings of discontent came predictably from the Baltic republics, the newest
members of the soviet "family of nations" and the most eager to leave. Both
glasnost and democratization led to the formation of popular fronts that
quickly captured control of the newly created democratic legislatures.
Popular fronts or pro-independence parties were created in all fifteen
republics by the summer of 1988. In the 1990 elections to the republic-level
legislatures, the local communist parties lost control in Lithuania, Moldova,
Estonia, Latvia, Armenia, and Georgia; in Central Asia, local communists
formally retained control, largely because they adopted much of the nationalist agenda.

In his 1990 campaign for a seat in the Russian legislature, Yeltsin fully
endorsed growing demands to weaken the authority of the central government and the right of secession of any republic. To the extent that a central
government remained, it would be limited to tasks of coordination and not
direct policy making. Its chief executive—Gorbachev—could remain only
in a ceremonial role.

Although each republic moved forward to the beat of a different drum-
mer, they all were playing the same tune. With remarkable consistency,
almost all went through the same progression from initial protests to eventual statehood. Perestroika and glasnost opened the door for reform and
gave a voice to those who wanted to move beyond Gorbachev's controlled
transformation. As Gorbachev himself radicalized in 1988 and 1989, democratic reforms were added to mix. Those who had found their voices—
and were now singing a very different tune from Gorbachev's original
melody—had real political power. As they began to flex their political
muscles, their demands began to radicalize. The progression typically
began with demands for greater latitude within the Soviet Union. Next
came a demand for sovereignty, which could mean a number of things: an
acknowledgment by the central government in Moscow that republic laws
took precedence over Moscow's enactments; a real acceptance on Moscow's
part that republics could exercise their right of succession; or that some
new formula might be found for a revised Union Treaty, embodying all or
some of these possible meanings and perhaps providing for different categories of membership in a revised version of the Soviet Union. The debate
over these possibilities was rancorous, driven forward by the radicalization
of opposition forces, the growing weakness of the central government, the
opportunism of political leaders at all levels trying to jump on a winning
bandwagon, and the inherent logic of the issue itself.[20]

Slowly at first, Gorbachev accepted the idea that the Union Treaty needed revision. In November 1990, he distributed a draft of a proposed new treaty to all the republics; the document envisioned a looser association of sovereign republics and the preservation of a weaker but still active central government. Events would soon derail this effort at compromise. On January 11, 1991, elite troops of the Ministry of Internal Affairs seized control of a television tower in Vilnius, the capitol of Lithuania, killing thirteen civilians. Yeltsin and the presidents of Latvia and Estonia quickly criticized the action and demanded that Lithuania and any other republic should be permitted to secede from the union if it chose.

The March 1991 referendum briefly muddied the waters. Its results seemed contradictory. Although it endorsed Yeltsin's proposal that an elected presidency be created within the Russian Republic, it also supported the preservation of the Soviet Union as a "renewed federation of equal sovereign republics, in which a full measure of human rights and liberties will be guaranteed to a person of any nationality." The question of the presidency won with 71 percent of the vote, and the endorsement of a continued but modified union won with 70 percent.[21]

Attempting to regain control of events, Gorbachev summoned the leaders of nine republics to a meeting at the government dacha in Novo-Ogarovo on April 23, 1991. Missing were Armenia, Georgia, Moldova, and the three Baltic republics, all of which had refused to participate in the referendum. Gorbachev seemed to yield on all of the issues, acknowledging that the republics were "sovereign states" with extensive (but poorly defined) control over their own affairs. A new Union Treaty creating a "Union of Soviet Sovereign Republics" was to be drafted and ratified by each of participating republics. Following ratification of the treaty, a new constitution would be drafted for the reconstituted nation, including the direct election of a national presidency. Gorbachev seemed to have saved his presidency, provided he could win it in a real election, a highly questionable proposition by this time. But he had surrendered on all the other points. As for the six republics that had boycotted the referendum, they would now go their own way as independent states. All that was needed was to get the new Union Treaty signed, an event scheduled for August 20.

Yeltsin was initially delighted with the Novo-Ogarovo agreement. He had won on all points except for the preservation of a national presidency. The agreement strengthened his hand considerably in the rapidly approaching elections for a Russian president, and he was now first-among-equals in the company of the leaders of the other republics. Although it was not a sure thing, the new Union Treaty perhaps signaled that Gorbachev had come to his senses and once more supported reform, if not as completely as Yeltsin might have hoped.

The Union Treaty was never signed, as you know from Chapter 2. A short-lived coup attempt destroyed any hope that either Gorbachev or the Soviet Union could survive. The coup had collapsed within days, but with lasting consequences. Gorbachev was destroyed and dispirited. His actions clearly indicated that he was out of touch with the reality of national politics, and his efforts to revive and renegotiate the Union Treaty came to nothing. They—and he—were too little, too late.

Yeltsin, by contrast, was the man of the hour. He deservedly got the credit for rallying the nation in a moment of crisis. The man who had been cast aside in 1987 was soon to be the president of an independent country. A day after Gorbachev's resignation on December 25, 1991, Yeltsin triumphantly took his place in the presidential office, shifting the center from the White House to the Kremlin. Now the president had a country—but a very troubled one.

Judicial Reform

For the most part, efforts at judicial reform were haphazard for the two-year interregnum between the demise of the Soviet Union and the 1993 constitution. On the one hand, the courts expanded their jurisdiction over constitutional, administrative, and commercial disputes, although the latter typically were handled through separate arbitration panels. Additional steps were taken to professionalize the status of judges and the legal profession in general, but implementation was slow and spotty because of limited funds and unqualified personnel. At the highest level, Gorbachev's Constitutional Oversight Committee evolved into a rudimentary Constitutional Court after the Soviet Union disbanded. As the confrontation between Yeltsin and the Congress of People's Deputies intensified, the Court increasingly sided with the legislature against the president. In a last-minute attempt to avoid a break between the two, the Court's chairman, Valery Zorkin, brokered a short-lived compromise providing for a referendum but then quickly withdrew his support and openly sided with the legislature. Now deeply mired in the conflict between Yeltsin and the Congress, the Court had clearly chosen its side in the dispute—the losing side.[22]

The President and the Legislature

Independence solved one issue—the relationship between the now-defunct Soviet Union and the newly constituted Russian Federation—but it intensified other problems. The new Russia was in fact governed by institutions that had been created in the old Soviet Union. The Russian Congress of People's Deputies and the smaller Supreme Soviet had been elected in 1990 before the fall of the communist regime. Even the presidency had been in large measure a copy of Gorbachev's post, different only in that its incumbent had been popularly elected. Created in haste, it left considerable ambiguity about the relationship between the legislative and the executive branches.

The overwhelming unity that prevailed between Yeltsin as president and the legislature until independence was won was a product of circumstance rather than constitutional design. At first, Yeltsin's executive role was merely an extension of the legislature itself; it was not until his popular election in June 1991 that the two "branches" technically responded to different constituencies. The old soviet-era conceptualization of the relationship between executive and legislative authority survived despite dramatic and revolutionary changes in the political reality that underpinned it. Strictly speaking, under that interpretation (which was clearly the mindset when the Russian Republic constitution had been amended to create the Congress of People's Deputies and the presidency), the legislative branch was vested with full authority. The government, in the form of the office of the prime minister and the Council of Ministers, was an extension of legislative authority, not an independent executive branch. Presumably, the new presidency fell, legally at least, into the same category. What made it all work during the soviet years was that real authority lay with the Communist Party, whose general secretary was the de facto national leader and whose Politburo was the de facto cabinet. The legislative and executive parts of the government (*branches* is too strong a term at this point in history) never got out of step because the party simply would not permit it. With the party's key role now abolished, there was nothing left to informally coordinate the executive and legislative branches or to broker agreement between the two.

The composition of the Russian Congress of People's Deputies also must be taken into account to understand its growing conflict with Yeltsin. From the beginning, it was dominated by the Communist Party of the Russian Federation. In 1990, the Communist Party made up 87 percent of all delegates. By 1991, Communist Party membership had fallen to 75 percent, largely due to defections, dropping further to 65 percent by 1993. The decline of Communist Party membership did not, however, lead to the emergence of a stable counterforce.

The emergence of blocs within the legislature initially provided some sense of order. In 1990, two major blocs dominated: the Communist Bloc and the Democratic Russia Bloc, which brought together proreform and pro-Yeltsin forces. But by 1993, the Democratic Russia Bloc had collapsed. A new bloc, Russian Unity, combined Communist Party delegates with the center-left Creative Forces group. Increasingly critical of Yeltsin, they commanded the clear majority but not the two-thirds majority needed for impeachment.

It did not take long for sharp differences to emerge between Yeltsin and the legislature.[23] Late in 1991, just before independence was won, the Congress had voted Yeltsin special emergency powers to initiate economic reform. Good for one year, these powers permitted him to implement the 500-day plan, which provided for a cold-turkey "shock therapy" adjustment. As the reforms took hold and brought increasing hardship, the Congress of People's Deputies became the sounding board for protest. Never as strongly committed as Yeltsin and his advisors to economic reforms, it had granted him emergency authority in the hope that he would overextend himself. Few within the legislature had any reason to support the reforms. Most of the Communist Party delegates, whose background placed them within the old soviet-era bureaucracy, lost power and influence in a new market economy. Others saw the growing opposition to economic reform as a way to weaken Yeltsin and assert the power of the legislature over the presidency. Regional leaders saw the conflict as a way to weaken the power of the center itself. Yeltsin, once the champion of regional over national power within the soviet state, now reversed himself on the question of Moscow's control over the regions within the Russian Federation and appointed presidential "emissaries" to increase the center's influence.

Open warfare began at the December 1991 session of the Congress, which refused to confirm Yegor Gaidar as prime minister. Defiantly, Yeltsin assumed the post himself, instructing Gaidar to implement the reforms nonetheless. Conflict intensified at the next session, in April 1992. Democratic Russia, the faction that had most strongly supported reform, was falling apart. Yeltsin lost majority control of the Congress at this time as the Communists and other deputies on the left and center gravitated toward the opposition.

As with all things in politics, the battle lines were being drawn for both policy-related and personal reasons. The old communist elite had been schooled in a different world, and change was difficult. For them it was easier to accept independence than to agree to the fundamental change in the nature of society itself. Others, of course, had more personal reasons to oppose Yeltsin. Ruslan Khasbulatov, once a close ally, had assumed the speaker's chair in the Congress when Yeltsin advanced to the presidency. He now thought it appropriate that he move up to the office of prime minister and bitterly resented Yeltsin's initial selection of Gaidar. Alexander Rutskoi, a general and a war hero, and Yeltsin's running mate as vice president in the 1991 election, now coveted the higher post. All of the delegates knew that reelection in the next congressional race was problematic in the rapidly changing world of Russian politics, and they wanted to hold on to their salaries, Moscow apartments, limos, and other perks of office as long as possible. The issue was so sensitive that even as he disbanded the Congress in September 1993, Yeltsin took pains to assure the dismissed delegates that their salaries and other perks would continue for the full term.[24]

Yeltsin quickly perceived the gathering storm and tried to mollify the Congress's opposition. During the last half of 1992, he slowed the pace of economic reform and began to make new appointments from among the old soviet *nomenklatura*. The Congress and the president continued to clash on a number of key issues, including an extension of Yeltsin's special economic powers, the scheduling of the next session of the Congress (Yeltsin wanted a delay), and the holding of a national referendum on the role of the president and the need for a new constitution. After long and unsuccessful talks, a compromise was brokered by Zorkin, head of the Constitutional Court.

Despite the compromise, the next session of the Congress opened an old wound. The legislature once again refused to confirm Gaidar as prime minister. Frightened by the ominous tone of the moment, Yeltsin and Khasbulatov agreed on a common platform that might have lowered the tone of the confrontation and resolved some fundamental issues in the executive-legislative relationship. The compromise included (1) a national referendum on writing a new constitution that would be held in April 1993, (2) an extension of most of Yeltsin's emergency powers until the referendum, (3) a congressional assertion of its right to nominate and vote on candidates for the prime ministership, and (4) a congressional insistence on its right to reject the president's choices for the ministers of defense, foreign affairs, interior, and security. In a major concession, Yeltsin accepted the Congress's rejection of Gaidar and nominated instead Viktor Chernomyrdin, a high-level official in the energy industry and a more centrist figure in terms of reform.

The compromise did not last long. A few months later, the Congress backed away from its commitment to the referendum and began to whittle away at Yeltsin's powers. By this time, a pernicious deadlock was in place. Any attempt by Yeltsin to pass formal legislation was blocked in the legislature. In response, Yeltsin attempted to implement policies by executive decree, which prompted legislative action to reduce his admittedly vague powers in this area.

The March 1993 emergency session of the Congress raised the stakes. At Khasbulatov's urging, it proposed to amend the constitution to reduce the president's powers and cancel the referendum. Yeltsin overplayed his hand in response. Never one to suffer opponents willingly, Yeltsin told a national television audience that he had just signed a presidential declaration establishing a "special regime" permitting him to assume extraordinary executive power. The precise meaning of "special regime" remained vague, but it suggested a presidential coup. The Constitution Court quickly labeled it unconstitutional, acting even before it saw the full text of the declaration. When it was published several days later, the "unconstitutional" provisions had been removed.[25]

With his bluff called, Yeltsin was in a perilous position. His opponents—now including his own vice president, Rutskoi—moved for impeachment, which would have brought Rutskoi into the presidential office until a new election could be called. Yeltsin took a step back and acknowledged that he had made mistakes. Only support from the never-certain centrist faction saved the day. The vote fell seventy-two short of the two-thirds majority needed to remove him from office.

The much anticipated national referendum finally occurred on April 25. Yeltsin won handily on the most important issues. Fifty-nine percent of the voters said yes to "Do you have confidence in Boris Yeltsin the President of Russia?" while 53 percent responded positively to "Do you approve the social and economic policy of the President of Russia . . . since 1992?"

"Do you consider early presidential elections necessary?" got a 50.5 percent no vote, indicating that a razor-thin majority wanted to leave the president in place. The final question asked "Do you consider early elections of the Congress of People's Deputies . . . necessary?" produced a 69-percent majority.

Yeltsin interpreted the results as an overwhelming popular endorsement. He chose to go on the offensive in the next stage of the battle, the drafting of a new constitution. The current constitution was mute on the question of how the nation could write a new one; amending the existing document was clearly a process that depended on legislative, not presidential, action. But writing a new one brought everyone into unfamiliar and dangerous territory. In June 1993, Yeltsin brought together a constitutional convention of his own making. It included over 700 delegates drawn from every element of Russian society: regional leaders, political parties, social organizations, and the like. They were asked to comment on and eventually to submit to the Congress a constitution based on an early draft that Yeltsin had released in April. Predictably, that version abolished the Congress of People's Deputies and created a bicameral legislature and, most important, a strong and independent presidency. Also predictably, the Congress of People's Deputies wanted nothing to do with Yeltsin's version of constitutional reform. It quickly rejected the draft, insisting that if constitutional reform were needed, the Congress itself would undertake the task. Their eventual draft was based on the soviet notion of the primacy of the legislature and a clearly subordinate executive branch.[26]

Over the summer of 1993, the two sides continued to snipe at each other. The next serious confrontation came early in September when Yeltsin attempted to suspend Vice President Rutskoi, now clearly an enemy hoping to ascend to the presidency. The move was justified by "accusations of corruption," a ploy that had been used by both sides to harass key leaders in the enemy camp. Little came of the effort, other than to worsen the already-acrimonious relationship. By early autumn, the very active Moscow rumor mill had it that it was only a matter of time before Khasbulatov launched another attempt at impeachment, with the outcome uncertain.

In mid-September, Yeltsin proposed a trade-off. If the Congress would agree to early legislative elections, the president would also once again stand before the voters. The legislature ignored Yeltsin, as he probably anticipated. More a tactical ploy to portray the Congress as dead set against any cooperation with the president, it underscored the increasingly irreconcilable nature of the deadlock.

On September 21, 1993, Yeltsin moved to break the deadlock. He dissolved the Congress of People's Deputies and its Supreme Soviet. The action clearly was unconstitutional; the existing constitution stipulated that any president who undertook such action would be removed from power "immediately" with no need for formal impeachment. To replace the old order, Yeltsin offered a new constitution calling for a bicameral legislature and a strong presidency. The new legislature would be elected in December, and the new constitution would be submitted to the people themselves as a referendum. He also promised an "early presidential election," the timing of which would be determined once the new legislature and constitution were in place.

In an emotional speech, Yeltsin justified his actions on two grounds. First, the presidency and the legislature were in gridlock; government had come to a standstill as each side found ways to nullify the actions of the other. Russia was at a precarious midpoint in its transition from a socialist to a capitalist economy, and delay and indecision only made things worse. Second, the president touted his legitimacy by reminding his listeners of his overwhelming victory in winning the presidency in June 1991 and the reaffirmation of the public's faith in him in the April 1993 referendum.

It was an incredibly risky move, but it was pure Yeltsin. The best defense was still a good offense. Had events gone as planned, the address to the nation would have followed the seizure of an empty White House, the seat of the Russian legislature since Yeltsin had decamped to the presidential offices in the Kremlin. But several hundred supporters of the legislature had gotten wind of the plan and had settled into the White House, demanding that they were still the only legitimate government since Yeltsin's action had instantly terminated his presidency and elevated Rutskoi to the top office. Rutskoi and Khasbulatov soon joined them. All dug in for a standoff, and a ragtag group of disgruntled politicians, soldiers and officers, and opportunists made its way to the White House to join the confrontation. What was to have been a fait accompli would become a bloody siege, a near civil war.[27]

The Constitutional Court sided with the Congress. Trying to carry on business as usual, the new "president" invalidated Yeltsin's decree disbanding the Congress and fired several ministers who sided with him. Just to be sure, a rump session of the Congress (638 delegates, below the required quorum of 689) formally impeached Yeltsin. The following day, Yeltsin announced that an early presidential election would be held in June 1994 (it wasn't), only to be countered by the Congress, which offered early legislative elections for March (which didn't happen, either).

The initial public reaction was hard to read. At first demonstrations occurred backing both sides, although public support would overwhelmingly swing to Yeltsin in the final days. The intelligentsia initially stood aloof, condemning both sides for the nation's problems. The military, whose role would be critical, maintained formal neutrality.

A week after the crisis began, the Interior Ministry surrounded and lay siege to the White House, which now contained an estimated military force of 600 as well as the original deputies. Despite efforts by the Russian Orthodox Church to broker an agreement, both sides steeled themselves for further clashes. On October 3, pro-Congress forces broke through the barricades and took control of the office of the mayor of the city and then marched to the television control facilities some distance away at Ostankino. A bloody clash occurred, but Yeltsin's forces held control of the television center.

It was now obvious that civil war was near, at least in Moscow. Public opinion began to shift in Yeltsin's favor, if for no other reason than his ability to frame the issue in terms of a struggle to prevent the return of communism. For Yeltsin, only two things were needed: confidence that the military—both officers and common soldiers—would follow his orders to seize the White House, and a plan of action. In fact, the top brass were divided and overly cautious; only slowly did they come to back the government, some demanding written orders before committing their units to action. But in the end, they accepted Yeltsin's actions as appropriate and necessary, albeit illegal.

The plan was easy, and a bit ironic. It took only one tank—the one on which he stood—for Yeltsin to defeat the coup attempt in August 1991. Now ten would be needed, some firing live rounds. In a room full of generals, the plan of action was devised by a low-ranking captain, who argued that troops should surround the White House and ten tanks be positioned in front of it. The tanks would fire a few rounds (mostly blanks) into the upper floors, largely for psychological effect and to discourage snipers. Loyal troops would begin to take the building floor by floor, with frequent breaks to permit those who wished to surrender to come forward. The only real hitch in the plan was reminiscent of life as it used to be; the tanks were easily available, but their crews had been deployed to a collective farm to help with the harvest.

By eight the next morning, October 4, the tanks (and their crews) were in place. After the initial shelling, troops began to enter the building. Resistance was minimal. Rutskoi and Khasbulatov negotiated a surrender and were taken off to prison. Eventually convicted of various offenses, they were pardoned by the newly elected legislature, as were the leaders of the 1991 coup.

About the future of Yeltsin's Russia, conventional wisdom waxed optimistic. Yeltsin was once again the man of the hour. He had written a new constitution tailored to his style of rule; he had created a completely new and much less powerful legislature; he had crafted a strong presidency, with no vice president to look over his shoulder; he had won endorsement in a referendum; he had defeated and discredited his opponents on both left and right; he was supported, at least at first, by a public that understood and approved of his actions, however unconstitutional; and he was touted by the international community as the savior of real democracy in Russia.

Foreign Policy

Although the end of the cold war fundamentally changed the nature of the international system, it did little to define a new role for Russia. Throughout his tenure as president, Yeltsin attempted to define that role in light of new international realities and the increasingly contentious world of Russian domestic politics. Not surprisingly, foreign policy was never at the top of his growing list of things to be done and crises to be managed, especially during the escalating confrontation with the legislature. Far less sophisticated and well-traveled than Gorbachev, Yeltsin drew heavily on his advisors whose own conflicting ideas about Russia's role in the post–cold war world fueled an intensifying debate about the nation's future.

Some realities seemed unavoidable. Russia was adrift in a new world largely of its own making. No longer a superpower—but still with a formidable military establishment and a sizable nuclear arsenal—Russia had to get used to the idea of wielding less influence in world affairs. But how much less, and what should it do with its diminished power provoked a fundamental debate. Was it still a global power, albeit in reduced measure? If not, was it primarily a European or Eurasian power, or both and perhaps a bridge between the two?

At first, Yeltsin's foreign policy closely followed the essential guidelines set forth by Gorbachev's new thinking. The new Russian foreign minister, Andrei Kozyrev, came to the task with long experience in the international organizations department of the soviet foreign ministry, hardly the central focus of Moscow's old foreign policy. Initial priorities included the promotion of human rights and universal values, a continuation of efforts to reduce the threat of nuclear war, and economic assistance from the West to shore up the Russian economy through its difficult transition to capitalism. Stress fell on (1) implementing these goals through Russia's membership in international organizations and (2) Russia's willingness to become a contributing member of the elite club of democratic and industrially advanced nations. Russia soon joined the Western-dominated forums such as the G-7, the Council of Europe, the Paris Club and the London Club (both specialize in debt reduction), and the International Monetary Fund, and it negotiated special relationships with the European Union and NATO. Relations with the United States remained close, in part because of Moscow's assessment that Washington's backing was the key to economic assistance and in part because the two "comeback kids"—Bill Clinton and Boris Yeltsin—established a close relationship. The details of START II, which promised a continuation of arms reductions begun with START I, were hammered out in June 1992, and the agreement was signed in January of the following year. For the first several years, greater emphasis was given to better relations with the United States and Europe, an orientation dubbed "Atlanticism" by its supporters and critics alike. By late 1992, growing criticism came from others who described themselves as "Eurasianists" or "pragmatic nationalists." Their challenge was driven by two realities: Russian politics was taking an increasingly confrontational and nationalist tone, and economic support from the West was far smaller than Moscow had hoped.

By early 1993, Yeltsin had softened his initial pro-Western bias and shifted to a more centrist position. Publishing a long-delayed formal statement on foreign policy priorities, Yeltsin now incorporated some of the demands of the pragmatic nationalists and Eurasianists, although he eschewed the more confrontational positions of the extremes of both camps. Primary focus fell on Moscow's relations with the near abroad and the protection of the 25 million Russians living there; the further integration of the Commonwealth of Independent States; and relations with Eastern Europe, which was claimed to be within Moscow's "historical sphere of interests." Consistent with the notion of Russia as the bridge between East and West, the doctrine also attached increased importance to Asia, especially China and Japan. A new military doctrine published later that year scaled down emphasis on nuclear weapons and parity with the West and emphasized the creation of rapid deployment forces more suitable to the maintenance of stability in the near abroad and Eastern Europe.[28]

Yeltsin as an Authoritarian Modernizer: A Preliminary Assessment

Although no complete assessment of Yeltsin as an authoritarian modernizer can be made at this stage of his presidency, some preliminary thoughts are in order. Given the way in which the era ended, it is difficult not to conclude that Yeltsin had few reservations about imposing his will when he thought it mattered. No matter how it was justified, and no matter how strong Yeltsin's earlier support in the public opinion polls, the June 1991 presidential election, and the March 1993 referendum, disbanding the Congress and the eventual assault to dislodge the rump government that had taken haven in the White House was a coup. Perhaps a necessary one, as most Russians and many in the West reluctantly concluded, but a coup nonetheless. But that's what authoritarian modernizers do, for the sake of the greater good as they understand it. They break the rules of the game as it is currently being played. Like Lenin or Stalin or any of the other authoritarian modernizers of the late nineteenth and twentieth centuries, Yeltsin chose ends over means, even if it meant violent confrontation. In this sense, he was far more typical of the model of authoritarian modernizers than Gorbachev, who sought to finesse his way through reforms that would rearrange and transform institutions. This is not to deny the reality that Yeltsin also sought compromise at times in his choice of prime ministers or his willingness to accept a de facto power-sharing agreement brokered by Zorkin, the head of the Constitutional Court. And it certainly is not to argue that the failure of these short-lived arrangements falls solely on his shoulders. But it is to accept the conclusion that Yeltsin was willing to risk all for the sake of breaking the gridlock that had stalemated Russian government for two years.

But how good a modernizer was he? Did he have a transformational agenda that would redefine the nation and not merely change the identity of those in power? Certainly he accepted the conventional wisdom of the day that democracy was the wave of the future. But as we will see more clearly in Chapter 4, he never seriously attempted to institutionalize his rule through the formation of a presidential party that could link the presidency to a controlling majority within the legislature, win control in regional legislative and executive elections, and form a network of party organizations throughout the nation. For him, the presidency was enough, an understandable point of view in a nation that had always personalized political power. But it also had serious implications about how presidential rule would evolve under his successors.

Yeltsin also accepted another element of global conventional wisdom that held that market economies, or mixed market-/state-regulated economies, were a part of what it meant to be modern in today's world. For this he had a plan—the 500-day program of structural reforms and privatization around which he had campaigned in 1991—although the outcome produced unexpected economic and political results. Unlike Gorbachev, whose cerebral vision of the future was short on details and hard to sell to the common citizen, Yeltsin thought in simpler terms—stability, prosperity, and democratic rule based on a strong presidency—and he had the street smarts to know how to sell it to the average person.

Notes

1. Leon Aron, *Yeltsin: A Revolutionary Life*, St. Martin's, 2000, 3–130; Timothy J. Colton, *Yeltsin: A Life*, Basic Books, 2008, 11–30; and George W. Breslauer, *Gorbachev and Yeltsin as Leaders*, Cambridge University Press, 2002, 108–318.

2. Colton, *Yeltsin*, 107–127; and Aron, *Yeltsin*, 131–217.

3. Mikhail S. Gorbachev, *Memoirs*, Doubleday, 1996, 241–251; Aron, *Yeltsin*, 201–217; and Colton, *Yeltsin*, 129–150.

4. Alexander Dallin, ed., *Political Parties in Russia*, University of California Press, 1993; Robert G. Moser, *Unexpected Outcomes: Electoral Systems, Political Parties, and Representation in Russia*, University of Pittsburgh Press, 2001; Andrey A. Meleshevich, *Party System in Post-Soviet Countries: A Comparative Study of Political Institutionalization in the Baltic States, Russia, and Ukraine*, Palgrave Macmillan, 2007; and Donald R. Kelley, *Politics in Russia and the Successor States*, Harcourt Brace, 1999, 227–246.

5. Shannon G. Davis, "The Unexpected Revolution: Gorbachev, Glasnost, and Nationalities Policy," in Donald R. Kelley and Shannon G. Davis, eds., *The Sons of Sergei: Khrushchev and Gorbachev as Reformers*, Praeger, 1992, 123–152.

6. Boris Yeltsin, *The Struggle for Russia*, Random House, 1994, 18–20; Aron, *Yeltsin*, 361-387; and Colton, *Yeltsin*, 116–176.

7. Breslauer, *Gorbachev and Yeltsin*, 108–40; and Colton, *Yeltsin*, 151–76.

8. Aron, *Yeltsin*, 308–19; and Colton, *Yeltsin*, 169–78.

9. Colton, *Yeltsin*, 178–92, 251–3; Aron, *Yeltsin*, 363–70; and Jerry F. Hough, *Democratization and Revolution in the USSR, 1985–1991*, Brookings, 1997, 293–305.

10. Thomas M. Nichols, *The Russian Presidency: Society and Politics in the Second Russian Republic,* St. Martin's, 1999, 49–63.

11. Aron, *Yeltsin,* 429–36.

12. Boris Yeltsin, *Midnight Diaries,* Public Affairs, 2000, 363–64; Aron, *Yeltsin,* 200–02, 221–22; and Colton, *Yeltsin,* 138–50,152–62,180–202, 194–96, 203–12.

13. Aron, *Yeltsin,* 419.

14. Aron, *Yeltsin,* 386.

15. Peter Reddaway and Dmitri Glinski, *The Tragedy of Russia's Economic Reform,* U.S. Institute of Peace,2001, 231–308.

16. Gorbachev, *Memoirs,* 372–400; and Hough, *Democratization and Revolution,* 103–39, 341–372.

17. Gorbachev, *Memoirs,* 373–436.

18. James Leitzel, *Russian Economic Reform,* Routledge, 1995; Marshall I. Goldman, *The Piratization of Russia: Russian Economic Reforms Go Awry,* Routledge, 2003; Andrei Shleifer and Daniel Treisman, *Without a Map: Political Tactics and Economic Reform in Russia,* MIT Press, 2000; and Peter Reddaway and Dmitri Glinski, *The Tragedy of Russia's Reforms: Market Bolshevism against Democracy,* U.S. Institute of Peace Press, 2001.

19. Gorbachev, *Memoirs,* 356–71.

20. Edward W. Walker, *Dissolution: Sovereignty and the Breakup of the Soviet Union,* Rowman and Littlefield, 2003; Roman Szporluk, *Russia, Ukraine, and the Breakup of the Soviet Union,* Hoover Institute, 2000; and Richard J. Krickus, *Showdown: The Lithuanian Rebellion and the Breakup of the Soviet Empire,* Brasseys, 1997.

21. Gorbachev, *Memoirs,* 584–93; Colton, *Yeltsin,* 191–92; and Aron, *Yeltsin,* 428–30, 505–08.

22. Peter H. Solomon, Jr. and Todd S. Foglesong, *Courts and Transition in Russia: The Challenge of Judicial Reform,* Westview, 2000; and Alexei Trochev, *The Role of the Constitutional Court in Russian Politics, 1990–2000,* Cambridge University Press, 2009.

23. Yeltsin, *The Struggle for Russia,* 183–284; Aron, *Yeltsin,* 494–553; and Colton, *Yeltsin,* 237–90.

24. Aron, *Yeltsin,* 496–524; and R.I. Khasbulatov, *The Struggle for Russia: Power and Change in the Democratic Revolution,* Routledge, 1993.

25. Aron, *Yeltsin,* 505–06.

26. Aron, *Yeltsin,* 510–12.

27. Yeltsin, *Struggle for Russia,* 217–84; Aron, *Yeltsin,* 515–53; and Colton, 275–92.

28. Robert H. Donaldson and Joseph L. Nogee, *The Foreign Policy of Russia: Changing Systems, Enduring Interests,* M.E. Sharpe, 1998; Neil Malcolm, Alex Pravda, Roy Allison, and Margot Light, eds., *Internal Factors in Russian Foreign Policy,* Oxford University Press, 1996; Leon Aron and Kenneth M. Jensen, eds., *The Emergence of Russian Foreign Policy,* U.S. Institute of Peace Press, 1994; Dmitri Simes, *After the Collapse: Russia Seeks Its Place as a Great Power,* Simon and Schuster, 1999; and Jeffrey Mankoff, *Russia Foreign Policy: The Return of Great Power Politics,* Rowman and Littlefield, 2009.

4

Yeltsin and Russia Reborn

B oris Yeltsin's action against the Congress of People's Deputies had been bold but not decisive. Russia got a new constitution, a stronger presidency, a new legislature, and a promise of immediate elections to the newly created Federal Assembly and, in the near future, new presidential elections as well. But in other areas, little changed. Some, but not all, of those promises would be kept. The Duma, the lower house of the new Federal Assembly, elected in December 1993, continued to be hostile to Yeltsin and his reform agenda; the next legislative election, held in 1995 when the truncated term of the first Duma ran out, was somewhat less hostile, but the legislative and executive branches remained strikingly at odds on most points. The promise to advance the date of the next presidential election was not kept.

The new draft constitution was ratified by a popular referendum held on December 12, 1993, and went into force on December 25, two years to the day since Gorbachev's resignation. Voter turnout was surprisingly low. A 50-percent turnout was required for the referendum to be valid. Only 55 percent of eligible voters went to the polls, and there were unsubstantiated claims that election officials had inflated the figure to avoid a second ballot. Of those who voted, just over 58 percent approved the new document.

Under the old order, there was no real distinction between the legislative and executive functions of government. In constitutional terms, Yeltsin was eager to separate the two. But he resisted the creation of effective checks and balances. The new constitution therefore created an institutional structure in which the presidency was given exceptional powers to run the country in the absence of agreement with the legislature. In a perfect world, agreement between the two branches was the preferred state of affairs. But the realities of post-communist Russia seemed to stack the deck against such accord, at least in the short run.

Relations between the central and regional governments were crafted to reflect the same balance of power and authority. Yeltsin, who had urged that the republics break away from the central government of the now-defunct Soviet Union, found himself facing regional authorities who demanded greater latitude within the Russian Federation. The undeniable reality was that Moscow was weaker in terms of its control over regional authorities than it had been for nearly two centuries.

After considering a number of possible constitutional models, including the U.S. presidential system, Yeltsin and his advisors chose the mixed presidential-parliamentary system of the French Fifth Republic. Created by Charles de Gaulle, who was its first and unarguably strongest president, the Fifth Republic was born in the midst of political crisis and near civil war and contained many of the features that Yeltsin wanted: a strong president, eventually directly elected and with reserve powers to rule in the case of legislative inaction or deadlock between the legislative and executive branches; a viable but presumably badly divided legislature, at least if the Third and Fourth Republics were any guide; an upper house, weaker but chosen to speak for the regions; a relatively weak judicial branch; and—or so everyone anticipated—a bitterly divided multiparty system that militated against the creation of stable majorities in the lower house of the legislature. As it turned out, only part of this vision was true. Although the institutional structure remained essentially the same, two unanticipated realities changed the way in which French politics operated, both during de Gaulle's tenure in office and under his successors.

First, the party system stabilized in a way never possible under the Third and Fourth Republics; although many smaller parties remained, the overall configuration gelled into a reasonably stable coalition between the center-right and the center-left. The former was led by the Gaullist party itself, which initially came together because of de Gaulle's personal dominance in the early years of the Fifth Republic but continued after his resignation in 1969 as a pragmatic alliance of center-right forces. To a lesser degree, the left fell into line behind (or at least grudgingly cooperated with) the Socialist Party, although the Communist Party found it difficult to reach any lasting accommodation.

The other unanticipated reality that shaped the Fifth Republic and made it an attractive model for Yeltsin to follow was the dominant role played by de Gaulle himself. What characterized the Fifth Republic was not just the creation of a strong presidency as an institution but also the fact that de Gaulle held the post for ten years. In retrospect, it seems that he was destined to play that role, but he had earlier abandoned the Fourth Republic and gone into self-imposed political exile largely because it failed to respond to his leadership. When the Fifth Republic was created, there were no guarantees that it would not produce the same results. What made the difference was de Gaulle's ability to reach beyond the conventional political establishment to create a new center-right coalition and to use the reserve powers of the presidency such as direct referenda to frame issues as a choice between stability or a return to the political gridlock of the past.[1]

For Yeltsin, of course, this sort of mixed presidential-parliamentary system offered attractive options. Beyond the institutional features of the system, this configuration fit his own concept of how he wished to lead the nation. Like the French presidency, its Russian counterpart was, in a way, "above" politics—at least in terms of narrow partisan interests and squabbling among parties and legislative factions. Yeltsin saw himself as standing apart from the day-to-day ebb and flow of political combat. It fit Yeltsin's style of dramatic confrontation and disinterest in the details of government. In *Midnight Diaries,* Yeltsin bragged that "[n]obody has ever been able to force me to play by his rules," an attitude that aptly summed up his hope to continue to play the dominant role, as had de Gaulle, in his republic.[2] Boris's constitution, Boris's rules. . . .

It didn't completely work out that way, of course, because there were major differences between the Russian and French experiences. Most important was the fact that Yeltsin wasn't de Gaulle. For a host of reasons discussed in this chapter, Yeltsin led with an unsteady hand. Whereas de Gaulle had been *above* politics, a posture that bespoke stability and disdain for partisanship, Yeltsin was frequently *away from* politics, which produced a vacuum in the nation's political life.

Just as significant was the reality that no stable party emerged to underpin Yeltsin's rule, either within the legislature or as a liaison to an institutionalized grassroots movement. The "parties of power" cobbled together for legislative or presidential elections were temporary affairs. Above politics, Yeltsin also was above party identity, a posture that permitted him greater latitude at key moments such as the 1996 presidential election but also cost him in terms of the practical advantages of a continuing grassroots organization, a significant liability since the newly reconstituted Communist Party of the Russian Federation retained a significant part of its old structure.

A word about Yeltsin the man also is appropriate. The old Boris was still there in many ways. Pugnacious, confrontational, and convinced that the best defense was a good offense, little of his style changed when he was on his game. But over the balance of his first term, and throughout his second term, he was less and less on his game. Less frequent would be those moments of focus and discipline, and more frequent would be long stretches of withdrawal, depression, ill health, and, by his own admission, excessive drinking, which he finally brought under control. At times he showed—at least for him—a remarkable willingness to compromise with the still-hostile legislature, especially over the appointment of mutually acceptable prime ministers like Viktor Chernomyrdin. Perhaps fearing another constitutional crisis, the Duma responded in kind, most of the time. And at times, despite ill health and depression, he roused himself to be the old Boris. If his finest moments had come atop a tank in 1991 and in standing his ground against the Congress of People's Deputies in 1993, he rose to stage an equally impressive last hurrah in his literally death-defying campaign for a second term in 1996.

He was a better underdog than winner. He knew that about himself and bragged repeatedly that he was at his best in moments of crisis or near defeat, whether in sports, the crisis-ridden construction industry, or politics.[3] He relied on this aspect of his personality to move mountains, a strategy that worked more often than not.

But with victory secured, Yeltsin frequently would retreat into isolation and disinterest. In his later years, some of this could be attributed to worsening health. But even if we allow for that, he still seemed to lose interest and focus, never moving to consolidate his victories or acquire lasting advantage, especially if it meant personally dealing with the day-to-day management of the state or the organization of an institutionalized political base. He never quite put it this way, but the truth was that he bored easily, leading him to hand over the lesser tasks of governance to others. Sometimes that worked quite well if the aides or prime ministers were talented (Yegor Gaidar, who implemented economic reforms) or smoothed the waters separating the president from his enemies (Chernomyrdin, who on two occasions brought both personal competence and political experience to the office of prime minister, and Yevgeny Primakov, probably the most talented and politically skilled of Yeltsin's prime ministers). But aides and prime ministers would come and go frequently, sacrificed as politics sometimes demands or sacked simply because Yeltsin lost confidence in them. But near the end, the quality of the new appointees seriously deteriorated, and Yeltsin, now less personally able to take control, countenanced the emergence of a strong kitchen cabinet of advisors, with his daughter, Tatiana Diachenko, and his own personal security chief, Alexander Korzhakov, playing key roles.

The Presidency and the Legislature

The 1993 constitution created a new political battleground whose institutional features were to shape Russian political life. Although the organizational chart presented in Figure 4.1 suggests a very simple division of power and responsibility, reality is far more complex. In a way, both the presidency and the legislature are still works in progress. The new legislature, the Federal Assembly, is bicameral. The upper house, called the Federation Council, is designed to reflect the federal structure of the Russian state; two delegates are selected from each of Russia's regions. At first, one delegate was chosen by the local legislature, the other by the local governor, although that arrangement would change in coming years. Delegates initially served a four-year term.

The Federation Council's primary responsibilities lie in the areas of interregional affairs and national security. It approves border changes between regions; approves presidential decrees on the creation of a state of emergency; "decide(s) on the possibility of using the armed forces of the Russian Federation beyond its territory," a purposely vague and hence meaningless charge; schedules presidential elections; appoints various federal officials; and, potentially most significant, hears impeachment charges brought by the Duma against the president.

The lower house, the popularly elected Duma, enjoys significantly greater powers. It contains 450 members. Initially 225 were elected in single-member districts and 225 from party lists. No party with less than 5 percent of the party list votes got seats. The original arrangement—a loose copy of the German system—was intended to reflect the reality that political parties had not yet taken hold by 1993. The result, at least in the early years, was the election of a significant number of independents drawn from local bailiwicks, making it difficult to cobble together majorities on the floor of the Duma.

On paper, the powers of the legislature seem impressive. The Duma must approve the president's choice for prime minister and may undertake a vote of no confidence against any incumbent (but if successful, the vote affects only the prime minister, not the president). If the legislature refuses three times to accept the nominee, the president may dissolve the Duma and call for new elections. Not surprisingly, this created an undefined sparring ground between the president and a willful legislature, although both would usually step away from confrontation at the last minute and find a compromise that left both claiming at least partial victory.

Figure 4.1   Russian Government

PRESIDENT

- Directly elected, with run-off if no candidate gets majority on the first round
- 6-year term (4-year term before 2012)
- Two consecutive term limit
- Names prime minister; Duma confirmation required
- Can dismiss prime minister
- Submits draft legislation
- Signs and vetoes bills
- Issues executive decrees
- May request referenda
- Can dismiss legislature and call for a new general election
- Commander-in-chief of the armed forces
- Has primary role in making and implementing foreign policy

PRIME MINISTER

- Serves as chief administrative officer of the government, working through the cabinet, ministries, and other agencies
- Serves at the pleasure of the president
- Subject to a vote of no confidence by the Duma, which the president may accept or reject
- Automatically resigns, as does entire government, upon the election of a new president
- Becomes acting president upon the resignation or death of a president until a new election is held

FEDERAL ASSEMBLY

DUMA	FEDERATION COUNCIL
• 450 seats, 5-year term (4-year until 2011) • 225 chosen by proportional representation • 225 chosen in single-member districts (in 2007 and 2011, all seats chosen by proportional representation) • Confirms prime minister in office • Can vote no confidence in prime minister • Introduces legislation • Can override presidential veto by two-thirds vote • Initiates impeachment against president	• 170 seats (two from each administrative unit plus presidential appointees) • One elected by local legislature • One selected by governor • Votes on all legislation • Votes on impeachment proceedings initiated by the Duma

SOURCE: Compiled by the author.

Should the Duma pass a vote of no confidence against the prime minister, the president has a number of options. He may simply ignore the legislature's action; the Duma's only recourse is to pass the same vote of no confidence three times within two months, which will force the president to take action. The president may then respond in one of two ways: He may either submit a new nominee, subject to the Duma's confirmation, or dissolve the legislature itself, resulting in new elections. Needless to say, cooler heads usually prevailed at the last moment, leading to a face-saving compromise.

The Duma's greatest powers emerge from its normal function of law making. As noted in the following, the dual executive system envisioned a division of labor between the president and the prime minister. The president would be responsible for the big picture, charting the nation's course of action and submitting important legislation, while the prime minister would be responsible for securing its passage through the Duma and its ultimate implementation through the government bureaucracy, of which he is the nominal head. Success therefore depended on two things: agreement between the president and the prime minister, and the latter's ability to get legislation through the Duma. That meant being an effective floor manager who could pull together enough votes in a badly divided and hostile legislature. Political reality therefore gave the Duma considerable leverage against Yeltsin, whose years in power were characterized by an internally divided Duma, a weak party structure, and continuing friction between the president and the legislature.[4]

Potential power also lies in the Duma's right to initiate the impeachment of the president, although the process is long and difficult. First, the Duma has to bring a charge of high treason or other serious crimes against the president. These charges have to be supported by two thirds of the deputies, based on the recommendation of a specially constituted Duma commission. Should the Duma vote to pursue impeachment, the Supreme Court has to affirm that the elements of a crime were present, and the Constitutional Court has to confirm that the Duma has followed the proper impeachment proceedings. The matter then goes to the Federation Council, which can convict the president by a two-thirds vote, provided that the action is completed within three months of the Duma's first indictment. Given this complexity, impeachment is hardly a sword of Damocles hanging over any president's head.

The Duma does have some constitutional protections against capricious presidential action. The president cannot dissolve it within the first year of its term, even if it twice votes no confidence in the government. Nor can he dissolve it until an impeachment process has run its course or during a period of emergency rule or martial law, states that may be invoked by the president.

It is the presidency, however, that is the real cornerstone of the 1993 constitution. It has evolved over its relatively short history toward a consolidation of power increasingly into the hands of the president and, in the broader federal context, the central government in Moscow.

Whatever the course of that evolution, it started with the 1993 constitution and Yeltsin's frustration with the leftovers of the soviet era. The presidency was to be his mechanism of rule. In the best of worlds, it would work in tandem with the legislature and with regional governments to sort through the issues and disputes involved in redesigning the nation from the ground up. But under less auspicious circumstances, the president would have the ability to force everyone to play the game by new rules. And, as recent history had confirmed, he was just the man to rise to such an occasion.

The list of presidential powers and advantages is impressive, with some limitations:

- The president is directly elected and thus receives a clear public mandate; in the event that no one wins a majority on the first round of voting, a runoff election is held between the top two, guaranteeing that a plurality-elected administration would never take office.
- The president "determines the basic guidelines for . . . domestic and foreign policy," thus confirming his far-reaching powers and his status as "above" politics.
- The president nominates the prime minister, who will function as his liaison to the Duma and director of the day-to-day administrative activities of government; if the Duma refuses to confirm the president's choice in three separate ballots, the president may dissolve the assembly and call for new legislative elections.
- The president may dismiss the government, including the prime minister and the cabinet, who serve at his pleasure.
- The president, in consultation with the prime minister, names the other members of the cabinet and the deputy premiers.
- The president names the director of the State Bank and may propose the director's dismissal.
- The president nominates justices of the Supreme Court, the Constitutional Court, and the Higher Court of Arbitration, subject to confirmation by the Federation Council.
- The president names the members of and chairs the Security Council, which plays an important but not exclusive role in determining foreign and military policy and the maintenance of public order at home.

- The president "confirms" the military doctrine of the nation and acts as commander-in-chief of the armed forces.
- The president appoints representatives to oversee regional and local governments, a mechanism that Yeltsin and Vladimir Putin used with increasing success to rein in the de facto devolution of power to the regions.
- The president may request public referenda, subject to certain restrictions imposed by federal constitutional law.
- The president may dissolve the Duma and schedule new elections, subject to certain restrictions.
- The president may submit draft legislation.
- The president signs all federal laws, thus granting the president veto power that could be overridden by a two-thirds vote of both the Duma and the Federation Council.
- The president may suspend the decisions of regional government if he judges them to be at variance with the constitution, subject to post facto confirmation by the courts.
- The president "exercises leadership" on foreign policy, thus becoming both the key policy maker and the top diplomat.
- The president may proclaim martial law or states of emergency, requiring "notification" of the Duma and the Federation Council.
- The president may issue presidential decrees and directives that, if constitutional, are binding on regional and local governments.[5]

The presidency clearly had significant powers, but using them was not always easy. All of these powers had to be exercised with the realization that the nation had just gone through a major political crisis and narrowly avoided a civil war. For a while at least, everyone would tread cautiously, posturing when it brought little real danger but drawing back just shy of all-out confrontation. Political realities limited risk taking. For its part, the Duma stopped short of provoking the president to a point at which he would exercise his power to dissolve the assembly and call a new general election. Yeltsin wisely declined to call for referenda, which he had used so successfully before. The dangers of a stunning, although symbolic defeat were just too great for Yeltsin, who had grown so cautious that he withdrew his promise, made during the 1993 constitutional crisis, to hold new presidential elections, now insisting that he would serve out his term until 1996.

Judicial Reform

The 1993 constitution established three types of courts. The Supreme Court serves at the apex of the courts of general jurisdiction, internally subdivided to deal with issues of civil, criminal, military, and administrative law, and to handle appeals from lower courts. Consistent with the handling of economic issues during the soviet era, now a growing problem with the privatization of the economy, a system of lower-level commercial arbitration courts and the Supreme Court of Arbitration were established to deal with business and contract disputes.

Most important in political terms is the Constitutional Court. It is responsible for cases dealing with conformity to the constitution; judicial disputes between federal bodies, including the presidency and the legislature; disputes between the central government and the regional authorities; and disputes between regional governments. It has the power of constitutional review of laws passed by the legislature, presidential decrees and directives, local constitutions and charters, and agreements between the central government and the regions, or between the regions themselves. Controversial from its inception, it did not begin its work until February 1995 because the Federation Council, the upper house of the legislature, repeatedly refused to certify the appointment of judges nominated by Yeltsin.[6]

The 1993 Duma Elections

The elections for the new Duma were paired with the constitutional referendum in December 1993. They were a sobering setback for Yeltsin, whose newly empowered presidency would face off against a distinctly hostile legislature. The biggest winner in the proportional representation voting was the Liberal Democratic Party, led by the charismatic Vladimir Zhirinovsky (Table 4.1). It was neither liberal nor pro-democracy, but it obviously was popular, drawing support for its nationalistic and anti-Yeltsin stance. It received 22.9 percent of the popular vote, nearly eight points ahead of its closest rival, Russia's Choice. That was enough for fifty-nine seats chosen by party-list voting. Adding another eleven from the single-member-district voting, it held a total of seventy seats in the 450-member Duma.[7]

Russia's Choice ran as the pro-Yeltsin party, although he refused to formally endorse it or to campaign openly for its candidates. It pulled only 15.5 percent of the popular vote, earning it forty seats among those chosen by party-list voting. It got fifty-six more seats in the district voting, for a total of ninety-six. Particularly disappointing was the low level of public support evidenced in the party-list voting. It did better in the district voting because local power brokers, anxious to jump on what they hoped was a winning bandwagon, backed what they thought would be the next party of power. But the diminished support among rank-and-file voters indicated that Yeltsin was in trouble.

Table 4.1   1993 Russian Legislative Election

Party	Proportional Representation	Single-Member-District Voting	Total Seats
Liberal Democratic Party	Votes: 12,318,562 Percentage: 22.9 Seats: 59	Votes: 1,577,400 Percentage: 3.0 Seats: 11	70
Russia's Choice	Votes: 8,339,345 Percentage: 15.5 Seats: 40	Votes: 3,630,799 Percentage: 6.8 Seats: 56	96
Communist Party	Votes: 6,666,402 Percentage: 12.4 Seats: 32	1,848,888 Percentage: 3.5 Seats: 33	65
Women of Russia	Votes: 4,369,918 Percentage: 8.1 Seats: 21	Votes: 309,378 Percentage: 0.6 Seats: 4	25
Agrarian Party	Votes: 4,292,518 Percentage: 8.0 Seats: 21	Votes: 2,877,610 Percentage: 5.4 Seats: 26	47
Yavlinsky-Boldyrev-Lukin bloc (Yabloko)	Votes: 4,223,219 Percentage: 7.9 Seats: 20	Votes: 1,849,120 Percentage: 3.5 Seats: 13	33
Party of Russian Unity and Accord	Votes: 3,620,035 Percentage: 6.7 Seats: 18	Votes: 1,443,454 Percentage: 2.7 Seats: 9	27
Democratic Party	Votes: 2,969,533 Percentage: 5.5 Seats: 14	Votes: 1,094,066 Percentage: 2.1 Seats: 7	21
Russian Democratic Reform Movement	Votes: 2,191,505 Percentage: 4.1 Seats: 0	Votes: 1,083,063 Percentage: 2.0 Seats: 8	8
Civic Union	Votes: 1,038,193 Percentage: 1.9 Seats: 0	Votes: 1,526115 Percentage: 2.9 Seats: 18	18
Independents		Votes: 25,961,405 Percentage: 48.7 Seats: 30	30

SOURCE: D. Nohlen and P. Stover. (2010). *Elections in Europe: A Data Handbook*. Baden-Baden, Germany: Nomos.

The Communist Party of the Russian Federation came in third, with 12.4 percent of the party-list vote, giving it thirty-two seats; it picked up another thirty-three from the districts, for a total of sixty-five. Newly reconstituted as a social democratic party, the Communist Party received the backing of the former party members who had not reconciled themselves to the new order of things and the growing number of ordinary citizens deeply affected by Yeltsin's economic reforms. It still had considerable advantages in terms of its grassroots organization.

A number of smaller parties trailed behind. Women of Russia got 8.1 percent of the party-list vote, for twenty-one seats, with four more seats from the districts. Next came the Agrarian Party, with 8.0 percent, also for twenty-one seats, with an additional twenty-six from district voting, for a total of forty-seven. It frequently followed the lead of the Communist Party, which it viewed as a natural ally in representing both urban and rural workers.

The pro-democracy parties fared poorly. Largest among them was the so-called Yavlinsky-Boldyrev-Lukin bloc, or Yabloko (all ardent democrats and former Yeltsin allies), with 7.9 percent of the vote, for twenty seats, with another thirteen from the districts. As always, other liberal parties, unable to form effective alliances, divided voters among themselves.

These vote totals fail to tell the whole story. Once seated, delegates sorted themselves into various parliamentary groups or factions that may or may not have been in strict accord with the party labels (if any) under which they ran. At first, an individual delegate could belong to many groups, further muddying the waters. Identification with a group was not necessarily stable over time, and a delegate could follow the lead of different groups on different issues. Party and group discipline was nonexistent. When examined from this perspective, the picture is even more complex. At any time, the Liberal Democratic Party faction could range from 53 to 64 votes, and the Communist Party from 45 to 47. Factions could be formed independently of party identity. Yabloko, with 27 to 29 votes, was never very successful in forging unity among pro-democracy forces. Odd bedfellows emerged frequently, as in the so-called red-brown alliance between the Communist Party and the Liberal Democrats.

The partisan divisions within the Federation Council were harder to discern. Most candidates had run as independents. The best estimates are that Russia's Choice held forty seats, with eight others held by pro-democracy delegates. Moderate reformers held another twenty-three, and moderate opponents of the regime, many identified with the former Civic Union, thirty-six. The Communist Party and other left-wing parties held twenty seats. The rest of the delegates were militantly independent.

In light of the election returns, Yeltsin moved cautiously. For their part, the leaders of both houses of the legislature responded in kind, and an uneasy peace descended over the land. Yeltsin named Chernomyrdin prime minister, stoking opposition from many in his early reform team who thought he was backing away from his commitments, but reassuring others that the president did not want to provoke another confrontation. In 1994, Yeltsin drafted a "Civic Accord," a political peace treaty committing all who signed to set aside their differences and seek agreement for two years. In April, almost all the parties signed, some undoubtedly with their fingers crossed behind their backs. Absent, however, were the Communist Party and its ally, the Agrarian Party, and Yabloko, the home of those who now criticized Yeltsin from the left.[8]

With the new constitution and a largely hostile legislature in place, Yeltsin moved to extend his reach through the creation of a larger presidential staff and a series of agencies that operated under his control, independent of legislative oversight. Most important was the Security Council, a sort of inner cabinet containing representatives of the "power" ministries that controlled national defense, foreign policy, intelligence, and internal security. Also significant was the expansion of the presidential apparatus, which by 1994 numbered over 2,000 people in Moscow alone, and extended its influence throughout the nation.[9]

If the office of the presidency were growing stronger, its incumbent was not. As he had done so many times before, Yeltsin withdrew into himself, shutting out all but a few trusted cronies like his security chief, Khorzhakov, and his daughter, Tatiana. Absences from his Kremlin office grew longer, and he did less and less even at his favorite dacha. He became increasingly despondent, potentially even suicidal. And he drank more and more, despite attempts by his inner circle to nudge him away from the bottle. Boris Yeltsin, who had willed himself to stand up against seemingly impossible odds in the past, was now on a downward spiral.[10]

The 1995 Duma Elections

In the spring of 1995, Yeltsin attempted to stabilize the field for the approaching legislative elections by fostering the creation of two broad coalitions. One would appeal to center-left forces and capture votes from Yabloko and the other reformist parties as well as the more moderate elements of the Communist Party. The other would be a center-right coalition that could lure votes from right-wing and nationalist groups like the Liberal Democratic Party and the new Congress of Russian Communities, led by Alexander Lebed, commander of Russian forces in Moldova, as well as from the growing business community. The center-left coalition would be led by Ivan Rybkin, speaker of the Duma, and the center-right group by Chernomyrdin, the prime minister.

The December elections were a confirmation of the growing disorder of Russian politics in general and of Yeltsin's declining popularity in particular. Over 270 political parties started out to collect the needed number of signatures to be included in the ballot, and 43 succeeded. These included the obvious players—Our Home Is Russia, which advanced Yeltsin's agenda of reform and would aid Chernomyrdin's hopes for eventually claiming the top post; the Communist Party, which led in the preelection polls and was critical of Yeltsin across the board; Yabloko, which argued for more rapid reform and an end to the war in Chechnya (discussed later in the chapter); the Congress of Russian Communities, which advocated nationalist causes and greater protection of the 25 million ethnic Russians now living in the other states created by the breakup of the Soviet Union; and the Liberal Democratic Party, which backed a nationalist and antireform platform (Table 4.2).

The results were a disaster for Yeltsin. The Communist Party was the biggest winner, taking 22.3 percent of the popular vote, for ninety-nine seats, and another fifty-eight in the single-member districts. Overall it went from sixty-five seats in the 1993 Duma to 157 in the new body, an increase of ninety-two seats. The Liberal Democratic Party came in second, dropping to 11.2 percent of the vote, for fifty party-list seats, and adding only one from the districts. It lost nineteen seats from the 1993 Duma. Our Home Is Russia, most clearly identified with the defense of the Yeltsin government, came in third, with 10.1 percent of the popular vote, for forty-five seats, with another ten from district balloting. Compared with Russia's Choice, the pro-Yeltsin party in the 1993 balloting, its popular support dropped by 5.4 percent in the proportional representation voting. Overall it lost forty-one seats. Yabloko got 6.9 percent of the popular vote, making it the last party to cross the 5-percent cutoff. That was enough to give it thirty-one party-list seats, with fourteen more from the district voting.[11]

Table 4.2   1995 Russian Legislative Election

Party	Proportional Representation	Single-Member-District Voting	Total Seats
Communist Party	Votes: 15,432,963 Percentage: 22.3 Seats: 99	Votes: 8,636,392 Percentage: 12.8 Seats: 58	157
Liberal Democratic Party	Votes: 7,737,431 Percentage: 11.2 Seats: 50	Votes: 3,801,971 Percentage: 5.6 Seats: 1	51
Our Home Is Russia	Votes: 7,009,291 Percentage: 10.1 Seats: 45	Votes: 3,808,745 Percentage: 5.6 Seats: 10	55
Yabloko	Votes: 4,767,384 Percentage: 6.9 Seats: 31	Votes: 2,209,945 Percentage: 3.3 Seats: 14	45
Women of Russia	Votes: 3,188,813 Percentage: 4.6 Seats: 0	Votes: 712,072 Percentage: 1.1 Seats: 3	3
Communists and Working Russia	Votes: 3,137,406 Percentage: 4.5 Seats: 0	Votes: 1,276,655 Percentage: 1.9 Seats: 1	1
Congress of Russian Communities	Votes: 2,980,137 Percentage: 4.3 Seats: 0	Votes: 1,987,665 Percentage: 2.9 Seats: 5	5
Party of Workers' Self-Government	Votes: 2,756,954 Percentage: 4.0 Seats: 0	Votes: 475,007 Percentage: 0.7 Seats: 1	1
Democratic Choice– United Democrats	Votes: 2,674,084 Percentage: 3.9 Seats: 0	Votes: 1,819,330 Percentage: 2.7 Seats: 9	9
Agrarian Party	Votes: 2,613,127 Percentage: 3.8 Seats: 0	Votes: 4,066,214 Percentage: 6.0 Seats: 20	20
Forward Russia	Votes: 1,343,428 Percentage: 1.9 Seats: 0	Votes: 1,054,577 Percentage: 1.6 Seats: 3	3
Power to the People	Votes: 1,112,873 Percentage: 1.6 Seats: 0	Votes: 1,345,905 Percentage: 2.0 Seats: 9	9
Independents		Votes: 21,620,835 Percentage: 32 Seats: 77	77

SOURCE: D. Nohlen and P. Stover. (2010). *Elections in Europe: A Data Handbook*. Baden-Baden, Germany: Nomos.

The creation of parliamentary groups sorted things out quite a bit, but certainly not to Yeltsin's advantage. The Communist Party bloc numbered 157 members, and its Agrarian Group ally, twenty, giving them the largest plurality in the Duma. Our Home Is Russia, the pro-Yeltsin coalition, and its allies came in second with only sixty-five seats. Zhirinovsky's Liberal Democratic bloc was third with fifty-one seats. That gave the "red-brown coalition" that frequently cooperated in the first Duma even greater power in the second. Yabloko, the only staunchly liberal party, was next, with forty-five seats.

The 1996 Presidential Election

Yeltsin made up his mind to run for reelection in December 1995, shortly after the Duma balloting.[12] It would be an uphill struggle, as the president and his advisors all knew. Despite the advantages of incumbency and the memory that twice before, in 1991 and 1993, Yeltsin had risked all to salvage his hopes for reform, the prospects were bleak. His popularity rating was in the single digits, a victim of the stalemated war in Chechnya and economic difficulties. He had withdrawn from public view, sulking in depression and growing alcoholism, with his absences unconvincingly explained away by a "cold" or a "sore throat." In truth, his health had deteriorated substantially and would continue to do so throughout the campaign. His few public appearances or trips abroad were filled with embarrassing lapses, a hardly reassuring omen that he could mount an effective comeback.

On February 15, 1996, Yeltsin journeyed to his home base in Ekaterinburg to announce his candidacy in the June election. From the beginning, his advisors were bitterly divided over campaign strategy or even whether the election should be held. First Deputy Prime Minister Oleg Soskovets was in charge initially. Working in tandem with Korzhakov, head of the president's security force and regarded as the éminence grise behind Yeltsin, they argued openly for a postponement of the election, perhaps coupled with a behind-the-scenes deal with the Communists to form a de facto coalition to rule the nation. On the other side of the issue were Anatoly Chubais, the moving spirit behind economic reforms who had been twice sacrificed for reasons of political expediency; Yeltsin's daughter, Tatiana; and a growing number of first-generation oligarchs who had made vast fortunes in the early economic reforms and were anxious to keep the Yeltsin ship afloat. Control over the campaign shifted gradually to the latter pro-election group, despite the risks. Under their guidance,

Boris would be Boris once again, dynamic, confrontational, and the harbinger of a frightening choice: It's me or a return to the past.[13]

The field of candidates was crowded. Seventy-eight candidates initially announced their intention to run, and seventeen actually collected the one million signatures needed to be listed on the ballot. Four of those were removed from contention by an election commission that allegedly found fraud in their applications, and others fell by the wayside. A number of the remaining eleven officially on the ballot were hardly serious choices, including a wealthy businessman who offered to run the country like a business, a former Olympic weightlifter and ultranationalist, and an eye surgeon.

Other candidates had more serious credentials. Zhirinovsky, whose Liberal Democratic Party had slipped in the Duma elections, was back again, as was Gennady Zyuganov, making another bid as head of the Communist Party. Grigory Yavlinsky, head of Yabloko, ran also. The most significant newcomer was Alexander Lebed, head of the Congress of Russian Communities and a strong supporter of nationalist causes, especially the fate of the large ethnic Russian communities now located in the former republics of the Soviet Union. Mikhail Gorbachev ran too in a last-ditch bid to salvage some level of public recognition and support.

Despite their common interest in blocking a first-round victory by Yeltsin, opposition candidates found it difficult to form an effective coalition. Long negotiations over the creation of such a coalition eventually faltered, primarily because no opposition leader was willing to stand aside in deference to another.

Yeltsin's most serious challenge came from Zyuganov, who ran at the head of a coalition called the People's Patriotic Bloc, a marriage of convenience linking the Communist Party with a number of smaller pro-communist or nationalist groups. Communist popularity had been demonstrated by the 1995 Duma elections, but it was another matter to translate it into a victory for the stiff and uncharismatic Zyuganov. Eventually Lebed clandestinely broke the deadlock; late in May he struck a secret deal with Yeltsin to throw his support to the incumbent in the second round, receiving in turn support for his campaign and a promise of a high-level appointment after the election. A similar round of talks with Yavlinsky, who was less likely to become the second-round kingmaker, collapsed over the issue of Chernomyrdin's continuing role in a postelection government.

In late spring, Yeltsin began to make a comeback in the public opinion polls. He was now vigorously campaigning, at considerable risk to his health. His central message was simple: It's me or a return to the Communists.

Combining contrition with old-fashioned pork-barrel politics, he made thirty-three campaign trips outside Moscow. He offered greater power to regional officials; loans to small businesses; payment of wage arrears to workers; increased pensions; aid to agriculture; compensation for inflation-riddled savings; in short, whatever it took, including a temporary cease-fire in Chechnya. He made a special effort to appeal to young voters, whose level of turnout might determine the race.

It worked. In the first round of balloting on Sunday, June 16, Yeltsin got 35.8 percent of the vote, with Zyuganov following at 32.5 percent, Lebed at 14.7 percent, Yavlinsky at 7.4 percent, and Zhirinovsky at 5.8 percent. Gorbachev, in his final bid for political redemption, got 0.5 percent (Table 4.3).

The stage was now set for a runoff between Yeltsin and Zyuganov, scheduled for Wednesday, July 3, a workday, which might cut back on blue-collar turnout. The choice was now black and white, and Yeltsin exploited it to the hilt. Television documentaries reminded viewers of the worst of the old soviet era—repression, stagnation, and Stalinism. Lebed publicly threw his support behind Yeltsin, receiving an even higher award in his appointment as secretary of the Security Council and special advisor on national security affairs, at least for a while. Korzhakov, the once-trusted

Table 4.3 1996 Russian Presidential Election

Candidate	Party	First Round Vote	Percentage	Second Round Vote	Percentage
Boris Yeltsin	Independent	26,665,495	35.8	40,203,948	54.4
Gennady Zyuganov	Communist Party	24,211,686	32.5	30,102,288	40.7
Alexander Lebed	Congress of Russian Communities	10,974,736	14.7		
Grigory Yavlinsky	Yabloko	5,550,752	7.4		
Vladimir Zhirinovsky	Liberal Democratic Party	4,311,479	5.8		
Mikhail Gorbachev	Independent	386,069	0.5		

SOURCE: D. Nohlen and P. Stover. (2010). *Elections in Europe: A Data Handbook*. Baden-Baden, Germany: Nomos.

head of Yeltsin's security team and a strong proponent of postponing the election, was sacked.[14]

But behind the scenes, things were going badly. While campaigning between the first and second rounds, Yeltsin began to experience chest pains. Three days later he was stricken by a full-scale heart attack, his fourth. His worsened condition was kept from the voters, however, and a few televised appearances from the hospital were staged to conceal their origin.

On Wednesday, July 3, Yeltsin won his second term in office. He received 54.4 percent of the vote, hardly a landslide, but good enough under the circumstances. Zyuganov got 40.7 percent. "None of the above" got 5 percent, up from 1.5 percent in the first round. By their own admission, Gorbachev and Zhirinovsky also voted "none of the above," but to little avail.

The Second Term: From Victory to Resignation

Yeltsin never recovered fully from the serious heart attack that struck him between the first and second rounds of balloting. Timothy Colton describes the beginning of Yeltsin's second term as a "reactive mode" in which he attempted, despite ill heath, to clean up the loose ends of the campaign and find a firm footing from which to govern the nation.[15]

In September 1996, Yeltsin publicly admitted the seriousness of his condition and alerted the nation that he would be undergoing an unspecified operation in the near future. Heart bypass surgery occurred two months later, with the president attended to by an international team of surgeons. Although he survived, as was expected, he was never quite the same. His convalescence was long and hard, and during his recovery the day-to-day affairs of the country were in the hands of Chernomyrdin, whom he had once again appointed prime minister; Chubais, now presidential chief of staff, largely because of his successful conduct of the campaign; Gennady Seleznyov, speaker of the Duma; and Yegor Stroev, speaker of the Federation Council. Chernomyrdin and Chubais clearly ran the show, with Yeltsin's daughter, Tatiana, never far away.

Everyone in the president's team was in agreement about the first task that lay before them: reining in Lebed, who was already overplaying his hand as the putative chief of national security policy. Lebed acted as if the next presidential campaign had begun, demanding additional powers and impudently suggesting that Yeltsin step down from office until he had recovered fully. Yeltsin appointed Lebed as his personal envoy to Chechnya, instructing him to find an end to the hostilities. He cobbled together an uneasy peace, temporarily ending the war. Ominously for Yeltsin, public opinion polls revealed that Lebed was the second most popular political leader in the country, with Yeltsin a narrow first. With less than four months of service in his new post, Lebed was abruptly dismissed late in September amid thinly veiled charges of insubordination. Major changes in the high command of the military quickly followed. Down but not out, Lebed reinvented himself as a regional leader, eventually winning election as governor of the Krasnoyarsk province.[16]

Upon his return to active political life in the spring of 1997, Yeltsin launched a major shake-up designed to get control of the fractious presidential staff and advance the stalled campaign for economic reform. Yeltsin named Chubais to the post of first deputy prime minister under Chernomyrdin. Once again Chubais was instructed to take the lead in further economic reforms. Opposition quickly emerged to his preeminence, and soon another first deputy prime minister was named. The newcomer was Boris Nemtsov, the up-and-coming governor of Nizhny Novgorod, which he had made into a successful testing ground for business-friendly economic reforms.

Despite his return to active politics, Yeltsin remained frail and marginally involved in day-to-day governance. In many ways, it was a predictable return to his earlier style of leadership—bold, decisive actions followed by withdrawal and a failure to consolidate his victory—only made worse by his declining health. While he would occasionally rouse himself to action, putting presidential staff and government officials under fire and dismissing them with increasing frequency, little seemed to change in the real world. The revolving door, especially among prime ministers and ministers, spun more quickly. As the administration edged toward its unexpected demise, it became far more reactive than proactive.

In March 1998, Yeltsin fired Chernomyrdin from his post as prime minister and named Sergei Kiriyenko in his place. Kiriyenko was a product of the Nemtsov reform team in Nizhny Novgorod, and Yeltsin hoped that he would emerge as the second-generation Chubais who could jump-start economic reforms. The Duma, still under the control of Yeltsin's critics, vigorously opposed the appointment, approving it in the last-ditch, third round of voting to avoid giving Yeltsin the opportunity to dissolve the assembly and call a new general election. Kiriyenko's inauspicious beginning as prime minister would soon be followed by an even greater shock, the crash of the Russian stock market and the devaluation of the ruble in 1998.

To his credit, Kiriyenko made all the right moves, at least at first. He secured the dismissal of key opponents to reform and said all the right things. But he could not forestall an economic crisis that began in Southeast and East Asia and quickly, like a tsunami, engulfed other nations. Efforts to get the Duma to authorize austerity measures failed. In truth, Yeltsin himself also bore a fair share of the blame, having promised budget-busting programs during the 1996 campaign.

The economic crisis gave the Duma the opportunity to launch a full-scale attack on the president. By a vote of 248 to 32, it passed a nonbinding resolution calling for his resignation. On August 22, Yeltsin dismissed the ill-fated Kiriyenko and, once again, nominated Chernomyrdin as a gesture toward the Duma and a symbol of cautious leadership. For once, the Duma made it clear it would reject Chernomyrdin, and that it intended to consider impeachment of the president. This presented Yeltsin with a dilemma. Under the 1993 constitution, the president could not dissolve the legislature once an article of impeachment had been voted by the Duma. This threatened to deprive the president of his most powerful weapon to force the acceptance of his nominee—to dissolve the Duma and call new elections.

Yeltsin backed down from the looming confrontation and withdrew Chernomyrdin's name. He now offered a compromise candidate, Yevgeny Primakov, the minister of foreign affairs. With roots in the last soviet and Gorbachev periods, he was minimally acceptable to everyone. At first he declined the nomination, but eventually he accepted under strong pressure to avoid a debilitating confrontation in the midst of an economic crisis. His nomination was approved on the first ballot, 317 to 63.

Primakov's nomination gave Yeltsin sorely needed breathing room in his confrontation with the Duma. Operating as a centrist with good relations with virtually all parties and factions within the legislature, Primakov ran a stable if unexciting coalition government. In truth, Yeltsin was increasingly withdrawing from public affairs, and the Primakov interregnum, coupled with good news as the economy rebounded in late 1998, led both the president and the Duma to let the sleeping dog lie undisturbed. Yeltsin's health again took a turn for the worse, leading to repeated absences from public view and increasing calls in the legislature and the media for him to step down with dignity.[17]

Yeltsin's declining physical and political fortunes led his staunchest enemies in the Duma once again to float the idea of impeachment. In May

1998, a legislative committee was created to draft charges against him, which under the constitution had to reflect "high treason or other serious crimes." By February of the next year, five counts had been offered: destroying the USSR by signing the treaty for its dissolution, abetting murder in 1993 in his action against the Congress of People's Deputies, exceeding presidential authority in sending armed forces into Chechnya, destroying the army, and causing the "genocide of the Russian people."[18]

On the eve of the Duma vote on the charges, Yeltsin once again roused himself to action, although not as dramatically as before. Reacting to the complex situation in Yugoslavia, where Serbian forces were under NATO-sponsored pressure to cease their attacks on Kosovo, Yeltsin named Chernomyrdin as his special envoy to the region and symbolically committed a small contingent of Russian troops to the area. Little came of the action in Yugoslavia, but in Moscow it was now clear that the sleeping dog had been awakened once again. It was enough to buy Yeltsin more breathing room.

More seriously, Primakov's growing popularity led Yeltsin to ponder his future. Touted as a serious candidate for the presidency in the next election, or before if Yeltsin's health should fail, Primakov was not acceptable presidential material in Yeltsin's eyes. Although competent and politically skilled, Primakov was too closely tied to the Gorbachev and soviet eras. Three days before the scheduled vote on the articles of impeachment, which would have made it impossible for the president to dissolve the Duma, Yeltsin fired Primakov and named Sergei Stepashin acting prime minister. Days later the startled Duma took the impeachment vote; not one of the five articles received the needed votes. Impeachment was a dead issue, and Stepashin was quickly confirmed as prime minister on the first ballot.

Stepashin, who had served as minister of the interior, was little more than a placeholder. But a placeholder for whom, or what? Yeltsin apparently considered a run for a third term, although the courts found that he was ineligible even though technically his first term began before the 1993 constitution was approved. Realizing that health and political reality militated against another last hurrah, Yeltsin undoubtedly pondered his legacy. In personal terms, he was concerned about forestalling any legal action against him as a private citizen. But more important was his concern that, although his years in office had brought democracy to Russia, he had failed to give it any lasting political order, especially a stable center that could withstand pressures from the more extreme elements of right and left. To be sure, much of the fault lay at Yeltsin's own doorstep. Repeatedly he had refused to create a presidential party or even to accept formal membership in the parties-of-power that had been cobbled together for each election. As the end drew near, Yeltsin became all the more willing to gamble on his successor, hoping to find a young, powerful figure with acceptable credentials as a democrat and an economic reformer on whom to stake the nation's future as well as the vindication of his years in office.

He eventually chose Vladimir Putin, although many others were on the initial list. Putin was a surprising choice, to say the least. Yeltsin offered few direct comments on the reason for his choice. But it seems apparent that, after marathon crises over the years, Yeltsin wanted someone who was capable of providing the highest of Russian virtues, *poryadok*—order, discipline, and rectitude. In Putin, the president thought he had found these qualities. Putin's democratic credentials were impeccable: He had served with Anatoly Sobchak, the first democratically elected leader of St. Petersburg. His credentials as an economic reformer were equally impressive: He had championed market-oriented reforms in that northern city and later in a number of posts in Moscow. His KGB background suggested that he had the discipline and backbone needed to bring order, consensually if possible; by other means, if necessary. Yeltsin appointed him chairman of the Federal Security Service, the successor to the KGB, in July 1998, and he did not disappoint. He was soon also named secretary of the Security Council. Putin's star was rising, and Yeltsin began to hint that he would be the aging president's anointed successor.

On August 9, 1999, Yeltsin dismissed Stepashin. Putin was designated as acting prime minister and subsequently confirmed in office by the Duma. For a number of reasons, Putin caught the public imagination, and his stock in the opinion polls rose quickly. He was a positive contrast to the infirm president and the colorless series of prime ministers who had preceded him in office. He did all the right things: increased pensions, campaigned vigorously for pro-Yeltsin candidates in the Duma elections in the fall of 1999; and stood tough when, allegedly, pro-Chechen terrorists set off a series of explosions in Moscow and other cities, sending Russian forces once again into their homeland in the Caucasus.[19]

Yeltsin's Economic Reforms: Phase II (1994–1999)

Yeltsin's economic policy from 1994 to 1999 was in many ways a replay of his earlier policies. Throughout most of 1995, the government maintained tighter control over the economy. As a consequence, government expenditures decreased (the good news), but wage arrears grew as both the government and private industries stopped paying workers on a regular basis and the safety net of social, medical, and educational services began to deteriorate (the bad news). Political reality soon created strong pressure to loosen economic controls; the next Duma elections were scheduled for 1995, and presidential elections followed the next year.

The second phase of the privatization program begin in 1994, focused on the direct sale of shares in the remaining state-owned industries. Particularly controversial were the so-called "loans for shares" transactions. Badly in need of increased revenues, the government struck a deal with many of the nation's top banks. The banks would lend the government the money it needed to pay wage arrears and run the state on a day-to-day basis; as collateral the banks were given extensive stock holdings in the larger state enterprises slated for privatization, including raw materials and energy giants. If the government failed to repay the loans (nobody really expected that to happen), the banks could then auction off these shares to the highest bidder. But in reality, the auctions were rigged; rather than bid the prices up to something approximating market value, the auctions sold off control of important industries to bank-favored insiders.

The primary beneficiary of these transactions was the first generation of oligarchs who built vast holdings as the economy shifted from state to private hands. Less pejoratively called "*nomenklatura* capitalists," these were the enterprising former managers of soviet-era industries who bought up their former bailiwicks or skilled entrepreneurs who built vast and diversified holdings on their own. In the early days, an oligarch's portfolio typically included at least one and more often a number of large industrial complexes, usually built around energy or raw materials industries, a bank or two, a newspaper and/or telecommunications facilities, and as time went on, increasing investment abroad. Not surprisingly, such wealth also quickly brought political influence. In his 1996 reelection bid, Yeltsin received extensive financial backing from a number of oligarchs, including Boris Berezovsky, who was particularly close to Yeltsin's daughter.

On August 17, 1998, a major crisis rocked the economy. Long in coming and rooted in the government's short-sighted policies, it brought the economy to near collapse for the next year. It began with an announcement that the government could not pay its debts. The government default quickly spilled over to the private sector. The Russian stock market lost 90 percent of its value in 1998 alone, and unemployment rose to nearly

18 percent of the total population, far exceeding even the worst years of the Great Depression in the United States. Ninety-nine percent of the value of private savings disappeared. Although there was plenty of blame to go around, the average Russian blamed the collapse on the self-serving oligarchs and on a government that was unwilling, or perhaps just too weak, to control them.[20]

Foreign Policy

The ratification of a new constitution in December 1993 radically changed the institutional setting of foreign policy formation. The presidency was vested with increased powers, including the right to "define the basic domestic and foreign policy guidelines" within boundaries established by the constitution, a purposely ambiguous formulation that Yeltsin and future presidents would cite as granting them virtually carte blanche. The president has the power to "supervise the conduct of foreign policy" and "conduct negotiations and sign treaties." The chief executive also serves as commander-in-chief of the armed forces and sets the military doctrine of the armed forces. In addition, the foreign minister and the other "power ministries"—defense, interior, and the heads of the intelligence and security agencies—report directly to the president and not the prime minister. Yeltsin strengthened the Security Council as an advisory body, although he refused to give it operational control, fearing that it could potentially challenge presidential power. Consistent with this concern, Yeltsin increasingly vested power in the hands of the Foreign Ministry and sustained an important role for the former KGB, which was divided operationally into as many as six separate agencies with different areas of responsibility. In contrast, the Ministry of Defense and the military establishment in general lost power under the new arrangement, in part because of the ineptitude of the high command and in part out of pique at the military's lackluster performance in the first Chechen war. More fundamentally, Yeltsin was intent on reforming the officer-heavy, corrupt, and wasteful military, pledging to cut the size of the armed forces, end conscription, and reduce the military budget to 3.5 percent of the gross national product, down from a 1991 level of 7.2 percent.

The pro-Western "Atlanticist" orientation that had dominated Russian foreign policy continued to deteriorate after the 1993 crisis. In part out of disappointment with scant Western economic aid, and in part out of resentment of what was perceived as Western paternalism, Yeltsin took a harder line. To be sure, the move also was motivated by domestic political concerns; the Dumas elected in 1993 and 1995 were dominated by critics on both the right and the left who advocated a more assertive foreign policy. Russia grew more supportive of Serbia's actions after the breakup of Yugoslavia and more critical of NATO, especially concerning possible membership for former Warsaw Treaty nations anxious to join in light of Moscow's assertion of a sphere of influence in the region. Although Russian diplomats openly accepted the argument that a new European security mechanism was needed, they favored its creation through the more neural Organization for Security and Co-operation in Europe rather than the cold war–tainted NATO. Eventually Russia settled in 1977 for the creation of a NATO-Russia Council, which provided a mechanism for ongoing consultation but left NATO free to act independently.

Relations with the former soviet republics also proved difficult. The Commonwealth of Independent States, created at the time of the breakup of the Soviet Union, was little more than a hollow shell. Yeltsin treated it as an instrument of Russian foreign policy, which offended other members. Efforts to merge Russia and Belarus produced little beyond meaningless platitudes about a "common economic space." Under pressure from Russian nationalists in the Duma who wanted to see these two Slavic peoples reunited, Yeltsin signed a treaty creating a formal union days before his resignation in 1999. In reality, the agreement clarified nothing about either the political or economic relations between the two nations. Relations with Ukraine were clouded by the status of the Crimea, formerly a part of Russia that Khrushchev had generously given to Ukraine, and the Russian Black Sea fleet, anchored in Sevastopol. In 1977, both sides reached an agreement that permitted Russia to lease port facilities for the fleet for twenty years.

In 1996, Yeltsin replaced Kozyrev, who remained as the lightning rod for opposition to his foreign policy, with Primakov, then director of the Foreign Intelligence Service. Primakov's credentials included long service in various foreign policy think tanks and close connections to the KGB. Trained as a specialist in the Middle East, he quickly emerged as a pragmatist who championed Moscow efforts to contain NATO expansion, reassert its influence over the former soviet republics and Eastern Europe, and restore its presence in the third world, especially the Arab world. As Yeltsin's health deteriorated after the 1996 presidential race, Primakov increasingly took control over a more assertive and nationalist foreign policy, winning respect from the Duma.[21]

The First Chechen War

Independence and national self-determination for the fifteen former republics of the Soviet Union was one thing, but the status of the administrative territories within the new Russian Federation was quite another. Like the former republics, they were deeply concerned with redefining their relationship with the "center," and the vast majority of them wanted to see Moscow's control over local affairs weakened. In fact, considerable devolution of power and authority had already occurred, and there was little that Yeltsin's new government in Moscow could do about it. By March 1992, a new format was reached that provided different categories of membership in the Russian Federation: republics, territories, regions, and autonomous areas, plus two "federal cities," Moscow and St. Petersburg. In reality, all but one of these new administrative units entered into bilateral negotiations with Moscow and eventually reached some agreement, at first usually involving considerable concessions to local autonomy. That one exception was Chechnya.

Gorbachev's reforms and the reawakening of national identity soon produced national independence movements throughout the Caucasus. In September 1991, members of the Congress of the Chechen People, a nationalist group led by a former soviet air force general, Dzhokhar Dudayev, seized control of the pro-Moscow legislature in Grozny, effectively establishing an independent government. Dudayev was named president and declared independence from the Soviet Union. Preoccupied with the final stages of his struggle with Gorbachev, Yeltsin dispatched troops to Grozny, quickly withdrawing them when he realized that Chechen forces had surrounded the airport at which they landed. The direct conflict with Moscow remained muted for the next several years as Chechnya slipped ever deeper into internal chaos and an increasingly authoritarian Dudayev faced growing opposition at home from other nationalists and local warlords. In 1993, Chechnya once again proclaimed its independence, this time from the Russian Federation.

Anti-Dudayev forces were quick to reach out to Moscow for support, and Yeltsin was more than willing to provide assistance, hoping to make an example of the breakaway regime to discourage others from similar action. In October and November 1994, Russian and anti-Dudayev forces struck against Grozny. Both attempts to dislodge Dudayev failed, and late in

November, Yeltsin issued an ultimatum to all forces in Chechnya to lay down their arms and submit to Moscow's control. Dudayev refused, and heavy aerial bombardment began on December 1, followed ten days later by an invasion of Russian forces. The military had promised Yeltsin a quick and easy victory.

They couldn't keep their promise. Many within the Russian ground forces opposed the attack, as did some of Yeltsin's own advisors. Poorly trained and demoralized Russian troops quickly fell victim to the tactical skill of Chechen fighters who engaged them in urban guerrilla warfare and then took to the hills when Grozny eventually fell after prolonged bombing and artillery attacks. Now occupying the bombed-out shell of the city, Russian troops slowly and painfully extended their control over the countryside. In March 1996, rebel forces infiltrated Grozny and launched a surprise raid on the city; more a propaganda victory than a military success, it reminded war-weary Russians that the conflict was far from over.

Those same war-weary Russians were about to go to the polls in the 1996 presidential election in which Yeltsin was waging an uphill fight for a second term. His prospects seemingly brightened when a Russian missile attack killed Dudayev on April 21, 1996. Yeltsin quickly proclaimed "victory" and negotiated a brief cease-fire. Whatever the military merit of the proclamation, it defused the conflict and undoubtedly contributed to Yeltsin's second-round victory. But Dudayev's eventual successor, Aslan Maskhadov, was already planning a second offensive to retake Grozny.

The attack came on August 19, shortly after Yeltsin had taken the oath of office for the second time. Fighting in Grozny was heavy, and the rebels rebuffed several attempts to relieve the stunned Russian army. In desperation, the Russian commander threatened the use of heavy bombardment and told the civilian population to flee for their lives. The Russian offensive was ended by a cease-fire brokered by Alexander Lebed, who had come in third in the presidential balloting and thrown his support to Yeltsin. The agreement that emerged from further talks led to the withdrawal of all Russian forces from Chechnya and de facto independence. Several months later, Yeltsin and Maskhadov signed a formal peace agreement. It was over—for now.[22]

The December 1999 Duma Elections

The December 1999 Duma elections were not so much the last event of the rapidly failing Yeltsin regime as the first event of the now-inevitable

Putin era. With Putin the designated heir apparent (although it was not yet evident how quickly Yeltsin intended to relinquish the presidency), all eyes turned to how the elections would play out for the future, not the current, leader. In many ways, the political landscape was familiar. The once-powerful "party of power," Our Home Is Russia, had already withered on the vine, as had its predecessors, a victim of presidential inattention and the regrouping of political forces for the post-Yeltsin era. Among the others, the Communist Party still held the lead as the likely centerpiece of a postelection anti-Yeltsin and anti-Putin coalition. Zhirinovsky's Liberal Democratic Party was still there, but continuing to slip away both because its base was being tempted by other parties and because of the bizarre actions of its leader.

At first there was an attempt to rebuild a viable middle ground not controlled by Yeltsin and Putin, although the effort was compromised by the ambitions of other presidential hopefuls. In the regions, individual governors launched their own parties, variously to promote their own candidacy, consolidate control over their bailiwicks, or play a role in brokering the selection of the next president. Moscow's ambitious mayor, Yuri Luzhkov, who had made no secret of his presidential aspirations, founded Fatherland Front in December 1998. Other regional leaders quickly followed. Samara's governor formed a bloc called Russia's Voice; Kemerovo's governor offered Revival and Unity; and Tatarstan's governor created United Russia. In August 1999, Fatherland Front and United Russia formed an alliance, Fatherland–All Russia, naming dismissed former prime minister Primakov as its head and establishing him as a likely candidate in the next presidential election, formally scheduled for June 2000. Another attempt to regroup the middle ground around a reformist and business-friendly coalition emerged in the Union of Right Forces, also created in 1999. Closely associated with reformers like Chubais, Nemtsov, and Gaidar, it offered itself as a pro-democratic and pro-market alternative to Putin.

Yeltsin's endorsement of Putin as heir apparent scrambled his opponents' plans. Under pressure to create an alternative centrist coalition more supportive of his bid for office, Putin invited a large group of regional governors to Moscow late in September. He forcefully informed them that he personally would back a new pro-Kremlin party now being formed by Sergei Shoigu, a Yeltsin loyalist. No strangers to the reality of political power, the governors quickly got the message and signed up for the new bloc, Unity, which fielded candidates for the upcoming Duma election and endorsed Putin's presidential bid. Following the Yeltsin tradition, Putin would indicate his personal preference for Unity candidates running for the Duma and accept its support in the presidential election, but not formally join its ranks.

Voting for the new legislature took place on December 19. The Communist Party again captured the largest plurality, with 24.3 percent of the party-list votes, for sixty-seven seats; it got an additional forty-six seats from the single-member districts (Table 4.4). That gave them an overall voting bloc in the Duma of 113 seats, down 44 from the previous election. Although it was still the primary party of the left and of opposition to Yeltsin's version of Russian democracy, it was in sharp decline.

Unity came in second in the party-list totals, getting 23.3 percent of the vote, for sixty-four seats. It picked up an additional nine seats from the districts, for a total of seventy-three seats, forty fewer than the Communists. Fatherland–All Russia followed with 13.3 percent of the party-list ballots, giving them thirty-seven seats, with another thirty-one from the districts. With sixty-eight seats, they were third in total Duma voting strength. The Union of Right Forces fared less well, with 8.5 percent of the party-list ballots, for twenty-four seats, and another five seats from the districts. The Liberal Democratic Party, now billing itself the Zhirinovsky Bloc, got just 6.0 percent, for seventeen seats, with none from the districts; overall it dropped thirty-four seats from the last election. Yabloko got 5.9 percent, for sixteen seats, and another four seats from district balloting. It had dropped twenty-five seats from the previous Duma. None of the other parties got past the 5 percent cutoff for party-list seats, although a few gained a small presence from the districts. As before, independent candidates did well, capturing 105 seats in district voting. "None of the above," still a token measure of resistance, got just over 3 percent.[23]

Overall, the results presented a mixed picture. Former opposition parties from left to right did less well, but as yet no overwhelmingly popular centrist "party of power" had captured a commanding lead. The collective heirs of the Yeltsin years had not yet agreed completely on how to pick up the pieces, even in light of his endorsement of Putin. Perhaps the next presidential election, now more than six months away, would sort things out, and in the interim the presidential hopefuls could continue their game.

That was not the way Yeltsin himself intended it.

Table 4.4   1999 Russian Legislative Elections

Party	Proportional Representation	Single-Member-District Voting	Total Seats
Communist Party	Votes: 16,196,024 Percentage: 24.3 Seats: 67	Votes: 8,893,547 Percentage: 13.7 Seats: 46	113
Unity	Votes: 15,549,182 Percentage: 23.3 Seats: 64	Votes: 1,408,801 Percentage: 2.2 Seats: 9	73
Fatherland–All Russia	Votes: 8,886,753 Percentage: 13.3 Seats: 37	Votes: 5,469,389 Percentage: 8.4 Seats: 31	68
Union of Right Forces	Votes: 5,677,247 Percentage: 8.5 Seats: 24	Votes: 2,016,294 Percentage: 3.1 Seats: 5	29
Zhirinovsky Bloc	Votes: 3,990,038 Percentage: 6.0 Seats: 17	Votes: 1,026,690 Percentage: 1.6 Seats: 0	17
Yabloko	Votes: 3,955,611 Percentage: 5.9 Seats: 16	Votes: 3,289,760 Percentage: 5.1 Seats: 4	20
Our Home Is Russia	Votes: 790,983 Percentage: 1.2 Seats: 0	Votes: 1,733,257 Percentage: 2.7 Seats: 7	7
Russian All-People's Union	Votes: 245,266 Percentage: 0.4 Seats: 0	Votes: 700,976 Percentage: 1.0 Seats: 2	2
Independents		Votes: 27,877,095 Percentage: 43 Seats: 105	105

SOURCE: D. Nohlen and P. Stover. (2010). *Elections in Europe: A Data Handbook.* Baden-Baden, Germany: Nomos.

Yeltsin's Surprise Resignation

Late in 1999, Yeltsin played his last hand. The 1993 constitution provided that in the case of the resignation of a president, the prime minister automatically became acting president, with a new election to follow within three months. On December 24, Yeltsin advised Putin of his intention to resign on New Year's Eve. He told his daughter on December 28, three days before the resignation, and his wife on the day of the event. His televised address to the nation on the last day of the twentieth century expressed sorrow for not doing more, closing with "I did all that I could." After a brief ceremonial toast, he took his leave of the Kremlin, which he had fought hard to reach and to retain. "Take care of Russia," he instructed Putin as he left.[24]

Citizen Yeltsin was now *na pensii*—on pension, retired, leaving an office and a nation as works still in progress.

Yeltsin as an Authoritarian Modernizer: A Final Assessment

Much of the preliminary assessment offered in Chapter 3 holds true for the remainder of Yeltsin's tenure in office. In many ways, his best days were behind him. His challenge to Gorbachev, his return from political oblivion to the presidency of the Russian republic in June 1991, his resistance to the coup attempt in August 1991, his role in the breakup of the Soviet Union, his support of rapid privatization of the economy, his coup in September 1993, and his role in drafting a new constitution—these were the actions of an authoritarian modernizer intent on transforming the nation he governed. But by December 1993, most of these elements were already in place. Only the second phase of privatization remained, and the general outlines of how it would be accomplished (but perhaps not its economic and political consequences) were apparent. The only new policy initiative after the ratification of the 1993 constitution was the growing war in Chechnya. Although the political and human costs were high for both sides, the conflict should be viewed against the larger backdrop of the negotiated relationship between the central government in Moscow and assertive local authorities in the regions. Chechnya was a bloody and costly exception, but an exception nonetheless.

These accomplishments clearly established Yeltsin as an authoritarian modernizer. He had addressed a host of issues that set the nation on a new course:

- A democracy, institutionalized in ways that revealed both the strength and the disorder of democratic rule, and one that he would defend against the 1991 coup attempt; a leftover communist-era legislature that had a different view of how power should be distributed within that democracy; and his own advisors, who suggested that he postpone the 1996 presidential election
- A market economy, going through a difficult period of privatization and adjustment

- A new international role for Russia, stronger and more assertive than Gorbachev's new thinking had implied, but less powerful and demanding than the former Soviet Union
- Above all, a new nation with a renewed sense of its Russian identity, despite its formal designation as a multinational federation

But there also were shortcomings. In his own way, Gorbachev had understood that transforming political institutions was only a part of consolidating democratic rule. Even his futile attempt to transform the Communist Party into a popular mass-based party contained the recognition that a viable party system was an important part of stabilizing democratic rule. But Yeltsin either did not understand or simply rejected the need to create a lasting presidential party. The jury-rigged entities cobbled together for each election hardly filled the void, especially since Yeltsin personally kept his distance from them. Yeltsin's strategy to reach out to the nation beyond Moscow's Garden Ring was to personalize, not institutionalize. To be sure, he was very good at it, and in 1996 it won him a second term against great odds. But it did not contribute to the creation of a broader party system or civil society that helped to stabilize and institutionalize democracy.

Notes

1. Sylvain Brovard, Andrew Appleton, and Amy Mazur, *The French Fifth Republic at Fifty: Beyond Stereotypes,* Palgrave Macmillan, 2009; and Nicholas Atkin, *The French Fifth Republic,* Palgrave Macmillan, 2005.

2. Boris Yeltsin, *Midnight Diaries,* Public Affairs, 2000, 222.

3. Boris Yeltsin, *Zapiski prezidena (Notes of a President),* Ogonek, 1994, quoted in Colton, *Yeltsin: A Life,* Basic Books, 2008, 305; and Leon Aron, *Yeltsin: A Revolutionary Life,* St. Martin's, 2000, 108.

4. Thomas F. Remington, *The Russian Parliament: Institutional Evolution in a Transitional Regime, 1989–1999,* Yale University Press, 2001; and Thomas F. Remington, *Politics in Russia,* Prentice Hall, 2011, 69–74.

5. Thomas M. Nichols, *The Russian Presidency,* Palgrave Macmillan, 2000; and Eugene Huskey, *Presidential Power in Russia,* M. E. Sharpe, 1999.

6. Peter H. Solomon, Jr., and Todd S. Foglesong, *Courts and Transition in Russia: The Challenge of Judicial Reform,* Westview, 2000.

7. Michael McFaul, *Understanding Russia's 1993 Parliamentary Elections,* Hoover Institute Press, 1994; and Stephen White, Richard Rose, and Ian McAllister, *How Russia Votes,* Chatham House, 1997, 107–130.

8. Colton, *Yeltsin,* 321–44; and Aron, *Yeltsin,* 558–78.

9. Huskey, *Presidential Power,* 43–97.

10. Colton, *Yeltsin,* 293–320.

11. Robert Ortung, Ralph S. Clem, and Peter R. Craumer, *The Russian Parliamentary Election of 1995: The Battle for the Duma*, M. E. Sharpe, 1997; Richard Rose, *Understanding Multiparty Choice: The 1995 Duma Elections*, University of Strathclyde 1996; and White et al., *How Russia Votes*, 175–240.

12. Colton, *Yeltsin*, 351.

13. Aron, *Yeltsin*, 579–633.

14. Michael McFaul, *Russia's 1996 Presidential Election: The End of Polarized Politics*, Hoover Institute Press, 1997; Jerry F. Hough and Susan G. Lehmann, *The 1996 Russian Presidential Election*, Brookings, 1996; and Peter Rutland, *The Russian Presidential Election of 1996*, M. E. Sharpe, 2002.

15. Colton, *Yeltsin*, 384.

16. Harold Elletson, *The General against the Kremlin: Alexander Lebed—Power and Illusion*, Little Brown, 1998; Alexander Lebed, *General Alexander Lebed: My Life and My Country*, Regnery, 1997; and Colton, *Yeltsin*, 394-398.

17. Colton, *Yeltsin*, 407–422.

18. Colton, *Yeltsin*, 426–427.

19. Colton, *Yeltsin*, 429-435; and Richard Sakwa, *Putin: Russia's Choice*, 2nd ed., Routledge, 2008, 1–37.

20. James Leitzel, *Russian Economic Reform*, Rutledge, 1995; Peter Raddaway and Dmitri Glinski, *The Tragedy of Russia's Reforms: Market Bolshevism against Democracy*, U.S. Institute of Peace Press, 2001.

21. Jeffrey Mankoff, *Russian Foreign Policy: The Return of Great Power Politics*, Rowman and Littlefield, 2009.

22. Olga Oliker, *Russia's Chechen Wars, 1994-2000*, RAND, 2001; Anna Politkovskaya, *A Small Corner of Hell: Dispatches from Chechnya*, University of Chicago Press, 2007; and James Hughes, *Chechnya: From Nationalism to Jihad*, University of Pennsylvania Press, 2008.

23. Timothy J. Colton and Michael McFaul, *Popular Choice in a Managed Democracy: The Russian Elections of 1999 and 2000*, Brookings, 2003; and Vicki L. Hesli and William M. Reisinger, eds., *The 1999 and 2000 Elections in Russia: Their Impact and Legacy*, Cambridge University Press, 2003.

24. Colton, *Yeltsin*, 433–435.

5

Putin I,
2000–2008

Vladimir Putin's elevation to the post of acting president virtually ensured his victory in the approaching general election. The mobilization of Boris Yeltsin's "family," including the oligarchs and other special interests that sought continuity, placed considerable resources at his disposal. The advantages of incumbency were many: access to the media, the ability to use the resources of the government to entice voters to his side, and the preeminence of the presidency placed Putin at the head of the pack. The financial support of the oligarchs, who had bankrolled Yeltsin's 1996 victory, carried considerable weight, as did the vast media resources they controlled. It also was important that the presidential aspirations of Moscow mayor Yuri Luzhkov and former prime minister Yevgeny Primakov had been dealt a serious blow through the forced merger of their parties and the emergence of a new party of power, Unity, which rapidly endorsed Putin's candidacy.

To his credit, Putin quickly rose to the occasion and stepped forward as a viable and dynamic candidate. He was a far cry from the debilitated and withdrawn Yeltsin. Like any good campaigner, he found the issues that produced support and made them his own. These included a renewed war in Chechnya and a series of never completely explained bombings of civilian targets in Moscow and elsewhere. Putin visibly took charge of policy toward the rebellious enclave and personal responsibility for the outcome. It played well to the voters.[1]

The voters had begun to warm to Putin even before Yeltsin's resignation. As prime minister, he clearly was on the list of possible candidates. During the last months of Yeltsin's rule, Putin rose dramatically in the polls. In August 1999, he was favored by a scant 2 percent of the voters. By the end of September, support had risen to 15 percent; by the end of October, to 25 percent; and by late November, to over 40 percent.[2]

The 2000 Presidential Election

Although Putin was clearly in the lead going into the presidential election, he still had notable opposition. Luzhkov and Primakov could have mounted strong candidacies, but both pulled out of the race rather than challenge the clear backing of the Kremlin and the advantages of incumbency. This left the usual suspects, who did their best in a familiar and predictable campaign. Gennedy Zyuganov was back as the candidate of the Communist Party, which was losing some of its support to Putin on both economic and internal security issues. Vladimir Zhirinovsky also was in the running for the Liberal Democrats. Grigory Yavlinsky again stood for Yabloko. Aman Tuleev, the leftist governor of the Kemerovo region who had stepped aside for Zyuganov in the previous election, now stood his ground, saying that he would throw his support to Zyuganov in the second round. In all, eleven candidates were on the ballot.

Putin's campaign was run by his friend and close associate from St. Petersburg, Dmitry Medvedev, who had also entered the world of democratic politics at the time Sobchak controlled the city. The campaign stressed several themes, including a return to a strong state capable of governing the nation; a sense of order and discipline within society; rapid, although undefined, advancement of a market economy; suppression of separatist movements in the provinces; and restoration of the power and glory of Russia in the international arena. Everything that had been abandoned, or lost, or merely slipped away in the Gorbachev and Yeltsin years would be brought back. All it required was strong leadership.[3]

Table 5.1   2000 Russian Presidential Election

Candidate	Party	Votes	Percentage
Vladimir Putin	Independent	39,740,467	53.4
Gennady Zyuganov	Communist Party	21,928,468	29.5
Grigory Yavlinsky	Yabloko	4,351,450	5.9
Aman Tuleev	Independent	2,217,364	3.0
Vladimir Zhirinovsky	Liberal Democratic Party	2,026,509	2.7

SOURCE: D. Nohlen and P. Stover. (2010). *Elections in Europe: A Data Handbook*. Baden-Baden, Germany: Nomos.

On March 26, 2000, the Russian people voted to choose their second president. Putin won in the first round, with 53.4 percent of the vote (Table 5.1). No runoff would be needed as in Yeltsin's 1996 victory, and therefore, no compromises would have to be made, at least at this point. Zyuganov came in second with 29.5 percent of the vote, slightly below the 32.5 percent he won in the first round of the 1996 balloting. Yavlinsky got 5.9 percent, a point and a half below his 1996 support. Tuleev got 3.0 percent and no opportunity to play kingmaker in a second round. Zhirinovsky had a really bad day, dropping to 2.7 percent, well below his 5.8 level of support four years earlier. "None of the above" got just under 2 percent.[4]

Vladimir Putin: From Spy Novels to the Kremlin

Who was this person that Russia had chosen as its second president? He was born in Leningrad on October 7, 1952, to modest beginnings, even for the Soviet Union at the time. His father was a conscript in the navy, where he served in the submarine fleet, and his mother was a factory worker. Good proletarian credentials, but hardly an auspicious starting point. The family's only real political connection, of a sort, was that his paternal grandfather was an occasional cook for both Lenin and Stalin. In school, he was uncharacteristically slow to join the communist youth organization. He did, however, develop an early interest in the martial arts, especially *sambo,* a Russian variation of judo. He became infatuated with spy novels and movies, an interest that would shape his later life.

He graduated from Leningrad State University in 1975 with a degree in international law. While there, he joined the Communist Party and studied under Anatoly Sobchak, an association that would later change his life. He joined the KGB upon graduation, undoubtedly benefiting from the agency's decision to broaden recruitment to diversify its ranks. He served first in Leningrad in various capacities that monitored foreigners. From 1985 to 1990, he was posted to Dresden, East Germany; it was hardly a choice assignment, since the agency sent its best prospects to enemy states, not allies. He returned to the Soviet Union and was assigned to the International Department of Leningrad State University. More important, he reconnected with his former teacher, Sobchak. Seeing the handwriting on the wall, Putin resigned from the KGB shortly after the coup attempt in 1991 to try his hand in the new world of democratic politics.[5]

VLADIMIR PUTIN

- Born October 7, 1952, in Leningrad (now St. Petersburg), Russia.
- Studied law at Leningrad State University from 1970 to 1975; joined the Communist Party while at university; studied under Anatoly Sobchak, who taught business law.
- Joined the KGB in 1975 upon graduation; initially assigned to minor posts in Leningrad, then transferred to Dresden, East Germany, from 1985 to 1990, where he worked undercover to recruit agents.
- Recalled to Leningrad in 1991, where he worked in the KGB office at Leningrad State University.
- Resigned from the Communist Party in August 1991 in protest to the attempted coup against Gorbachev.
- In May 1990, was appointed advisor on international relations to Anatoly Sobchak, the city's first democratically elected mayor; advanced to higher posts within the city and became active in Our Home Is Russia, a pro-Yeltsin political party.
- Transferred to Moscow in June 1996, to become deputy head of the Presidential Property Management Office under Yeltsin.
- In March 1997, appointed deputy chief of the presidential staff.
- In July 1989, appointed head of the Federal Security Service, the internal affairs wing of the former KGB.
- In August 1999, appointed as one of three first deputy prime ministers and then advanced to acting prime minister; named as Yeltsin's chosen successor.
- Named acting president upon Yeltsin's resignation on December 31, 1999; won election to the post on March, 26, 2000, with 53.4 percent of the vote on the first round.
- During first presidential term, gradually weakened the power of the oligarchs and the Yeltsin "family," the remaining supporters of the first president.
- On March 14, 2004, reelected to a second term with 71.9 percent of the vote.
- Increasingly emerged as the broker among a growing number of factions in the government.
- Barred from a third consecutive term, Putin and prime minister Medvedev switched places for the 2008 presidential race; Medvedev is elected president on March 2, 2008, with 70.3 percent of the vote and named Putin as prime minister, beginning a four-year "tandem."
- During the run-up to the 2012 presidential election, Medvedev and Putin announced their intention to switch posts once again.
- Putin won election to a third term on March 4, 2012, with 63.6 percent of the vote; named Medvedev as prime minister; deepened presidential control over the government, the media, civil society, and opposition groups; began a more assertive foreign policy, including annexation of the Crimea.

Sobchak emerged as the leader of democratic forces in Leningrad. As the newly elected mayor, he appointed Putin as his advisor on international affairs. Until 1997, Putin served in a number of other posts in city government, some dealing with the sensitive and profitable question of property transfers in the emerging capitalist economy. Sobchak lost his bid for reelection in 1996 and soon fled the country with Putin's help in the face of corruption charges. In June 1996, Putin was summoned to Moscow to become deputy chief of the Presidential Property Management Department. Yeltsin soon advanced him to the posts of deputy chief of the presidential staff and director of the Presidential Property Management Department; the first brought him closer to the man who would eventually designate him as his successor, and the second deepened his connections with the murky world of property distribution to Yeltsin's chosen allies. He was soon named first deputy chief of the presidential staff. In 1998, he became director of the Federal Security Service, the new designation for the domestic affairs wing of his old home, the KGB. In August 1999, Yeltsin named him as one of three first deputy prime ministers. That same day, upon the dismissal of prime minister Sergei Stepashin, Putin was advanced to the post of acting prime minister and eventually designated as Yeltsin's chosen successor.

The Putin Formula

As he came to office, Putin faced a complex legacy from his newly acquired patron. In many ways, Yeltsin had finished the Gorbachev revolution. The Soviet Union was gone, and a Russian Federation had emerged. Yeltsin's 1993 coup against the remnants of the soviet institutional order had completed the process and created a new presidency and legislature, but they were still mired deeply in the problems and mindsets of the old order. His episodic involvement in public affairs, in part because of illness and in part because of willful inattention to the details of using power left many problems unsolved. The economic transition was stalled in mid-course, and considerable economic and political power had fallen to the first generation of oligarchs, who had underwritten Yeltsin's successful political comeback in the 1996 election and now supported Putin's candidacy. A number of factions had gelled into place in the Kremlin and in the broader context of regional politics, including Yeltsin's family, led by his daughter, Tatiana, and powerful oligarchs such as Boris Berezovsky as well as a number of hangers-on and hopeful future claimants to power.

From Putin's perspective, this questionable legacy created daunting tasks. The first dealt with a political question: How could he take command in what was still a volatile political system and protect his flanks against present or potential opponents? It was common knowledge that Yeltsin had a number of names on his list of potential successors, and Putin's was not the first. His selection might be interpreted as confirmation of his weakness in one sense; he would remain pliable to Yeltsin's continuing influence, especially in protecting the president and his entourage against potential indictment for economic or political crimes, and he would be heavily dependent on the family as a counterweight against other factions within the Kremlin. At the least, he could be seen as everyone else's second or third choice, and probably the least threatening to those who wished little change to come from the succession. Moreover, he had no power base at his disposal at the time of his appointment. Though a member of the *siloviki* because of his earlier career in the KGB, he was hardly its chief spokesman within the Kremlin hierarchy. Eventually the *Pitery*—St. Petersburg-based officials usually with an earlier career connection to Putin—would rise to greater (although probably overestimated) significance, but they were not viewed as a major faction at the beginning of Putin's first term in office.[6]

In seeking consolidation, Putin chose at first to rely on the ever-diminishing strength of the Yeltsin family and gradually to shift to the role of broker among the other contending factions (discussed at length later in this chapter). Although he was eventually able to place an increasing number of his personal allies or people with whom he shared past career links into positions of power, it is inaccurate to argue that he set out to create a Putin faction per se. In a milieu in which increasingly numerous and powerful factions compete for dominance, real power and indispensability lie not in heading the largest faction (which is changing constantly) but in being the one person to whom they turn to mediate their differences. Putin's real political skill became his ability to finesse this sort of floating balance, never letting any one faction rise to disproportional power.[7]

Less directly, Putin also moved to consolidate another aspect of his presidential power through the creation of United Russia, the party of power (but again, not in the usual parliamentary sense of "in power") that dominated his first two terms in office and the four-year Medvedev interregnum. Far more durable than its brief-lived earlier counterparts, United Russia was meant to serve as a link between the presidency and what might be called the periphery. As with Washington, D.C.'s Beltway, a distinction is commonly made between what occurs inside or outside Moscow's Garden Ring. Putin's ability to manipulate the various factions empowered him to control most of what happened inside the Garden

Ring, but what happened outside was a different matter in two ways. First, during the Yeltsin period, regional leaders had created virtual fiefdoms. One of United Russia's first accomplishments was to bring the provinces into line just as the Yeltsin succession was beginning, and Putin used it to strengthen his hand once in office.

Second, the vast majority of the voters who select a president or the legislature lie outside the Garden Ring. Despite earlier efforts, Yeltsin had never been able to create a presidential party that had any sticking power. In truth, he offered at best only token support for such efforts; he regarded the presidency as "above politics," at least in the narrow partisan sense, setting a precedent that both Putin and Medvedev would follow in the narrowest legal sense. But in reality, Putin devoted considerable attention to building a party that would turn out the vote and impose a greater degree of control over political life in the provinces. A certain degree of reciprocity was inevitable. In return for accepting the party line and national candidates chosen in Moscow, regional party elites would receive support from the center; close association, it was hoped, with popular presidential candidates with long coattails; and a degree of autonomy to do what they wanted at home, unless over-the-top local corruption and malfeasance made it impossible to ignore their transgressions.[8]

That brings us to a fundamental feature of the Putin and Medvedev years that is essential to understanding how Russian politics works. In any complex political system, there are always many games in progress. The Western term for this is "nested games." Like a three-ring circus, each "game" offers the viewer a different act, each seemingly localized to one of the rings, but in reality somehow related to and sequenced within the larger picture taking place under a single tent. Something, or someone, connects these competing realities and orchestrates them toward a common end.[9]

In the Russian context, the first "game" is common to all presidential systems—the rivalry between the presidential apparatus and the permanent government housed in the vast bureaucratic leviathan of the state. Each has a different sense of mission and purpose, responds to a different constituency, has a different sense of life trajectory (a single presidential administration versus the continuing mission of a ministry or agency), and competes for the never adequate resources of the state.

The second "game" revolves around the factions that represent various institutional, economic, or geographic interests or a particular cohort experience (the *siloviki* or *Pitery*, for example) or a particular political orientation (the statists or the liberals). At their most effective, they play a closed

game among players already familiar with the rules and costs of engagement, eventually hammering out a compromise among themselves or turning
to an acceptable even-handed broker to facilitate agreement and lower the
costs of the game to all players. The problem in post-communist Russia is
that it has taken a long time for the game of factions to fall into place and
for the terms of engagement to be clearly defined and accepted.

The third "game" is the most recent to emerge. It lies in the still-
incomplete task of connecting what Richard Sakwa calls the two realms of
Russian politics, one inside the Garden Ring, where the playing field and
the rules are increasingly well defined for presidents, bureaucrats, and
factions, and one outside the Garden Ring, involving the linkage between
the byzantine realm of Kremlin politics and the broader role of parties and
public opinion.[10] In well-functioning democracies, that connection is
provided by two elements: the personalized, idiosyncratic, and charismatic
connection between national candidates and the public and/or the role of
organized political parties. The personalized dimension has always been
there from the beginning and is perhaps even more important today
because of the all-pervasive communications grid that can bring everything
to everyone in a matter of seconds. A cult of the personality has never
depended on rapid communication, but it surely is facilitated by it.

In most established democracies, that connection is supplemented by
the more prosaic role of political parties, performing both mobilization
and communications tasks, and playing an important role in brokering
agreement within parties or among factions that accept internal compromise as the price of victory and meaningful participation. But in the
Russian context, that is a poorly established link between the insiders and
the outsiders. As long as they can cobble together a working majority
within the legislature, national leaders are tempted to regard the mundane
world of grassroots action as a secondary priority, except in the run-up to
national elections, when the time-honored practice of "storming" occurs—
intense last-minute round-the-clock activity, a term taken from the common
practice of soviet-era factories to slack off until just before the production
deadlines of the current economic plan. For their part, the factions have
little motivation to colonize political parties; from their perspective, the
lower the involvement of the public and the legislature, the greater the
potential for the factions to exert influence.

As noted earlier, Putin needed both to consolidate and to validate his
victory. Validation in this context means to develop his own agenda and
plan for the future. In many ways, Yeltsin had an easier time in validating

his rule; the mere survival of democratic institutions was enough. But in Putin's case, more was required. The new leader needed a new platform, much as in the soviet era each new leader offered a revised version of the ever-present "plan" to establish his own identity and confirm the wisdom of his selection to rule. For Putin, that meant synthesizing elements from several different aspects of his earlier experiences.

The earliest of those experiences came, of course, from his years of service in the KGB. He was drawn to the agency because of a youthful fascination with espionage. Had the soviet regime not self-destructed, he was probably headed for a successful career in the KGB's middle to upper echelons, but nothing beyond. That said, what would he have taken away from the experience? Like most *chekisti*, he shared in their paternalistic sense of responsibility for the fate of the nation and the sense that they were the last bastion standing between Mother Russia and its enemies. Their role as "the sword and the shield" of the nation was an important part of their corporate identity. Putin probably also took away a strong sense of self-discipline and pragmatic professionalism. In his years as KGB director, Yuri Andropov, who himself briefly ruled the nation after Brezhnev's death, had extensively transformed the agency, broadening its recruitment to diversify the staff and turning it into a highly professional intelligence service with a strong sense of tell-it-as-it-is pragmatism.[11]

Putin's second formative experience came as a consequence of his association with Sobchak, first at Leningrad State University and then more significantly in the early democratic reforms in their native city of Leningrad. There is every reason to believe that Putin's conversion to the still imprecisely defined idea of Russian democracy was genuine. The two men were very close, and the early democratic reforms brought hope to pragmatists like Sobchak and Putin that they might awaken the nation from its stagnation. But there also was a dark side to democracy, as both men would soon learn. Sobchak's career as the first democratically elected mayor of Leningrad was soon compromised by unfounded charges of corruption, and Putin assumed great personal risk to have him spirited out of the country into safe haven.

Soon after Sobchak's demise, Putin moved to Moscow and eventually into the Yeltsin entourage, although he never was a full-fledged member of the family. Not surprisingly, the transfer would offer a new formative experience. Now close to the real center of power, he saw the increasing weakness of the Yeltsin presidency and the growing power of Kremlin factions. Ultimately anointed as the heir apparent and thrust into office by

Yeltsin's end-of-millennium resignation, Putin was now called upon to reconcile all of the elements of his past into a comprehensive political identity, a persona that would define him and his tenure in office.

Every long-serving leader develops what might be called a "political formula" that defines both the formal and informal rules of the game of politics during his or her tenure. Janus like, it looks in two directions. Gazing inward, it defines the world of elite politics; who gets to play, what are the rules of the game, and what is the role of the mutually acknowledged leader? Gazing outward, it defines the relationship with the rest of society; how is that relationship institutionalized, how much power is really exercised by the public as opposed to the political elite, and how is the stability of that relationship maintained? In the Brezhnev era, the answer to the first set of questions was corporatism; a closed but internally pluralistic elite collectively exercising power under the guidance (but not control) of a conciliatory general secretary. The answer to the second set of questions was welfare state authoritarianism; a closed and selectively repressive regime bought public support through relatively egalitarian programs and by assuring its politically powerless citizens of an increasing standard of living and pride in the accomplishments of a global superpower.

Viewed from this perspective, what is Putin's political formula? Like any leader's agenda, it is a moving target. Certain core elements can be identified as running consistently throughout his first two terms, surviving in slightly different form through the Medvedev interregnum, and reemerging in altered form in the third (and maybe fourth) term. Yet the core remains, as described in the sections that follow.

A commitment to a distinctly Russian form of democracy. All powerful nations have claimed such exceptionalism at some point in their history. In the Russian case, these claims fill the pages of the nation's history: Moscow as the Third Rome; for the Slavophiles of the nineteenth century, Russia's mission to show the world an alternative to industrialization and secularization; and for the communists, the Soviet Union's mission to implement and share with the world a Leninist form of domestic and eventually world revolution. In its present incarnation, such exceptionalism initially took the form of *sovereign democracy,* an imprecisely defined and controversial doctrine that is meant to set post-communist democracy apart from its counterparts elsewhere. In many ways, sovereign democracy is little more than a buzzword. From the start, its meaning has purposely been vague, and little scholarly discussion has taken place to resolve its place in the pantheon of types of democracy or to note its precise implications. Some, including Medvedev, have even questioned the need for its existence,[12] and Putin has backed away from the term, without openly disavowing it, since his reelection to a third term in 2012.

At its core, sovereign democracy asserts the right of the state to block external attempts to influence the evolution of an indigenous form of democratic rule. Thus, sovereign democracy is not only "different," it is also fragile and the target of well-meaning or less-well-intentioned efforts to shape the future of Russian politics. "Hands off" is both an extension of the notion of sovereignty itself and a useful slogan denoting the willingness of domestic elites to stand up to foreign intervention.

A commitment to the creation of a powerful state, encapsulated in the concept of the "vertical of power" or other formulations that stress hierarchy. Consistent with the Russian concept of the state from tsarist rule onward, the idea of a centralized, powerful, and proactive state is central to the concept of post-communist democracy. A strong state is not seen as antithetical to democratic rule; quite the opposite, a strong state, itself democratically elected, is a necessary prerequisite, at least in theory, to the preservation and functioning of democracy.[13]

Putin's insistence on restoring the "vertical," as everyone called it, was a response to the nature of democratic rule at the end of the Yeltsin era. Putin's response was both traditionally grounded and politically prudent. Treading lightly at first because of the power of the holdover Yeltsin family, the oligarchs, the factions, and the regional barons, he gradually moved to reinforce the role of the central government and to bring those who opposed him into balance, if not under complete control.

A structuring of political competition both among the increasingly contentious factions within the Garden Ring and in the larger arena of electoral politics. "Structuring," of course, is the key word and has many different meanings. Any viable democracy must find a balance between "contestation," as the theorists usually call it, and structured governance. Finding that balance is never easy, even under the best of circumstances. Putin took the oath of office as president not quite eight years after his fellow Russians were shooting in the streets over just that question. Although no one expected a replay of 1993, none of the political questions that had brought them to that conflict had been resolved. The role of the president and his relationship with the legislature and other important power centers like the oligarchs and regional leaders were still largely undefined.

Putin's initiatives took two forms. The first was directed at political forces within the Garden Ring. These included the president's family, which combined Yeltsin's daughter and other close associates, including a number of oligarchs like Berezovsky; other oligarchs less personally involved with Yeltsin but supportive of his administration; and various factions like the *siloviki*, the statists, and the economic reformers. The details of their struggles are described later in this chapter, but the essential strategy was simple and direct: Neutralize the most threatening elements (the family and its entourage, and then the first generation of oligarchs) and orchestrate and balance the influence of the others, leaving Putin as the arbiter of intraelite conflict.

The second initiative sought to restructure the mechanisms of open political competition, including both political parties and the media. The expansion of United Russia—which first appeared late in the Yeltsin years as just another party *of*, but not *in*, power—was to be the lynchpin of bringing order to the cacophony of Russian politics. During the first Putin term, it expanded into an effective network at both the national and regional levels, growing in part because of the recentralization of central power through the vertical and in part because Putin's growing popularity created a coattails-and-bandwagon effect. This centrist and highly personalized extension of Putin's power was frequently supplemented by other officially sponsored parties slightly to the right or the left designed to siphon off support from the few remaining independent parties such as the Communist Party or the Liberal Democratic Party. Smaller parties were simply harassed into submission as the requirements for nominating candidates or getting seats in the legislature were altered to raise the bar ever higher.

The once-lively media also was brought under control. In most cases, control was imposed as Putin-friendly oligarchs or megacorporations like Gazprom, the nation's largest gas producer, bought up newspapers or television stations and maneuvered critical editors and journalists out of the mainstream. In other cases, the response was more draconian; overly aggressive reporters would be beaten into submission or, as in the case of Galina Starovoitova, murdered, most likely as an example to others.[14]

A loosely defined commitment to economic reform. Putin's economic agenda was rooted in the political and economic realities of the day. In the short run, democratization had not been kind to the standard of living of the average Russian. Industrial output tumbled, and workers once assured of jobs for life soon found themselves out of work. Government cutbacks destroyed the safety net of health and retirement programs, and rapid inflation shrank what little had been put aside by private citizens. In sharp and visible contrast, a small minority prospered. They came from many sources. Most were former managers who had gotten rich buying up undervalued assets while others leveraged early successes in the private sector into vast diversified holdings. But they all had two things in common: They were grim reminders to the average citizen of the growing income gap in Russian society and confirmation of the government's failure or unwillingness to deal with corruption.

Putin's full economic agenda is discussed later in this chapter, but it is sufficient for now to observe that it focused on three elements, all closely tied to his understanding of what it meant to transform and modernize the post-soviet economy. First, the role of the state was to be increased, especially in key areas such as energy and raw material production. Second, the oligarchs were to be brought under control, usually through government-sponsored "adjustments" to the size and power of their empires, still leaving them with vast holdings, and sometimes through the blunt force of government intervention or prosecution. Once again offering a deal that was discussed briefly late in the Yeltsin era but never put in place, Putin assured the oligarchs that their vast fortunes would be largely secure and immune from adjustments to the sweetheart deals they negotiated in the 1990s, provided that they withdrew from political life. Most gladly accepted the arrangement, while others, like the soon-to-be-imprisoned Mikhail Khodorkovsky, learned the hard way that the carrot was accompanied by a stick.[15] Third, consistent with eventual Russian membership in the World Trade Organization and Putin's efforts to make it a part of the growing global economy, greater attention was to be given to technological modernization and the diversification of an economy centered on energy and raw materials, although the political weight of the energy sector and the importance of its profits made it difficult to wean the nation away from such exports.

A commitment to restoring a global role for Russia. Empires die hard, especially in the memories of their once-proud citizens. The breakup of the Soviet Union left Russia as a shadow of its former self. Putin set out to change that. Motivated both by his KGB-rooted sense of stewardship over the fate of Mother Russia and by the realization that a healthy dose of Russian pride would strengthen him at the polls, he launched a charm offensive to convince the world that the uncertainties of the Yeltsin years had ended. He professed a commitment to the integration of Russia into the global economy and the World Trade Organization and, after September 11, 2001, to the global struggle against terrorism, as he now defined Russian actions in Chechnya. At first the charm offensive worked well, convincing Western leaders like U.S. president George W. Bush that they had found, as British prime minister Margaret Thatcher had said of Mikhail Gorbachev a decade earlier, someone with whom they could work. The luster soon faded as Russia and the West found themselves at odds over issues such as the enlargement of NATO, U.S. plans to create a missile defense system in Eastern Europe, the spread of the European Union, growing Western criticism of the treatment of journalists and other critics of the regime in Russia, and the impact of military engagements in places like Georgia and Chechnya.[16]

The Putin Presidency Emerges from Yeltsin's Shadow

Yeltsin was a hard act to follow. Putin was initially surrounded by the holdovers from the Yeltsin era and moved cautiously to advance his own agenda. He named Mikhail Kasyanov as his first prime minister. Close to the Yeltsin family, Kasyanov held the post for three years before Putin was able to push him aside. Early attempts to name his own choices to top posts were thwarted. He was never fully accepted by the Moscow elite, especially the powerful Yuri Luzhkov, who became the mayor of the city during Yeltsin's tenure and survived until near the end of the Medvedev presidency.[17]

Putin's first task was to free himself from the control of the family and those oligarchs closest to it. The family's hold remained strong even after Yeltsin's resignation. Putin gradually distanced himself from Yeltsin's inner circle, at first pushing aside lesser members and finally, in February 2004, sacking Kasyanov. He replaced them with his own appointees or drew some of the second-tier players—like Vladislav Surkov, who would become his key political strategist—into his own growing entourage.[18]

In many ways, moving against the oligarchs was an easier task. Many, including Berezovsky, had come under investigation during Yeltsin's second term. Pressure against him intensified after Putin's inauguration, and in

2001 he fled to self-imposed exile in London, turning his energies toward overthrowing the Putin regime. In July 2000, just six months into his first term and not yet completely free of the pressure exercised by the family, Putin met with a large number of the oligarchs and offered them a clear choice. Their wealth would be secure, and they would be free from any investigation of how they acquired it if, and only if, they stayed out of politics. Putin's presidency, Putin's rules. Most got the message.

But not all. Or at least that is the way the story of the prosecution of Mikhail Khodorkovsky, one of Russia's richest oligarchs, would be spun by the Putin administration, which moved against him in 2003. Khodorkovsky was in many ways typical of the first generation of oligarchs. He began his entrepreneurial career as an official of the Komsomol, or Communist Youth League, in the early days of perestroika. Like many budding capitalists, he used the connections he made there to build an economic empire that began modestly with a private café and expanded to include banking and import–export interests. The crown jewel was Yukos, an oil company acquired at a bargain price when state-held resources were privatized. It specialized in developing vast Siberian reserves and rapidly rose to become one of largest corporations in Russia.

Unlike most of the other oligarchs, Khodorkovsky began to cross the line that Putin had drawn in the sand. He was often publicly critical of Putin, sometimes directly to his face in meetings between the president and business leaders. Although he professed no personal political ambitions, he endorsed and funded a number of programs that ran counter to Putin's agenda of the vertical and sovereign democracy.

In October 2003, Khodorkovsky was arrested and charged with fraud and tax evasion. His trial was a throwback to the worst of the communist era, when party officials dictated to the prosecutors and the courts who should be indicted and convicted. Yukos was broken up, sold off to a largely fictional holding company, and Khodorkovsky was stripped of most of his other assets. The show trial, offered up for public consumption as a lesson to the other oligarchs, concluded in 2005, resulting in a nine-year incarceration in Siberia. As the sentence neared its end during the Medvedev years, Khodorkovsky was again indicted on largely trumped-up charges. Conviction again was certain, and his prison term was extended until 2017.

With the family and the oligarchs in retreat, Putin now faced a new political reality. Political life within the Garden Ring was still dominated by a series of factions, each deeply rooted in some aspect of the government bureaucracy, a particular sector of the economy, a geographic region, or some general policy orientation. Now the strategy was to learn to play each against the other to maintain balance.

The cast of characters was large, as described in the sections that follow.

The siloviki. The term *siloviki* is based on the Russian word for "force." In institutional terms, it includes an exceptionally broad assortment of agencies, all sharing a common perception of their special role in defending the nation but also internally divided by their own unique missions and bureaucratic rivalries. Included are the KGB and its post-communist incarnations in the Federal Security Service and the Federal Intelligence Service, the former focusing on internal affairs and the latter on foreign intelligence; elements of the Ministry of Internal Affairs that deal with the national police force; the Federal Narcotics Service; elements of the military dealing with intelligence and internal security issues; the newly created Investigative Committee, which deals with corruption and politically sensitive issues; and the recently created National Guard, under the command of a close Putin associate. Their shared concerns with the power of the state and the preservation of social order predispose them to support many elements of Putin's agenda, including the vertical and the notion of sovereign democracy, but their institutional diversity commits them to vastly different priorities in the constant intra-bureaucratic struggle over jurisdictional and budgetary issues. Although they share a common point of view with Putin on many issues, the president was clearly never regarded as the leader of a unified *siloviki* faction.

Although the *siloviki* may have become more important during Putin's first and second terms, there is considerable dispute over the scope of that expansion. Estimates range from a threefold to a sevenfold increase in their numbers, with considerably higher representation in key government ministries, the seven federal regional administrations, and Putin's personal kitchen cabinet, which met weekly.[19]

The democratic statists. The democratic statists focus primarily on domestic political issues. Their primary concern is the creation of a stable political system, formally democratic in nature but operating within the parameters of the doctrine of sovereign democracy. As Richard Sakwa puts it, they were "democratic but not liberal."[20] In many ways, Putin's initial views on state building are closest to the democratic statists, although he is careful to maintain a sense of formal neutrality in order to balance factional interests. For him, under the circumstances he inherited from Yeltsin—a divided and

combative Duma and a seemingly strong but largely untested presidency—
the first order of business was to strengthen his office. Most of his actions,
at least in the first term, were directed at increasing the power of the presidency vis-à-vis the legislature and regional leaders, creating a supportive
party in United Russia, and finding ways to outflank his opponents, such as
through the use of presidential decrees.

The democratic statists quickly emerged as the technicians of political
power. Much like the political consultants, spin masters, and professional
campaign managers that dominate democratic politics in other nations, they
stood just a step behind the leader, crafting strategies and issues that would
lead to victory. Most prominent among them during the Putin era was Surkov,
the reputed guiding spirit behind the president's consolidation of power.

Another major concern among the democratic statists was the creation
of a controlled civil society. Although nongovernmental organizations
(NGOs) are acknowledged as playing an important role in a pluralistic and
democratically governed society, the democratic statists argue that they too
must operate within parameters set by the state. Accordingly, the more
than half a million such organizations functioning in Russia must be registered and file regular financial reports, and those with foreign connections
are subjected to intensified scrutiny.

Guiding an active political debate, another major concern of the statists,
was further institutionalized by the creation of two quasi-state bodies, the
State Council and the Public Chamber. The State Council was created in
September 2000 and included all of the still popularly elected governors of
the regions that made up the Russian Federation.[21] On paper it looked
good; the president himself chaired the body, and the creation of a smaller
seven-member rotating presidium made it seem possible that the otherwise
large and unwieldly body might be taken seriously. In reality, it came to
nothing, except as good public relations to argue that the Putin presidency
was reaching out to a broader audience outside the Garden Ring.

The creation of the Public Chamber in 2005 was yet another mechanism to organize political discourse. Numbering 126 members, it suppos-
edly represents a microcosm of Russian society. The president names one
third of the members from among prominent citizens, usually a hodgepodge of academics, business people, athletes, lawyers, public intellectuals,
and the like. An additional third are named as representatives of national
public NGOs, and the final third are chosen by regional and interregional
NGOs. Despite its wide-ranging mandate, there is little evidence that the
Chamber has played an important role.[22]

Economic reformers and technocrats. The economic reformers have emerged as a counterweight to the *siloviki* and the democratic statists through their insistence on the continuation of economic reforms and integration into the global economy. Most prominent among them during Putin's first two terms was Alexei Kudrin, the finance minister who is credited with maintaining stability after the 2008 global stock market debacle. But even he was not immune to the vagaries of factional and personal rivalries; he was dismissed by Medvedev in 2011 after a public dispute over Kudrin's refusal to serve under Medvedev as prime minister in a future administration.

Business interests. It is hardly surprising that business interests have become major players in the world of Russian politics. The story of the relationship between Russian big business and the government goes far beyond the role of the oligarchs, whichever generation is under the microscope. Although the oligarchs grab the headlines, the other story is frequently ignored.

As Richard Sakwa points out, there are really two different groups of corporate actors. The first is composed of the remnants of the old soviet-era megacorporations in which the state still holds a controlling, although not necessarily exclusive, interest.[23] Most are the well-known giants such as Gazprom, Russian Railways, Rosoboronoexsport (Russian Arms Export), Rosneft (Russian Oil), and others mostly in the energy, raw material, or transportation sectors. Between two worlds, these giants must respond both to the market (domestic and international) and to government influence, if not direct control.

The second group consists of large corporations that increasingly have gone global. Frequently associated with the second- or third-generation oligarchs, they lack direct state involvement in the day-to-day management of their affairs, although on occasion the Kremlin will intervene to keep the overall picture in balance. There is little doubt that these seemingly independent corporations receive favorable treatment and de facto government assistance in building larger market share in an increasingly global economy.

In broader perspective, Putin also attempted to orchestrate the broader lobbying environment for the business community as a whole. Shortly after assuming office, he let it be known that an already existing body, the Russian Union of Industrialists and Entrepreneurs, should become the major mechanism of communication between the business community and his regime; virtually all industries were instructed to join and channel all proposals, suggestions, and complaints through that body, but only after having worked out a common group position. Soon thereafter, he designated two other groups, *Delovaya Rossiya* and United Entrepreneurs' Organizations of Russia, to reach out to medium and small business interests. Yevgeny Primakov, a former foreign minister and prime minister who briefly considered a run for the presidency against Putin, was selected to head the Chamber of Commerce and Industry. Despite the formalization of channels, most effective lobbying still occurred through the time-honored face-to-face ties that linked political and economic leaders, confirming the Russian proverb that it is better to have a hundred friends than a hundred rubles.[24]

Regional power centers. The de facto decentralization of power in the 1990s led to the emergence of a host of regional barons not only in the provinces but also in key cities like Moscow. For them, local autonomy and a weak central government were the keys to keeping tight control over local government and enriching themselves through exploiting local resources and homegrown corruption. The creation of seemingly untouchable fiefdoms was especially blatant in the Caucasus, although certainly not limited to this region. While the seven federal districts with their Moscow-appointed leaders could do little to bring the barons into line, the shift to the central appointment of regional governors in 2005 began to erode their power. Still, it sometimes took exceptional efforts to push aside the last of the provincial strongmen.

The Moscow and St. Petersburg fiefdoms were a different story, primarily because each played a double game. They sought not only to maintain an independent political base within each of these cities, complete with the sort of patronage and widespread corruption needed to maintain control, but also to colonize and win influence within the central government. During the Yeltsin years, Moscow had the upper hand. Its powerful local boss, Yuri Luzhkov, was initially close to Yeltsin, although not a part of the official family. A rift eventually developed when Luzhkov entertained presidential ambitions in his own right. St. Petersburg's turn came second, coincident with the rise of Putin and the *Pitery*, a faction loosely defined by its members' close association with Putin's earlier career in that city rather than by any institutional or policy-related ties. Putin's choice to lead the city after his departure was Valentina Matvienko, who unified the city's machine under her control and remained in charge until the Medvedev era, when she was transferred to Moscow. As noted many times over, Putin's reliance on his early associates brought future influence for the *Pitery* over national affairs and undoubtedly worked to the benefit of the city itself.

Outside the Garden Ring: "Managing" the New Democracy

As noted, Putin set out to put the two worlds of Russian politics in order and somehow to connect them. Following the Gaullist approach in France, he sought to develop a mass-based political party to mobilize support and to connect the center with the provinces. The president never was truly dependent on United Russia for election, and it did not control the selection of prime minister. The party's popularity peaked after the 2007 legislative elections, which gave it 64.3 percent of the vote and a potential constitution-changing majority in the Duma. It fell to 49.3 percent after the 2011 Duma vote, although it cobbled together a working majority with the support of other parties. Even in decline, United Russia remains the largest party in the legislature.

United Russia's most important impact came in two ways. First, it became Putin's link to the general population beyond the Garden Ring. Even in a world of television and social networks, it played an important role, sustaining a sense of connection and commitment, even as Putin himself maintained a posture of neutrality and distance, as had Yeltsin. It gave Putin a label that could be translated into political action at all levels: If you like Putin, and most Russians did, then vote for the United Russia candidate. It was that simple, and out in the provinces, simple was good.

Second, it changed the focus of Russian politics. In the 1990s, political life had been about defending the democratic revolution against the possible return of communism (or, less likely, a form of right-wing authoritarianism). Now the goal changed, redefining the battle lines. The intertwined ideas of stability and economic improvement took hold. Simple ideas with deep resonance in an exhausted and impoverished nation, they offered hope. Yet "stability" did not necessarily mean more or better democracy, and "economic improvement" did not necessarily mean structural reform or more equitable income distribution. They just meant that, for a while, things would seem to get better. But for a while, that would be enough. . . .

The Presidency and the Legislature: The 2003 Duma Elections

Even though Putin's overall strategy was clear, its implementation in the real world was mired in the vagaries of elite and electoral politics. The 2003 Duma elections provided the first opportunity to test the strategy outside the Garden Ring. Eighteen political parties and five blocs took part in the December balloting. Overall turnout was comparatively low, at just under 55 percent. Seemingly confirming the wisdom of Putin's strategy, United Russia was the big winner, getting 37.6 percent of the party-list vote (Table 5.2). That gave it 120 seats from the party list, and an additional 103 from the single-member districts, for a total of 223 seat—just three short of a controlling majority in the Duma. Sixty independents soon joined the party, giving it a controlling edge.[25]

Other parties fared far less well. The Communists pulled in 12.6 percent of the party-list vote, for forty seats, with another twelve seats selected in the districts. The Liberal Democrats continued their decline; with 11.5 percent of the party-list votes, they got thirty-six seats, with no additional seats from district balloting. A new party, Rodina (Motherland), got 9.0 percent of the party-list vote, for twenty-nine seats, with another eight seats coming from the districts. No other party crossed the 5-percent threshold for party-list seats. Yabloko pulled only 4.3 percent but did get four seats from the districts. The Union of Right Forces got 4.0 percent in the party-list voting but picked up three seats from the districts. The Agrarian Party, still allied with the Communists, got 3.6 percent of the party-list votes and two seats in district voting. All the other parties, sixteen of them, collectively got twenty-three seats in district voting, and independents captured sixty-seven district seats. "None of the above" did exceptionally well this time, with 4.7 percent, nearly raising the sticky question of what to do if it had crossed the 5-percent eligibility requirement. In three districts, the "noners" actually won, forcing another round of voting.[26]

Meanwhile, inside the Garden Ring, Putin's consolidation continued. Now far less hemmed in by the surviving elements of the Yeltsin family, he was finally able to sack Kasyanov as prime minister in February 2004, appointing Mikhail Fradkov to replace him. A surprising choice to many, Fradkov was a highly regarded economist with long experience in foreign economic relations. Perhaps more important, he was not closely identified with any of the major Kremlin factions. His appointment permitted Putin

Table 5.2   2003 Russian Legislative Election

Party	Proportional Representation	Single-Member-District Voting	Total Seats
United Russia	Votes: 22,776,294 Percentage: 37.6 Seats: 120	Votes: 14,123,625 Percentage: 24 Seats: 103	223
Communist Party	Votes: 7,647,820 Percentage: 12.6 Seats: 40	Votes: 6,577,598 Percentage: 11.2 Seats: 12	52
Zhirinovsky Bloc	Votes: 6,944,322 Percentage: 11.5 Seats: 36	Votes: 1,860,905 Percentage: 3.2 Seats: 0	36
Rodina	Votes: 5,470,429 Percentage: 9.0 Seats: 29	Votes: 1,719,147 Percentage: 2.9 Seats: 8	37
Yabloko	Votes: 2,610,087 Percentage: 4.3 Seats: 0	Votes: 1,580,629 Percentage: 2.7 Seats: 4	4
Union of Right Forces	Votes: 2,408,535 Percentage: 4.0 Seats: 0	Votes: 1,764,290 Percentage: 3.0 Seats: 3	3
Agrarian Party	Votes: 2,205,850 Percentage: 3.6 Seats: 0	Votes: 1,104,974 Percentage: 1.9 Seats: 2	2
People's Party	Votes: 714,705 Percentage: 1.2 Seats: 0	Votes: 2,677,889 Percentage: 4.5 Seats: 17	17
Independents		Votes: 15,843,626 Percentage: 26.9 Seats: 67	67

SOURCE: D. Nohlen and P. Stover. (2010). *Elections in Europe: A Data Handbook*. Baden-Baden, Germany: Nomos.

to maintain the balance among the factions and escape the difficult choice of seeming to favor one over another.

Judicial Reform

Significant reform in the judicial system occurred during Putin's first two terms in office. Much of it was motivated by a desire to further professionalize the courts and other aspects of the legal system. Putin had been trained as a lawyer, and he understood the importance of law—and particularly legal reform—as both a symbol of social change and a mechanism of social transformation.

Putin also knew Russian history well enough to understand that law could be used as a mechanism of social transformation as well as control. The reassertion of a strong transformational role for the courts was an important aspects of Putin's vertical of power. There would be both a positive side and a dark side to these changes. On the positive side, ten new legal codes were written in areas dealing with the creation of a market economy, property and land ownership, taxes, labor, and criminal procedure. The latter reduced the once-dominant role of the procuracy, created the option for jury trials (little used), and strengthened the rights of defendants, although the return of politically motivated trials compromised these rights in a small number of high-profile cases. Set against these changes, of course, was the momentum of the vast weight of those elements of the legal profession that remained in place. Changing the laws was one thing; changing how the system worked was quite another.[27]

But there was a dark side, too. More aggressive prosecution of economic crimes became an important political weapon. Threats of prosecution for economic crimes also became a frequent tool to rein in regional leaders who had built their own corrupt bailiwicks in the Yeltsin years. The first to fall was Yevgeny Nazdratenko, governor of the Primorsky Krai region in the Pacific Northeast, who was afforded a soft landing in an appointed position in the area once he agreed to step down in the face of potential prosecution. Others, like Moscow's mayor Luzhkov, whose wife had become Russia's wealthiest woman largely as a result of real estate transactions in the city and elsewhere, survived until the Medvedev years.[28]

The 2004 Presidential Election

The 2004 presidential election was a cakewalk for Putin, who was returned to office with 71.9 percent of the vote.[29] In what will probably be remembered as the high point of his career, Putin won with the open support of United Russia, whose spreading organization was beginning to make a difference. But more broadly, he also won widespread grassroots support that had rallied to his call for economic and social stability and national pride. His dismissal of Kasyanov before the election seemingly cleared the

Table 5.3   2004 Russian Presidential Election

Candidate	Party	Votes	Percentage
Vladimir Putin	Independent	49,558,328	71.9
Nikolai Kharitonov	Communist Party	9,514,554	13.8
Sergei Glazyev	Independent	2,850,610	4.1
Irina Khakamada	Independent	2,672,189	3.9
Oleg Malyshkin	Liberal Democratic Party	1,405,326	2.0
Sergei Mironov	Russian Party of Life	524,332	0.8

SOURCE: D. Nohlen and P. Stover. (2010). *Elections in Europe: A Data Handbook.* Baden-Baden, Germany: Nomos.

deck of the last vestige of the Yeltsin era, and the appointment of a techno-crat like Fradkov suggested that the political strife of the past had been replaced by the calmer "management of things," as soviet leaders used to say to reassure the masses. In truth, factional conflict still raged just below the surface and would rear its head in the run-up to the 2008 election, which faced the more difficult question of choosing a successor to Putin at a time of economic uncertainty.

Putin's opponents in 2004 seemed to do everything wrong. Some tried to organize a boycott of the election itself, since a turnout of less than 50 percent would have invalidated the result. Their resolve soon weakened, and the coalition disintegrated amid acrimonious charges of betrayal of the common cause. Grigory Yavlinsky, who had once been the standard-bearer of the dwindling liberal opposition, refused to run. The perennial Communist candidate, Zyuganov, also refused to take the field; the Communist Party was led into battle by the little-known Nikolai Kharitonov, himself not even a member of the party but of its junior partner, the Agrarian Party. He got just 13.8 percent of the vote. Zhirinovsky also chose not to run on the Liberal Democratic ticket, designating his personal body-guard, a boxer named Oleg Malyshkin, to stand in for him, for an embar-rassing 2.0 percent of the vote. Sergei Glazyev, who along with Dmitry Rogozin, led Rodina (Motherland) in the recent Duma race, broke from the party and ran as an independent, for 4.1 percent of the vote. Irina Khakamada, cut off from her previous association with the Union of Right Forces, ran an independent wild card candidacy, winning 3.9 percent. And Sergei Mironov, speaker of the Federation Council, the upper house of the legislature and past Putin loyalist, got less than 1 percent running on the

Russian Party of Life ticket. In its last hurrah (the category would be removed before the next election), "none of the above" got 3.5 percent.

The Rules and the Game Change

In 2004 and 2005, a number of important changes were made in the electoral system. Although complicated, they all pointed in the same direction—toward diminishing the potential role of small parties and further consolidating the institutionalized hold of what was clearly then the dominant party, United Russia. Introduced in the wake of a deadly terrorist seizure of a school is Beslan, they were ostensibly justified as anti-terrorist measures designed to strengthen the unity of the nation, although few believed such a transparent explanation.[30]

Balloting for the 450-member Duma was changed to provide for the election of all members from party lists. Gone was the 225 member bloc of seats elected in single-member districts, which had provided a second opportunity for small parties or locally popular independent candidates to gain a seat. Two lists of potential delegates appeared on each ballot. The first consisted of the party's nationally prominent candidates for the Duma itself, now limited to three names. The second list contained the prioritized names of delegates seeking to represent the party at the regional level in at least 100 regions. The creation of such elaborate lists was virtually impossible for the smaller parties, leaving only United Russia (the largest party by far), the Communists, and the Liberal Democrats positioned to dominate the ballots.

The threshold point for entry into the Duma was raised to 7 percent, two points higher than before. In the past, some smaller parties formed blocs to pool their votes to jump the hurdle. Now that avenue was closed. A complicated set of new rules also affected the 7-percent barrier. Since 60 percent of the ballots cast in any election had to be represented in the Duma, parties that initially fell below the 7-percent cutoff might still receive seats until the 60-percent requirement had been satisfied. The new rules also generously required that at least two parties had to be represented in the Duma, no matter the voting results.

The bar was raised in other ways as well. Requirements to get candidates on the ballot were increased. More signatures in more districts were now required, and challenges by the less-than-neutral election board were now more frequent and effective. The 50-percent turnout requirement to validate national elections was dropped, ending the use of boycotts as opposition tools. And "none of the above" disappeared from future ballots.

In a further effort to control the regions, the popular election of governors ended. In 2004, the procedure was changed to permit the president to nominate the governor, who must be confirmed by the regional legislature. But if that body rejects the nominee three times, the president may dissolve the local assembly and force a new election, while simultaneously appointing an acting governor who may rule for six months. In light of the political risks to local lawmakers associated with such a confrontation and United Russia's ability to capture control at the regional level, presidential "nominees" were virtual shoe-ins, at least for a while.

The potential for using public referenda as a mechanism of grassroots rebellion against the government also was restricted. Initially understood as possible presidential leverage against a recalcitrant legislature (the way de Gaulle successfully employed it), such referenda originally could also be initiated by public action. While technically still possible under the tightened restrictions approved in 2004, such action was now far more difficult.[31]

The Run-Up to the 2008 Presidential Election

Political rivalries inside the Garden Ring ramped up during Putin's second term, especially in the run-up to the 2008 presidential elections, which would pick his successor or find some ploy to keep him in office despite the constitutional provision that a president could serve only two consecutive terms. Putin periodically shuffled the lineup of the government and the presidential staff to maintain a balance among the factions, thus preserving his ability to maneuver. In November 2005, the pro-Putin defense minister, Sergei Ivanov, was also named a first deputy prime minister. The head of the presidential administration, Dmitry Medvedev, also was advanced to first deputy prime minister. A close associate from St. Petersburg, Medvedev was also placed in charge of a number of high-priority national projects, giving him a new level of public visibility. Both were regarded as viable choices to follow in Putin's footsteps, and it is hardly surprising that the president chose to play them off against each other.

The game was soon joined by others. The *siloviki* were still important players, their cause forcefully pressed by Igor Sechin, who had worked with

Putin since his days in the mayor's office in St. Petersburg. But he personally was not regarded as presidential material, and the *siloviki* lacked any
serious candidate for the top office. Although he had extensive KGB experience, Ivanov was too close to Putin to be accepted unquestioningly by the
siloviki as a reliable kindred spirit. In the aftermath of the Khodorkovsky
affair, the remaining oligarchs wisely kept their heads down, while the
more traditional business and entrepreneurial lobbies sided cautiously with
Medvedev, who reached out to such modernizing forces. The military was
virtually cut out of the game; Ivanov, the defense minister and strong con-
tender for the presidency, was never regarded by the uniformed military as
a strong advocate of their cause. His eventual successor, Anatoly Serdyukov,
was a civilian who had made a fortune in the furniture industry and eventually served as head of the Federal Tax Service, preparing him for his
mandate to crack down on corruption within the military. Greater influence seemingly accrued to the democratic statists, largely because they still
most closely represented Putin's views about the need for order and stability and the necessity to gracefully manage the 2008 transition from Putin
to his anointed successor.

In mid-September 2007, Putin further complicated the waiting game.
Previous experience, limited though it was, suggested that the president
would remove Fradkov as prime minister some time prior to the election
and that his choice to replace him would be the de facto designated successor. Remove Fradkov he did, but instead of choosing between the supposed
front-runners, Ivanov and Medvedev, Putin selected a wildcard: Viktor
Zubkov, head of the Federal Financial Intelligence Agency. Zubkov seemingly had no close ties to the contending factions, although he originally
hailed from Leningrad. He also had no background in the intelligence
community, presumably distancing him from the *siloviki*. His appointment
prompted widespread speculation. Had Putin copied Yeltsin in naming an
unexpected successor, a dark horse whom he would quickly advance to the
front of the pack?[32]

Putin was now confronted with the need to assert control over the
succession. With no clearly acknowledged front-runner, the field was
open to several strategies. Since no single faction seemed likely to capture
control of the succession, an alternative strategy would be to preserve the
balance by amending the constitution to permit Putin to run for a third
consecutive term. United Russia's control of the legislature made this
legally possible. Alternatively, Putin could choose a nominal successor,
who would quickly step down from the presidency, permitting Putin to

run for the office since the constitution banned three *consecutive* terms in office. Although perfectly legal even under the existing constitution, it still carried political risks. Or he could select a full-term successor and attempt to exercise continuing influence from behind the scenes, perhaps as prime minister with enhanced powers. That option would demand two things, a compliant successor, himself free of close ties to any of the major factions, and the continuing ability to balance the competing factions as prime minister.

In one sense, Putin was fortunate. It proved relatively easy to get control of the factions; the *siloviki* were internally divided over questions of policy and personal rivalries, and other factions could be brought into line through a series of new appointments or criminal investigations into their alleged corruption. Putin also advanced a new group, the *financisti* as a counterweight to more conventional groups. Best understood as financial managers rather than conventional oligarchs or business interests, they exercised increasing influence and were visibly represented at the top by the new prime minister, Zubkov.

The 2007 Duma Elections

The 2007 Duma was the first to be chosen under the new election law, the cumulative impact of which was, if you accepted the most generous interpretation, to bring order to the party structure. If you accepted the generally held and far less generous point of view, it was to stack the deck in favor of United Russia. In fact, it did both. Under new registration requirements, now only fifteen parties qualified to post candidates, fewer than half the number in the 2003 election. The other changes—party-list voting for all seats, the 7-percent rule for entry into the Duma, the end of a "none of the above" option, and others, all discussed earlier—now focused the game on a handful of larger parties in which United Russia was best positioned to win.[33]

In a surprise move, Putin agreed to place his name at the head of United Russia's list of candidates. He still insisted that he would not formally join United Russia, prompting the party congress to pass a new rule permitting the ticket to be headed by a nonmember. The move was probably intended to head off factional divisions within the party, in which regional and policy differences, as well as differences over the selection of Putin's successor, had begun to take their toll. Putin also implied that he might serve as prime minister under his not-yet-named successor if the party won a clear victory and the new president were someone with whom he could work, a disingenuous comment from the man who would ultimately name his own successor.

A new party, Just Russia, took the field. Formed in 2006 to fill a center-left niche, it was intended to bleed off support from the communists and liberals such as Yabloko. Led by Sergei Mironov, it soon sought to acquire a separate political identity of its own, not atypical of past Kremlin-created parties with delusions of grandeur. The Communist Party, with Zyuganov once again in the lead, ran virtually the same campaign it had in the past, calling for the renationalization of key industries and efforts to rebuild as much of the former Soviet Union as possible. The Liberal Democratic Party offered its usual assortment of oppositional and nationalistic slogans, and Zhirinovsky did not disappoint as the party's most visible representative. The Union of Right Forces, a center-right grouping of serious reformers who had been friendly to Putin's economic agenda, also fielded candidates, and Yabloko continued its liberal criticism of the regime.

Russians went to the polls on December 2, 2007, not yet knowing whom Putin would name as his successor. The results surprised no one. United Russia won 64.3 percent of the vote, giving it 315 seats in the new Duma and increasing the margin by which he held an unchallengeable constitution-changing majority. The Communists got 11.6 percent, for fifty-seven seats; continuing its decline, it fell from 12.6 percent of the party-list vote in 2003. The Liberal Democratic Party came in with 8.1 percent, dropping from 11.5 percent of the party-list vote in 2003. That was enough to win forty seats. Just Russia was the last party to rise above the 7-percent cutoff point; with 7.7 percent, it got thirty-eight seats. Yabloko got 1.6 percent of the vote, and no seats, and the Union of Right Forces got just under 1 percent.

Table 5.4   2007 Russian Legislative Election

Party	Vote	Percentage	Seats
United Russia	44,714,241	64.3	315
Communist Party	8,046,886	11.6	57
Liberal Democratic Party	5,660,823	8.1	40
Just Russia	5,383,639	7.7	38

SOURCE: D. Nohlen and P. Stover. (2010). *Elections in Europe: A Data Handbook.* Baden-Baden, Germany: Nomos.

Even as United Russia celebrated its victory and prepared for the upcoming presidential race, several bothersome realities did not bode well for the future. The level of support for United Russia fell far below that of its primary candidate and spiritual leader, President Putin himself. In the 2004 presidential election, Putin pulled in 71.9 percent of the vote, and his popularity ratings just before the 2007 balloting put him at around 80 percent, yet the party itself got just over 64 percent. Clearly the Putin magic was not completely transferable. United Russia also did poorest in the nation's two major cities, Moscow and St. Petersburg, where it pulled only 54 percent and 50.3 percent of the vote, respectively, a harbinger of things to come.

Putin's Economic Reforms

Putin's first two terms in office were marked by improvement in the economy. In many ways, it was a fortunate coincidence for the man to whom the luckless Yeltsin had entrusted the future of the nation. In all fairness, some of the credit legitimately belonged to the new president. His strengthening of the state and the imposition of the vertical brought order to the disarray of the Yeltsin era. Whatever their negative political consequences, these actions provided a more stable foundation for an economic recovery. Putin also attempted to bring the oligarchs into line, or at least to limit their direct influence over political life. To the average Russian, he was a strong leader who knew the value of *poryadok*—order and discipline—qualities deemed essential to putting the country back to work.

The numbers looked good, especially if one ignored the underlying political and social realities. During Putin's first two terms, from 2000 to 2008, gross domestic product increased by 70 percent, industrial output by 75 percent, and investment (both foreign and domestic) by 125 percent. In 2007, the gross domestic output reached the 1990 level, signaling at least a formal return to the nation's benchmark level at the end of the communist era. Over the same period, real income more than doubled, while poverty was cut in half. Average income increased from 2,200 rubles (US$90) to 12,500 rubles ($500) per month, while the average pension climbed from 823 rubles ($90) to 3,500 rubles ($140) per month. Both rose more rapidly than inflation over the same period. In broader terms, the middle class grew sevenfold, from 8 million to 55 million. The number of people living below the official poverty line dropped from 30 percent in 2000 to 14 percent in

2008. In 2004, a Stabilization Fund was created largely from revenues from the oil industry to cope with emergencies. Within two years, the fund had accumulated sufficient resources to pay off Russia's sovereign debt. In 2008, it was split into the Reserve Fund, to be used to shield the nation from global financial shocks, and the National Welfare Fund, designated for pension reform and other social services.

Problems still remained. The first wave of privatization had shifted much of the nation's manufacturing and the service sector into private hands, but many state-owned or state-controlled large corporations remained, especially in critical sectors such as energy or raw materials production. An oft-promised second wave of privatization was delayed repeatedly, more for political than economic reasons. Little was done to diversify the nation's economic profile to move it away from continuing dominance on extractive and export-oriented industries. Although lip service was rendered to the importance of technological innovation, the development of a stronger domestic market, and the creation of an entre-preneur-driven development model to move the economy to the next stage, little was done to put these notions into action.

Putin's first two terms also brought significant changes in the identity and role of the oligarchs who had emerged during the Yeltsin years. As noted earlier, Putin promised that the oligarchs would remain free to pursue their own economic interests (subject to occasional "adjustment" of their holdings to somewhat level the playing field, and a willingness to tolerate the emergence of a new generation of oligarchs waiting in the wings), if they were willing to remain politically neutral. For most of them, the deal was a good bargain. A few who resisted or who had already fallen under attack before the 2000 presidential election were still at risk. Boris Berezovsky, still close to the Yeltsin family, decamped to London to avoid prosecution on charges of tax evasion, and Vladimir Gusinsky, whose interests had suffered during the 1998 economic crisis, soon fol-lowed into self-imposed exile.

A new generation of oligarchs began to emerge during the Putin years. Some were linked with the president, either through service in Leningrad/St. Petersburg or through KGB ties. Now numbered among the oligarchs were newcomers like Mikhail Fridman, Alexander Smolensky, Vladimir Lisin, Alexei Mordashov, Mikhail Prokhorov, Vladimir Potanin, Alisher Usmanov, Oleg Deripaska, Vagit Alekperov, Viktor Vekselberg, German Khan, and others. Most built economic empires rooted in raw materials extraction, media and banking interests, and manufacturing, all with increasing attention to investments abroad as well as at home, but none overtly overplayed his hand either in seeking to acquire dominance over the others or in overtly challenging the increasing centralization of state power over the economy.[34]

Foreign Policy

Putin's first two terms in office were marked by a more assertive role for Russia in the international community. He sought recognition for Russia as a major actor, if not a superpower, on the world stage, to oppose real and perceived efforts on the part of the United States and NATO to encroach on Russia's traditional diplomatic and security interests, and to reassert Moscow's interests in Eastern Europe and the independent states created by the breakup of the Soviet Union. Such efforts enjoyed mixed success at best. Russia's new activism prompted increased Western efforts to shore up its defenses against growing Russian assertiveness, and efforts to increase and institutionalize Russian influence over the former union republics produced a backlash against a de facto resurrection of the post-communist Russian sphere of influence. Whatever else may be said of Russia's more activist role in the world, it certainly reminded the world that Russia was still a nation that could not be ignored.

Escaping from a massive national inferiority complex was no small part of Putin's foreign policy agenda. In the 1990s, it was jokingly said that Russia was ruled from Spasso House, the official residency of the U.S. ambassador. Although that was far from the truth, even as a joke it understandably offended many Russians, who were constantly reminded that Western scholars like Michael McFaul (himself a future ambassador to Russia) would refer to their democratic revolution as "unfinished" or that Western economists and businesspeople were publicly critical of the slow progress toward creating a market economy. Seldom content to tolerate Western criticism or to accept other nations' blueprints for economic and political change, Russians across the political spectrum longed for the world to accept their version of national exceptionalism.

Not surprisingly, relations with the United States became an important testing ground for Russia's more assertive stance. Although Moscow and Washington would occasionally seek common ground, especially in areas such as resistance to terrorism, Putin was increasingly critical of American initiatives abroad. When President George W. Bush withdrew the United States from the Anti-Ballistic Missile Treaty to pursue American deployment of a missile defense system in Poland and the Czech Republic, Moscow was quick to charge that the system was really aimed at Russian interests in the region and to threaten "countermeasures" such as the deployment of Russian missiles. In 2007, Russia resumed long-distance patrol flights of strategic bombers that had been suspended in 1992; largely a symbolic move, it nonetheless was interpreted in the West as an effort to remind the world of Moscow's capabilities.

Moscow and Washington also traded increasingly barbed criticism of each other's policies. The Russian government openly opposed the American-led invasion of Iraq, noting the absence of United Nations authorization and questioning the existence of weapons of mass destruction. Moscow also bridled under an increasing barrage of criticisms from the West of its treatment of the media and critics of the regime. For its part, Washington was quick to condemn Moscow's efforts to influence the Ukrainian presidential election in 2004–2005, which eventually led to the selection of the strongly anti-Russian Viktor Yushchenko, whose rise to power had been billed as the "orange revolution" and a grassroots victory over the communist old guard. Similar concerns motivated Moscow's opposition to developments in Georgia, where Putin openly opposed the election of a pro-Western government under the control of Mikheil Saakashvili. Already troublesome disputes over the status of two small non-Georgian enclaves escalated quickly during Putin's second term and led to a brief but nasty war in the first months of Medvedev's presidency. Events in Ukraine and Georgia fueled Moscow's growing suspicion that such revolutions might occur elsewhere within what it still regarded as a Russian sphere of influence and that the West, and especially the Americans, had a hand in encouraging the creation of anti-Russian regimes in the region.

Relations with NATO soured quickly over the expansion of the alliance. An initial basis for consultation had been established in 1997 and strengthened, at least on paper, through the creation of the NATO-Russia Council in May 2002. Like the earlier body, it provided for mutual consultation in the hope of developing a consensus among its members over NATO's role in the post-cold war world. The Czech Republic, Hungary, and Poland joined NATO in 1999, followed by Bulgaria, Estonia, Latvia, Lithuania, Romania, Slovakia, and Slovenia in 2004. Continued suspicion about U.S. efforts to deploy a missile defense system in the Czech Republic and Poland, the establishment of U.S. and NATO bases in central Asia for operations in Afghanistan, and the creation of temporary NATO bases in Bulgaria and Romania stoked fears in Moscow that the West was once again contemplating encirclement of Russia. In 2007, Putin responded by suspending Russian adherence to the provisions of the Conventional Forces in Europe treaty until all NATO members, old and new, confirmed their willingness to subscribe to its provisions. For its part, Moscow failed to implement an earlier commitment to withdraw Russian troops from Moldova, where they were stationed in support of a breakaway enclave of ethnic Russians who constituted themselves as the Trans-Dniester Republic.

The expansion of the European Union into Eastern Europe and the former union republics of the Soviet Union also caused problems. The Czech Republic, Estonia, Hungary, Latvia, Lithuania, Poland, Slovakia, and Slovenia joined in 2004, followed three years later by Bulgaria and Romania. Others would follow during Medvedev's term as president, and later when Putin returned to office in 2012. Moscow's economic ties to the European Union became increasingly complex. Russia supplies the European Union with more than one quarter of its total gas and oil; such dependency had been expected to increase over the next 20 years, giving Moscow added leverage. Russia has become the European Union's third-largest trading partner, behind the United States and China. At the same time, Russia is increasingly dependent on the European Union as a trading partner and as a source of three quarters of its foreign direct investment.

Moscow increasingly has attempted to institutionalize its influence over the post-soviet republics. It continued to view the Commonwealth of Independent States, formed at the time of the breakup of the Soviet Union, as an instrument of Russian foreign policy rather than as a partnership of equals. Fearing Western encroachment, Moscow strengthened its influence on the Collective Security Treaty Organization (CSTO), which includes Russia, Belarus, Kazakhstan, Kyrgyzstan, Armenia, and Uzbekistan; Georgia, which had joined in 1994, withdrew five years later. Russia also strengthened its ties to the Shanghai Cooperation Organization, which included most of the same nations that had joined the CSTO as well as China.[35]

The Second Chechen War

Although the second Chechen war began in the waning months of Yeltsin's second term, it would be left to Putin, as the nation's new acting prime minister and future president, to shape its outcome. A formal cease-fire had been in place for several years, but periodic flare-ups, some beyond the borders of Chechnya itself, reminded everyone that a second round of fighting was likely. In late August 1999, the Islamic International Peacekeeping Brigade, one of an increasing number of self-styled and poorly coordinated rebel groups springing up all over the Caucasus, invaded neighboring Dagestan. On October 1, Yeltsin ordered Russian troops back into Chechnya, ending the de facto independence of the region that had been tolerated grudgingly since 1996.

The new conflict was different in two important ways. First, the Chechen forces fighting against Moscow increasingly were joined by Islamic militants from elsewhere. The attack in Dagestan that launched the second war was undertaken by forces combining Chechen, Dagestani, Arab, and other international mujahideen and Wahhabi fighters. Second, the conflict was brought to the Russian heartland outside the Caucasus by an increasing number of terrorist attacks. In September 1999, apartment bombings occurred in Moscow and other Russian cities. Chechen terrorists were blamed for the attacks, although a number of skeptics alleged that they were false-flag operations undertaken by Russian authorities themselves to stoke public anger. Moscow responded with increasingly brutal tactics in Chechnya aimed at both military and civilian targets. The winter siege of Grozny virtually destroyed the already-damaged city. Once the city was taken by Russian forces in the early spring of 2000, equally brutal fighting shifted to the mountains, a terrain more suited to the guerrilla tactics of the rebels.

In May 2000, direct Russian rule was established in Chechnya. A month later, Putin appointed Akhmad Kadyrov as head of an interim pro-Russian government. Guerrilla fighting continued, however, and Kadyrov was killed in a 2004 bombing. He was replaced by his son, Ramzan Kadyrov, who ruled as the de facto leader of the nation until officially confirmed as the president, with Putin's blessing. While his elevation brought a measure of peace to this war-torn nation, terrorist acts continued both in the Russian heartland and across the Caucasus.

The 2008 Presidential Election

On the eve of the 2008 presidential race, there was no doubting Putin's continuing popularity. Polls showed an approval rating over 70 percent, with

42 percent of the public supporting a third term.[36] Within the Garden Ring, the factions remained divided, with the *siloviki* inclined toward Zubkov (who himself had no direct connections with the group), and the democratic statists favoring Ivanov. Zubkov's announcement that he would consider running for the presidency briefly prompted speculation that Putin might resign prematurely, advancing him to acting president before the next general election. It would have been a replay of Yeltsin's resignation, but instead of leaving the political stage, Putin would continue to manage affairs from the background.

On December 10, Putin ended the suspense. He announced that Medvedev was his intended successor. United Russia, of which Medvedev was not formally a member, also endorsed him, as did Just Russia, the Agrarian Party, and Civic Force, the other very junior partners in the de facto governing coalition. The next day, Medvedev dropped the other shoe. To no one's surprise, he announced his intention to name Putin as his prime minister, and Putin formally accepted the arrangement a week later at the United Russia convention. The "tandem," as it would later be called, was now in place.[37] Putin had maintained control without formally amending the constitution.

In an effort to reassure the factions within the Garden Ring, Medvedev also pledged to keep in place "the team created by the incumbent president." While he was not the first choice of any of the major factions, Medvedev was an acceptable second choice, with no close associations with the powers that be except Putin himself. Although inclined toward the democratic statists and the reformers, he maintained his own identity. Possessing no independent power base, Medvedev was not viewed as a threat to anyone. With him in the presidency, and Putin as prime minister, there was a good chance that the balance of forces within the Garden Ring could be maintained.

With the outcome all but decided long before the election, other candidates considered their options. Zyuganov stepped forward once again to run as the leader of the Communist Party, reversing his decision in the 2004 election to stand aside. Always hopeful, Zhirinovsky tried again as leader of the Liberal Democrats. Andrei Bogdanov of the Democratic Russia party joined the field as a dark horse. Boris Nemtsov ran briefly as a candidate of the Union of Right Forces, eventually withdrawing in favor of Mikhail Kasyanov of the People's Democratic Union, whose candidacy was rejected by the election commission.

Table 5.5   2008 Russian Presidential Election

Candidate	Party	Vote	Percentage
Dmitry Medvedev	United Russia	52,530,712	71.2
Gennady Zyuganov	Communist Party	12,243,550	18.0
Vladimir Zhirinovsky	Liberal Democratic Party	6,988,510	9.5
Andrei Bogdanov	Democratic Party	968,344	1.3

SOURCE: D. Nohlen and P. Stover. (2010). *Elections in Europe: A Data Handbook.* Baden-Baden, Germany: Nomos.

On March 2, 2008, Russia voted, confirming that Putin's popularity could easily be transferred to his anointed successor (Table 5.5). Medvedev won with 71.2 percent of the vote, respectfully just below Putin's 71.9 percent in 2004. The vast majority of Putin's supporters had shifted easily to the less-well-known Medvedev, who had never served above the rank of first deputy prime minister. Medvedev carried Moscow with just over 71 percent, and scored one point higher in his native St. Petersburg. Nationally, Zyuganov got 18 percent, followed by Zhirinovsky with 9.5 percent. Bogdanov got 1.3 percent.

The "tandem" was about to begin.

Putin as an Authoritarian Modernizer

Any assessment of Vladimir Putin as an authoritarian modernizer is admittedly premature, even within the context of a narrative at the end of his second term in 2008. In 2012, he was once again easily elected president for a six-year term, and under a revised constitution, he is eligible for a second six-year term after the 2018 election. That would put him in office until 2024. A tentative assessment, however, presents a mixed picture. Few would dispute the presence of a trend toward increasing authoritarianism, clearly at the expense of the intent if not the form of democratic rule. Russians still go to the polls in national and local elections, some genuinely to support and others to vote against Putin and the system he created. And few would argue against the admission that the deck is increasingly stacked against opposition forces. The advantages of incumbency, control over the media, the support of almost all of the new generation of oligarchs, and control over a system of patronage at all levels, plus the undisputed presence of the usual assortment of dirty tricks and bogus vote counts—all testify to the increasingly authoritarian nature of Putin's Russia.

Little in that assessment challenges Putin's categorization as an authoritarian modernizer. More often than not, history shows us that authoritarian modernizers—even those who at first attempt to create their own version of democracy—become more authoritarian over time. The rationalizations may vary: Authoritarian rule is needed to complete the transformation of society, the revolution faces enemies at home or abroad, or, more typically, the public is willing to tolerate increasing authoritarian rule for the sake of social order and greater prosperity. But the result usually is the same: institutionalization of an authoritarian system that combines elements of old patterns of behavior and some, but not all, of the initial hopes and promises of those who tried to break with that past to create a new and better society. At least by 2008, that combination had taken the form of increasing manipulation of how Russian democracy works rather than an outright suppression of the essential institutional features of the 1993 constitution. Some observers would argue that the distinction is meaningless, and their case gains credibility as the tandem and Putin's third term play out in future chapters. But in 2008, when a critical turning point had been reached, Putin turned away from the opportunity to amend the constitution to grant himself a third successive term, just as Yeltsin at a similar turning point in 1996 chose not to postpone the presidential election. In both cases, those actions confirmed the reality that a new and updated version of a "modern" Russia required the preservation of pro forma but clearly flawed democratic institutions, creating what contemporary theorists have termed "electoral authoritarianism." As the literature on this hybrid form argues, even the seemingly most controlled and manipulated examples of electoral authoritarianism can, under certain circumstances, rise up against their creators.[38]

An assessment of Putin as a modernizer is more ambiguous. Certainly he initially accepted the criticisms of the old soviet order that labeled it economically backward, isolated, and increasingly out of step with the modern world. And he accepted the broad outlines of Gorbachev's and Yeltsin's reform agendas, which included some form of democratization, economic and social reform, and increasing integration into the global community. But even these benchmarks were qualified. Postcommunist democracy always fell short of Western notions of liberal democracy, as witnessed by the limits to popular rule inherent in Gorbachev's Congress of People's Deputies and Yeltsin's willingness to disband the Russian legislature in 1993. Economic and social reform played out against the backdrop of the efforts of the former party elite to retain control of the new levers of power and the empire building of the oligarchs. Any definition of the new Russia's place in the post-cold war international community was always tainted by the memory of the old Russia's power and assertiveness. The point is that there was never any clear definition about what "modern" should mean, except at the level of platitudes and generalities. When it came to the details, Gorbachev, Yeltsin, and now Putin made it up as they played the game.

In Putin's first two terms, his policies and personal style of leadership had much in common with the modus operandi of authoritarian modernizers. He restored a strong Russian state, reversing the flow of power from the center to the regions. More broadly, he restored a distinct sense of Russian identity to replace the patina of the "new soviet man." He positioned the presidency at the center of a complex network of political and economic relationships that increased its power and control. He used both the presidency and the state apparatus as transformational mechanisms to staunch the drift and malaise of the Yeltsin years and to win acceptance, however temporary, for his version of strong central leadership. He posited an idiosyncratic and distinctly Russian path to economic and political reform, borrowing from but selectively reinterpreting the experiences of other economically advanced democracies, whose tutelage he rejected. In the notions of sovereign democracy and the vertical, he reinterpreted the role of the state in the crafting of a new political and social order, drawing from and updating traditional themes such as Russian exceptionalism, hierarchy and subordination, and the guiding role of the state in ways that, at least for a while, seemed new and modern. He presided over the creation a presidential party that began to tie the pieces together and bridge the gap between those within and those beyond the Garden Ring. And he built a cult of the personality, in part the normal projection of any successful politician in a democracy and in part a growing manifestation of his own sense of destiny and the sycophantic behavior of his followers and acolytes.

Notes

1. Lilia Shevtsova, *Putin's Russia,* Brookings, 2005, 134–162; and Richard Sakwa, *Putin: Russia's Choice,* Routledge, 2008, 21–35.
2. Sakwa, *Putin,* 20–21.
3. Timothy J. Colton and Michael McFaul, *Popular Choice and Managed Democracy: The Russian Elections of 1999 and 2000,* Brookings, 2003; and Vicki L. Hesli

and William M. Reisinger, eds., *The 1999–2000 Elections in Russia: Their Impact and Legacy,* Cambridge University Press, 2003.

   4. Sakwa, *Putin,* 30–35.

   5. Vladimir Putin, et al., *First Person: An Astonishingly Frank Portrait by Russia's President,* Public Affairs, 2000; and Angus Roxburgh, *The Strongman: Vladimir Putin and the Struggle for Russia,* I. B. Tauris, 2012.

   6. Sakwa, *Putin,* 47–69.

   7. Sakwa, *Putin,* 70–76; and Richard Sakwa, *The Crisis of Russian Democracy,* Cambridge University Press, 2011, 132–137.

   8. S. P. Roberts, *Putin's United Russia Party,* Routledge, 2011.

   9. George Tsebelis, *Nested Games: Rational Choice in Comparative Politics,* University of California Press, 1991.

   10. Sakwa, *Crisis,* 1–51, 85–86.

   11. Amy Knight, *The KGB: Police and Politics in the Soviet Union,* Unwin Hyman, 1990.

   12. Sakwa, *Crisis,* 124–127, 206–238.

   13. Ivan Surkov, "The Power Vertical and the Nation's Self-consciousness," *Russia in Global Affairs,* 2, April-June 2008.

   14. Stephen White, *Media, Culture, and Society in Putin's Russia,* Palgrave Macmillan, 2008; Anna Arutunyan, *The Media in Russia,* Open University Press, 2009; Laura Belin, "Politics and Mass Media under Putin," in Cameron Ross, ed., *Russian Politics under Putin,* Manchester University Press, 2004, 133–154; and Maria Lipman and Michael McFaul, "The Media and Political Developments," in Stephen K. Wegren and Dale R. Herspring, eds., *After Putin's Russia,* Rowman and Littefield, 2010, 109–132.

   15. Martin Sixsmith, *Putin's Oil: The Yukos Affair and the Struggle for Russia,* Continuum Publishing, 2010; and Edward R. Miller-Jones, *Mikhail Khodorkovsky: The Fall of an Oligarch,* Fastbook, 2011.

   16. Jeffrey Mankoff, *Russia's Foreign Policy: The Return of Great Power Politics,* Rowman and Littlefield, 2011; Robert H. Donaldson and Joseph L. Nogee, *The Foreign Policy of Russia: Changing Systems, Enduring Interests,* M. E. Sharpe, 2009; and Peter J. S. Duncan, *Russian Foreign Policy from El'tsin to Putin,* Routledge, 2011.

   17. Sakwa, *Putin,* 74–76.

   18. Sakwa, *Putin,* 72–73.

   19. Sakwa, *Crisis,* 117–123.

   20. Sakwa, *Crisis,* 124.

   21. Thomas F. Remington, "Parliament and the Dominant Party Regime," in Wegren and Herspring, *After Putin's,* 39–58; and Ross, *Russian Politics,* 157, 164.

   22. Remington, "Parliament," in Wegren and Herspring, *After Putin's,* 52–54.

   23. Sakwa, *Crisis,* 127–129.

   24. Peter Rutland, "The Oligarchs and Economic Development," in Wegren and Herspring, *After Putin's,* 159–182.

   25. Sakwa, *Putin,* 109–113.

   26. Sakwa, *Putin,* 113–115.

   27. Peter H. Solomon, Jr., "Assessing the Courts in Russia: Parameters of Progress under Putin," *Demokratizatsiya: The Journal of Post-Soviet Democratization,* 16, 1, winter, 2008: 63–74; and William Partlett, "Putin's Artful Jurisprudence," *The National Interest,* January 2, 2013.

28. William Sixsmith, *Putin's Oil: The Yukos Affair and the Struggle for Russia,* Bloomsburg Academic, 2010; and William Alex Pridemore, ed., *Ruling Russia: Law, Crime, and Justice in a Changing Society,* Rowman and Littlefield, 2005.

29. Sakwa, *Putin,* 115–117.

30. Edwin Bacon, "Russia's Law on Political Parties: Democracy by Decree," in Ross, *Russian Politics,* 39–52; Luke March, "The Putin Paradigm and the Cowering of Russia's Communists," in Ross, *Russian Politics,* 53–75; and Stephen White, "Russia's Disempowered Electorate," in Ross, *Russian Politics,* 76–94.

31. Sakwa, *Putin,* 124.

32. *Sakwa, Crisis,* 184–209.

33. Sakwa, *Crisis,* 210–262.

34. Anders Aslund and Andrew Kuchins, *The Russian Balance Sheet,* Peterson Institute for International Economics/Center for Strategic and International Studies, 2009; Stephen Fortescue, *Russia's Oil Barons and Metal Magnates: Oligarchs and the State In Transition,* Palgrave, 2006; David E. Hoffman, *The Oligarchs: Wealth and Power in the New Russia,* Public Affairs Press, 2002; Anders Aslund, *Russia's Capitalist Revolution: Why Market Reforms Succeeded and Democracy Failed,* Peterson Institute for International Economics, 2007; Pekka Sutela, *The Political Economy of Putin's Russia,* Routledge, 2012; and Robert Orttung and Anthony Latta, eds., *Russia's Battle with Crime, Corruption, and Terrorism,* Routledge, 2012.

35. Nicholas K. Gvosdev and Christopher Marsh, *Russian Foreign Policy: Interests, Vectors, and Sectors,* SAGE/CQ Press, 2014; Jeffrey Mankoff, *Russian Foreign Policy: The Return of Great Power Politics,* 2nd ed., Rowman and Littlefield, 2011; and Maria Raquel Freire and Roger Kanet, eds., *Russia and Its New Neighbors,* Palgrave Macmillan, 2012.

36. Sakwa, *Crisis,* 265.

37. Sakwa, *Crisis,* 270.

38. Andreas Schedler, ed., *Electoral Authoritarianism: The Dynamics of Unfree Competition,* Lynne Rienner, 2006.

6

The "Tandem"

Although Dmitry Medvedev's victory surprised no one, it created considerable ambiguity about what would come next. Medvedev had scored an impressive first-round victory, receiving a slightly smaller percentage of the vote than Vladimir Putin four years earlier. There was a clear message in the returns. Medvedev was a winner, but Putin had outpaced him in his second bid for the presidency. It also was clear that the new president elect had won because of Putin's support, manifested both in his personal endorsement and in the efforts of United Russia to turn out the vote.

What was not as clear was what lay ahead. How long would the arrangement of dual power last? Quickly dubbed "the tandem," this power-sharing dualism raised both legal and political issues. How would power and responsibility be divided between the two? The political realities of the moment suggested that Putin would remain the dominant figure, despite the formal power and institutional preeminence of the presidency. As the Russian saying goes, the devil lies in the details. Even if Putin and Medvedev had already agreed on the big picture, there were surely a host of such "details" that would have to be resolved.

How and when the tandem could potentially end also presented intriguing possibilities. Although Medvedev had committed himself to naming Putin as his choice for prime minister during the campaign, he retained the constitutional power to dismiss a prime minister at will, although no one anticipated such action. But two or three years down the line, if Medvedev seriously intended to launch an independent bid for the job, it was a possibility. Hindsight, of course, is a wonderful thing. We now know that Putin and Medvedev apparently intended to preserve the tandem for the full four-year term and to accept a fairly straightforward and constitutionally rooted division of labor and authority, at least for day-to-day governance.[1]

But on the terra incognito of postelection speculation of 2008, other possibilities seemed worthy of consideration. After a respectable waiting period, Medvedev might step down, elevating Putin to the post of acting president and requiring another presidential election. A replay of Boris Yeltsin's action on New Year's Eve in 1999, it would have led to a new independent term for Putin, who would now be eligible for reelection to a second term, since the constitution prohibited no more than two *consecutive* terms.

And what of a potential role for the Duma itself? It seemed unlikely that it could play a make-or-break role in 2008, but there were some intriguing possibilities. United Russia controlled the Duma, enjoying a constitution-changing majority with its few allies. What if the unity of United Russia faltered? It had been cobbled together as another party of, but not in, power at the end of the Yeltsin era, and its success seemed linked to Putin's growing popularity. But United Russia always ran behind Putin in the polls, suggesting that the party needed him more than he needed it. What if Putin's popularity slipped? Or what if Medvedev's approval ratings grew and it seemed possible that he could challenge his former mentor? It would be possible, at least theoretically, for the Duma to stage a vote of no confidence in the prime minister. Under the constitution, a single vote to reject the prime minister would not lead to his removal. But if three successive votes were passed, the president would have the choice of nominating a new prime minister for legislative approval, or of dissolving the chamber and calling a new general election. What if a president wanted to dismiss his prime minister, using the opportunity to name a new prime minister more friendly to his cause? The scenario was farfetched, but it was possible.

The longer Medvedev remained in office, the more likely it became that others might try to play Putin and Medvedev off against one another. Although the various Kremlin factions accepted the necessity that a fair-handed Putin remain in power in some capacity, their support might shift if any faction thought it could play one against the other. As things were going in 2008, the *siloviki* were in greatest danger, already divided among themselves and facing a new president who wanted to advance technocrats, soon to be called *tekniki* as they became a recognized faction in their own right. But what if the balance of factions were upset by the demise of an important group or the rise of another, especially if Putin were no longer viewed as capable of maintaining balance?

Another, less Machiavellian scenario also was possible. By 2008, Moscow was like most other major capitals: filled with a growing number of think tanks and advocacy groups that vied for public attention and, far more important, for the ears of key leaders. Some, like the Institute of the World Economy and International Relations, had been around since the soviet era and had earned a reputation for a degree of intellectual integrity even under communist rule. Most were newcomers, representing a variety of points of view and not infrequently linked, both politically and financially, to commercial or industrial groups or to political figures who used them as extensions of their own political agendas and aspirations. Near the end of Medvedev's four-year term, a growing number of them directly or indirectly advocated for him to do more to establish a separate political identity, and even to consider seeking a second term. Medvedev himself closely identified with one of the most active of them, the Institute of Contemporary Development, headed by Igor Yurgens. In many ways, the institute became regarded as the president's intellectual voice on key issues such as economic and political reform, and a source of a well-developed campaign agenda, if Medvedev chose to use it.[2]

Putin also faced a mixed reality. The good news, of course, was that he had maintained his de facto power without resorting to amending the constitution. Medvedev's election seemed to give him the best of all worlds. A seemingly reliable ally—and a genuinely like-minded friend, by all accounts—had agreed to a constitutionally correct solution. As prime minister, Putin could continue to shape national policy, and even though he reputedly abhorred the administrative details of day-to-day governance, he and his aides could fill in the details of policy decisions and control the inner workings of government. Behind the scenes, he could also influence the big picture. Even as a degree of distance emerged between Medvedev and Putin over the four years of tandem rule, there is no convincing evidence that the two were fundamentally out of sync or that they failed to consult one another on major decisions. The new arrangement permitted Putin to continue to play the role of faction balancer and mediator. Although there were some changes in the relative power of the major factions from 2008 to 2012, there were no major shifts, and change came gradually.

There were also some lighter moments in sorting out the meaning of a government in tandem. For a while, the artisans who painted *matrioshkas*, the traditional Russian nested dolls, were faced with a dilemma of artistic and political proportions. In the past, the politically inspired dolls portrayed the current leader on the largest, outside doll, with past leaders pictured on the smaller interior dolls. But in the new setting, that would be politically incorrect, placing Medvedev on the larger doll and Putin on the next smaller. After a brief period of indecision, a solution was found. Both would appear on the outside doll, same expression, same height (which they weren't), and both staring at each other or straight ahead (but never back-to-back looking in different directions). The boldest artistic license came later, with Putin on one side and Medvedev on the other (but again, same expression and height). On any given day, you could choose one over the other but quickly rotate the doll to a new reality if the sands shifted. Politics and art were once more in tandem in a new form of post-socialist realism.

Dmitry Medvedev: Putin's Friend from Leningrad

Like all political leaders, Medvedev was a product of his upbringing and times. His upbringing had been very traditional, at least for the latter years of communist rule; the times, however, had been nothing of the sort, reflecting the disorder, failures, and new opportunities of the post-communist era. He was born on September 14, 1965, in Leningrad to parents who taught at the university level, his father a chemist and his mother a linguist. He was a smart but otherwise normal kid; the obligatory quote from his first-grade teacher portrays him as a "dreadful why-asker," and he was very interested in dinosaurs. In the seventh grade, he met Svetlana Linnik, his future and only wife. By his own admission, his grades suffered when his mind wandered from dinosaurs to other things, and he had to work very hard in his final year to salvage any hope of admission to university.[3]

DMITRY MEDVEDEV

- Born September 14, 1965, in Leningrad.
- Enrolled in Leningrad State University in 1982 to study law, graduating in 1987; studied under Anatoly Sobchak, as did Putin.
- In 1988, led Sobchak's campaign for election to the USSR Congress of People's Deputies; after the campaign, joined the faculty of Leningrad State University law school, teaching civil and Roman law until 1999.
- After Sobchak's election as mayor of Leningrad, joined the city's foreign affairs committee, working under Putin's direction.

- In November 1999, brought to Moscow by Putin, who had been appointed prime minister in August.
- Appointed deputy head of the presidential staff by Putin on December 31, 1999, after Yeltsin's resignation.
- Served as campaign manager in Putin's 2000 presidential election.
- Advanced to presidential chief of staff in October 2003.
- In November 2005, was appointed first deputy prime minister, positioning him as a possible successor to Putin.
- In December 2007, Putin named him his chosen successor, soon after announcing that he would serve as prime minister in the "tandem."
- Elected president on March 2, 2008, with 71.2 percent of the vote; named Putin prime minister.
- Advocated slightly more rapid social and economic reforms during his presidency and a "reset" of Russian–U.S. ties.
- In the run-up to the 2012 presidential election, briefly considered a bid for a second term.
- On September 24, 2011, announced to the United Russian party congress that he would recommend the party nominate Putin for the presidency, and that the two would serve in a reverse "tandem."
- Named prime minister immediately after the presidential election, serving in a much diminished role as power shifted back to the presidency.

He entered Leningrad State University in 1982 to study law, not a particularly impressive major in the late soviet years, and certainly not an assured ticket to political or economic advancement. He graduated in 1987, two years into the Gorbachev era, and took up graduate studies in civil law, probably headed toward an academic career. While in school, the otherwise very conventional Medvedev took up politics of a sort; he was the de facto campaign director of Anatoly Sobchak's successful bid for a seat in the newly created Congress of People's Deputies.

In 1990, Sobchak returned from Moscow to head the St. Petersburg city council. He hired a number of his former law students to assist him, Medvedev and Putin among them. The next year, Sobchak was elected major, and Medvedev became a consultant to the city's Committee on Foreign Affairs (typically a KGB-dominated venue), headed by Putin. The two men became both colleagues and close friends through that association.

In 1996, Putin joined Yeltsin's presidential administration in Moscow, advancing to prime minister in 1999 only months before Yeltsin's resignation. Putin brought Medvedev and a number of the other *Pitery* to Moscow in November 1999, and a month later Medvedev was appointed deputy head of the presidential staff. He served as campaign director for Putin's first bid for office in 2000. In October 2003, he was promoted to the top post in the presidential administration (which, like the White House staff and the Executive Office of the President in Washington, is different from the formal cabinet). In November 2005, he shifted from the presidential administration to the government itself, henceforth to serve as first deputy prime minister until his election to the presidency in 2008.

During Medvedev's service in Moscow, his connections to industry deepened. Gazprom had become an increasing problem. Like most soviet-era giants that had ventured into the new capitalist world, Gazprom was not exactly forthcoming in paying its taxes. Even worse, it was hostile to Putin and his entourage. The solution was simple: Charge Gazprom with tax evasion and appoint friendly managers to its board of directors, which brought Medvedev first to its board and then to its chairmanship, a position he held until becoming president.

What did Medvedev take away from that career and his friendship with Putin? At the least, he and Putin developed a real friendship that went beyond political convenience. Both have described themselves as "like-minded." The two men shared a sense of political pragmatism, with Putin probably more inclined to stress political pragmatism and Medvedev more inclined to stress technical or means-to-the-end pragmatism. But both acknowledged the limits that such pragmatism imposes: There can be only one leader at a time; compromises, especially among factional interests, must be reached, no matter the concessions; the politics of getting elected is different from the politics of governing on a day-to-day basis; and Russia would soon face a critical choice between a political and institutional reality that brought stability after the Gorbachev and Yeltsin years and potentially very different political and institutional realities that had to be accepted if the nation were to move forward.

Governing the Nation in Tandem

Writing at the beginning of the Medvedev presidency (and without the obvious benefit of hindsight, which the present author enjoys), Richard Sakwa argued that there were two ways forward for the new president to assert his authority within the restrictive confines of the new tandem.[4] As it turned out, by the end of Medvedev's four-year term, there were three.

The first was very conventional. Medvedev could advance his own supporters into positions of increasing power within the presidential administration and the government (remember, these are different powers centers)
and/or seek to convert other former Putin supporters or fence-sitters to his
cause. But there were a number of problems with this strategy. Medvedev
had always been in Putin's shadow. He initially had no independent power
base and little of a separate identity on which to build one. Although
United Russia had mobilized to support him in the election campaign, it
remained far more loyal to Putin. St. Petersburg hardly was an independent
regional power base; the *Pitery* remained loyal to Putin, who continued to
support their advancement (and enrichment). Medvedev also enjoyed at
best only scant support from the factional interests within the Garden
Ring. His only initial backing came from the few surviving elements of the
old Yeltsin family. But their support was based more on their anybody-
but-Putin logic, and their days were numbered. Although it appeared
increasingly evident that Medvedev was gaining support among the new
financisti—a new breed of financial managers increasingly in vogue in both
government and the private sector—they clearly were still the newest players in the game, and the personal hostility between Medvedev and their
most prominent member, finance minister Alexei Kudrin, compromised
any real connection.

The second strategy that Medvedev might employ potentially could
change the nature of the tandem itself. It involved formalizing the division
of responsibility and, to a lesser degree, power between the presidency and
the office of prime minister. In a strictly legal sense, the two offices were
tasked to do different, but interrelated, things. The popularly elected president provided overall leadership, especially in key areas like foreign and
defense policy and the broader question of maintaining public order. The
prime minister, appointed by the president and confirmed by the Duma,
was tasked with the more mundane functions of day-to-day government,
which he would undertake within parameters set down by the president. In
one sense, the relationship was not unlike the former realities of the soviet
era—the party's general secretary was really the "decider," to borrow a term
from a recent U.S. president, while the chair of the Council of Ministers
and his associates filled in the details and ran the bureaucracy of the state.

But in the new reality, with Medvedev in the primary post and Putin
in the second slot, form and substance seemed out of line, at least in those
rare cases in which they might differ. For obvious reasons, both worked
hard to reduce and manage those situations, with the two sometimes

offering different emphasis on points like Western action in Libya or the "reset" of ties to Washington. But as Medvedev grew more confident, the tone changed, if not the substance. The new president put forth a bolder reform agenda, focusing on high technology, diminished emphasis on energy extraction and export, and the centerpiece role of Russia's Silicon Valley, located in an internationally sponsored research center in Skolkovo, just outside Moscow.

This approach led Medvedev to stress the formal roles of the president and the prime minister, which worked to his advantage in most cases. He also offered a different political agenda—the sort that linked both policy and strategy in a way that constitutes a distinctly presidential "political formula." To be sure, it was never fully confrontational. Despite the occasional urgings of an admittedly small element of the political and intellectual establishment that he be more aggressive in endorsing reforms, Medvedev remained in the background, especially in those roles in which the presidency did not give him the upper hand or, in this case, the better bully pulpit.

In the reality of post-communist politics, the two offices, and hence the two functions, had melded together. That was probably inevitable given the disorder of the moment, and perhaps desirable given the need to bring order from chaos. But the emergence of the tandem now created at least the possibility that the two very different roles could be sorted out, perhaps to the advantage of both. To be sure, nothing in the tandem arrangement suggested that they would be completely separated. Political realities were still political realities; both men were still, by their own admission, "like-minded." They were still friends and colleagues who had worked together as superior and subordinate in the past. But from Medvedev's perspective, such a delineation of the two roles would clarify his own responsibilities and give him his own space in which to function. It also would simplify Putin's role as prime minister, especially if it were accepted—as apparently it was—that they would consult on all-important questions and that Putin would continue to work behind the scenes to keep the ever-changing role of factions in acceptable balance.[5]

By the middle of the Medvedev presidency, a third strategy emerged, one with much broader ramifications. This option had serious implications both within the Garden Ring and in the broader arena of electoral politics, although its impact did not emerge until the Duma elections in December 2011, when the depths of popular dissatisfaction with United Russia and, by implication, with the Putin–Medvedev team became dramatically apparent. In many ways, it addressed the old dilemma of soviet-era leaders, who needed both to consolidate their power in institutional terms and to put forward a "platform," for want of a better word, that legitimated their leadership. In the soviet era, the limits of that broader audience were defined by the membership rolls of the Communist Party itself, and especially its bureaucracy of *apparat-chiki*. But in post-communist Russia, that audience now reached out well beyond a relatively small community of political activists, and far beyond the Garden Ring. In even the least perfect of democracies, a fair characterization of Russia at the time, it now included the voting (or the potentially voting) public that could be mobilized by whatever combination of hopes, fears, or resentments that moved them to action.

This was perhaps an area in which Medvedev could move independently, albeit cautiously, to suggest that the nation should address these problems before it was too late. The Medvedev political formula, to return to our way of describing it earlier, contained three elements, each of which was to play out within the tandem but, in doing so, stretched the boundaries of its dualism toward a more inclusive and modernizing agenda. The first element was technical and economic modernization, considered more fully later in this chapter. It was a shibboleth that everyone supported, if they could spin it to their immediate political advantage. But in Medvedev's hands, it had more far-reaching impacts, carrying the nation away from dependence on raw material and energy exports and toward the outlines of a knowledge- and research-intensive economy and a place in an increasingly globalized world. That discussion also raised important questions about who would be best prepared to lead such an economy and about the criteria to guide economic and social decisions.[6]

The second element dealt with moving a political process born in the chaos of the Gorbachev and Yeltsin years toward a more stable and institutionalized way of doing business. More than anything else, the Putin agenda had been about the need to establish the vertical of power. There is no question that he succeeded in that endeavor. But perhaps now that could be treated as a temporary necessity, not to be abandoned but rather to be loosened, corrected, and modified in light of the changing nature of the society and the growing maturity and self-confidence of both the leaders and the led. That hardly meant that Medvedev advocated a reform agenda counterpoised to Putin's vertical agenda. But it did mean that there were growing differences of opinion over how much of the old order needed to be preserved and how quickly cautious change should be initiated.[7]

The third element lay in Medvedev's well-meaning but largely unsuccessful attempt to deal with the inordinately visible corruption at all levels of political and commercial life. It was his least successful effort to forge a distinctive political identity and to restore some level of respect for the state among rank-and-file citizens. Attempts to reform the police and the courts bounced off the thick hide of a corrupt reality. Show trials like the second, conveniently timed conviction of Mikhail Khodorkovsky, who was about to be released from prison, confirmed that "telephone justice," a soviet-era practice in which the Communist Party allegedly phoned the courts to dictate the outcome of a trial, was alive and well. The petty but annoying corruption of everyday life continued unabated. The growing reach of email and social network communications spread the realization that, as a protest chant after the 2011 Duma elections put it, the nation was led by a "regime of crooks and thieves."

Medvedev and Putin in Tandem

In most ways, the tandem worked rather well. In personal terms, the two men seemed to have sorted out the division of authority and functions in line with the constitutional separation of powers and the political realities that guided their actions. One of the most important realities was the relative decline in the power of the *siloviki* and the subsequent elevation of the so-called *civiliki,* or civilians, set in distinction from those who had been associated with the security and defense ministries. Even Putin acknowledged the need to rein in the *siloviki* and the tactical wisdom of letting them enrich themselves through "mercantilization," the euphemism that described their growing penetration into the economy. As president, Medvedev now had greater if not complete control over the power ministries, and his different work style and absence of any past association with the *siloviki* as a group gave him the ability to set a new tone. Putin continued to work behind the scenes to maintain the balance, but the important point was that the balance was now easier to achieve.[8]

The appointment of the cabinet was a compromise, and a substantial portion of Putin's key advisors left the Kremlin (the seat of presidential authority) and migrated to the White House (where the prime minister's office is housed). Putin dramatically increased the number of deputy prime ministers and created a fifteen-member presidium, which met weekly and had the authority to act for the full cabinet, which met monthly. Reputedly not a fan of the detailed work of government, Putin delegated most of the day-to-day tasks. He also maintained careful balance among his staff, cutting people like Igor Sechin, once the acknowledged leader of the *siloviki*, down to size while retaining his services and promoting reputed reformers like Alexei Kudrin as counterweights. For his part, Medvedev also sought to maintain the balance in his choice of the presidential staff, although he did continue to weaken the *siloviki*.

United Russia's unchallenged control of the Duma, of the Federation Council, and of most regional legislatures also stabilized political life. In the day-to-day business of government, the cabinet and the Duma were closely in sync. It still was not a party in power, but it was a party that had voting power when it counted. It held 385 out of 450 seats in the Duma, controlled 111 out of 166 seats in the Federation Council, and, by 2009, held 78 out of the nation's 83 regional governorships.[9]

Factional Realities

Early into the Medvedev presidency, the game of factional politics took a potentially disruptive turn. Prior to the election, the tide had seemed to turn against the *siloviki;* Putin himself acknowledged the need to rein in their growing power. For his part, Medvedev was already inclined to cut back on *siloviki* influence, and his own background and presidential style held them more at a distance. Instead, he advanced the *civiliki* and the *financisti*—the first defined by their lack of service in the military and security branches, the second by their greater sophistication in business and financial management. Both groups were more in tune with Medvedev's own style of leadership and responsive to his vision of economic and social reform. Moreover, the *siloviki* had fallen into squabbling among themselves, sometimes over their divided authority in competing agencies and sometimes over the division of spoils associated with mercantilization. All things being equal, time did not seem to be on their side.

But things are not always equal. The global financial crisis of 2008 deeply affected the Russian economy. Within a matter of months, the Russian stock market lost 70 percent of its value. For at least a while, everyone was forced to play a zero-sum game. Much of Putin's ability to play the various factions off against one another depended on having continually increasing resources at his disposal; now that reality was seriously threatened. Compounding the complexity of the game, the eventual rescue of the economy was credited to Kudrin, the finance minister in Putin's cabinet, who had also taken the lead in cutting back on government generosity to factions like the *siloviki* and the business interests with which they were associated. Further complicating the situation was the always-uneasy personal relationship between Medvedev and Kudrin. Putin's support is credited with keeping Kudrin in office until an eventual confrontation between Medvedev and the finance minister forced his de facto dismissal shortly before the 2012 presidential election.[10]

This contretemps clearly revealed the fragile nature of the factional balance. Putin was successful in keeping the contending forces in line, but his power was not absolute. Like any politician trying to keep the ducks in a row, he needed resources with which to work. Playing one faction off against another was a successful strategy, one that he used with considerable skill. But the ability to deliver resources, either in the form of support for agencies and programs, or in the form of compensation for the personal economic interests of the players, also was critical. Fortunately, at least for Putin, the Russian economy bounced back, permitting the conventional game to resume, albeit at a lower level.

Medvedev and Economic Reform

Although Putin and Medvedev never clashed publicly on the issue of economic reform, there were clear differences between them. Perhaps understandably, given his need to stabilize the nation after the Yeltsin years, Putin stressed stability and the least disruptive approach to moving the economy forward. At least in the short run, that meant focusing on Russia's current economic strengths, primarily in raw materials and energy. Given global energy prices and the sunk costs that had been incurred in developing the extractive sector and the vast network of pipelines to carry energy to European markets, it was an understandable and politically correct, if short-sighted, approach. The privatization of the energy sector meant that vast reserves had fallen under the control of politically powerful second-generation oligarchs who were unwilling to step aside in the interest of a still-vague image of a modern and technologically sophisticated Russia. Conventional wisdom, which always seems right in the short run, dictated caution.

Medvedev knew all this. He was as much a political realist as Putin. But for him there was an equally compelling reality: Today's good solution was

tomorrow's bad answer. And that meant he had to set forth another economic model, not in contradiction to the Putin energy model, but rather as
a revision of the general business model of the past decade. During that
period, the engine of development had two components: vast profits from
the energy sector, creatively distributed both to restore a degree of prosperity and to buy political balance among the factions, and a strong and direct
role for the state, not as a direct planner, but as a guiding and regulating
force. Whatever its potential problems, it worked—or seemed to work—for
Putin's first two terms in office. The concentration of economic power and
corruption that accompanied it were deemed acceptable in the short run
and even carried some political advantages in terms of providing leverage
that the regime could use to buy off opposition and reward its supporters.

Given that reality, Medvedev could not directly assault such seemingly
validated conventional wisdom. His course had to be more subtle, to set
forth a series of priorities that expanded on such conventional wisdom,
directing it toward a more sophisticated version of a future and a far more
diversified economy, and to provide an institutionalized mecca that
embodied and demonstrated the value of the new business model. The
first took the form of his new high-tech and innovative priorities for
future development, and the second, the Russian equivalent of a Silicon
Valley in Skolkovo.

Medvedev was quick to put the new economic model before the
nation. Although much of it had been expressed even in his first comments upon assuming office, it took an almost manifesto-like quality in a
sweeping indictment-cum-cure article published on the presidential
website in September 2009.[11] Titled "Forward, Russia" in Russian
(a distinctly Leninist turn of phrase) and "Go, Russia" in the English
translation, it dealt with a wide range of the nation's economic, social, and
political problems. It offered "five vectors of economic modernization":
efficient energy production and utilization (a real problem given energy
wastage at home, but also a sop to the powers-that-be in that powerful
sector); nuclear power engineering, but only for peaceful purposes; information technologies; space and telecommunications; and medical technology and pharmaceuticals.

Medvedev's decision to take his argument directly to the nation
through a website article was not accidental. Putin had done the same thing
at the beginning of his presidency. In most other cases, Medvedev followed
tradition and vetted policy proposals through institutional channels such
as the state of the nation address to the Federal Assembly or comments to

the St. Petersburg International Economic Forum or the Krasnoyarsk Economic Forum, both high-level annual meetings of business, government, and academic figures. But in this case, he went directly to the people, or more correctly to the growing attentive public who were beginning to engage Internet-based information sources and the social network.

"Forward, Russia" also engaged another important issue critical to future economic growth: Who was to lead it? Underpinning Medvedev's argument was the argument that the business model needed to change. Russia was beginning to enjoy the emergence of a new middle class and, even more important, a significant cadre of younger, better trained, and business-savvy technocrats whose talents and energies were wasted. Entrepreneurship was an undervalued skill, at least at home, and for many younger or simply more ambitious Russians who possessed it, the answer was to take their talents abroad.

Medvedev's response was to link an idea and a place. The idea was the encouragement of a far larger entrepreneurial role for the private sector, including international investors and economic giants like Siemens, IBM, and Nokia, which would collaborate on a wide spectrum of joint activities. Their association would go far beyond mere collaboration on specific (and, it was hoped, mutually profitable) projects; it would be an institution-changing and culture-changing catalyst that would redefine the idea of where innovation originated.

The place that was to embody this vision of the future was the Skolkovo Institute of Science and Technology, or SkolTech. After a brief and probably always rigged competition among different locations throughout Russia on which would host this new engine of growth, to no one's surprise, Moscow won. Putin and Medvedev had a brief public tug of war over who should be regarded as its creator and guiding spirit, but to the academic and business constituencies that would take part, it always was Medvedev's child. Probably best thought of as a research park, a teaching program in business and entrepreneurship, and an incubator for high-tech businesses, it sits in its own version of Silicon Valley not far from Moscow. Its faculty and student body are international; its first director was Edward Crawley, a Russian-speaking American with long experience in the U.S. space program (he dropped out of astronaut training to complete his Ph.D. in aerospace studies at MIT). Crawley's track record was strong in the commercialization of cutting-edge science. The teaching and research programs are a joint venture between SkolTech and MIT, and its board of corporate collaborators and sponsors includes over

350 members, some the most important high-tech industries in the global economy. It is billed as the primary mechanism through which research funding will be channeled to Russian academic and commercial programs, although that probably will be compromised by political necessity.[12] Its fate would signal whether the new economic model and its political implications would gain traction or merely slip away in the face of a safer conventional wisdom.

From the very beginning, any hope of fundamentally reforming the Russian economy ran headlong into the reality of the 2008 global economic downturn. Fortunately the government had set aside a stabilization fund from earlier budget surpluses and was able to prop up the economy. It directly bought stock in endangered businesses (a form of "soft" renationalization), recapitalized most but not all of the failing banks, and released up to US$50 billion of its dwindling foreign currency holdings to the oligarchs to service their foreign debt. A separate welfare fund of US$49 billion, also set aside from earlier surpluses, was used to reduce the impact of unemployment.[13]

By the spring of 2009, the worst was over. As the recovery took hold, Medvedev announced plans for a second round of privatizations designed to raise capital and speed the transfer of government-owned or -controlled industries, including some of the large oil and energy giants, into private hands. Consistent with his overall hopes for structural reform and contrary in many ways to Putin's preference for continued state control, these proposals met with strong resistance.

Medvedev and Political Modernization

Medvedev also began to articulate a cautious agenda for political modernization. *Reform* would be too strong a term; once again, he and Putin were essentially in agreement, differing only in terms of the nuances of how the jointly shared goals of stability and modernization should be accomplished. In his "Forward, Russia" missive, he linked the further development and technological modernization of the economy with the evolution of Russian political institutions, suggesting that the modernization of the attitudes and mindsets of the former was a prerequisite to the liberalization of the latter. Democracy needed both the social and the economic consequences of the modernization of the economy, which would—or so Medvedev argued— liberate and empower the increasing entrepreneurial spirit of the emerging middle class. Referring to the current state of Russian democracy as "immature," he argued that although democratic institutions had been "established and stabilized, their quality remains far from ideal. Civil society is weak, and levels of self-organization and self-government are low." The implications were hard to miss: The first task—creation and stabilization— had largely been completed. The current task was now quite different: to fine-tune those institutions to work better through animating civil society to take the initiative in the next stage of modernization. It was hardly a frontal assault on the past, but it was a different agenda for the future, one that Medvedev sought to make his own.

Medvedev also cautiously advocated a higher level of competition in political life. He was cautious enough never to launch a direct attack on United Russia, but he clearly viewed the return to a dominant single-party system as dangerously close to a revival of the dynamics of the old soviet order. The concern was not so much that the single party side-lined legitimate competition (although that was happening at the end of Putin's second term) but rather that a dominant single party that controlled all resources and incentives revived the old soviet mindset that discouraged entrepreneurship and the emergence of an independent civil society.

In reality, Medvedev's concern with broadening and deepening the political space for legitimate competition also was motivated by other factors. United Russia's support was broad but perhaps very shallow—a mile wide and an inch deep, as they say. It was cobbled together during the Putin era to create the appearance of stability. Its popularity was based on its close association with Putin, as least in the minds of the voters. Putin personally always got a far higher percentage of the vote than other United Russia candidates, confirming the continuing propensity for Russian voters to identity with people, not parties.

Medvedev's hopes to broaden political competition also reflected the reality that the opposition parties of the Yeltsin and Putin eras had run their course. The conventional opposition consisted mainly of the Communist Party of the Russian Federation and the Liberal Democratic Party. The former was seen as a political dinosaur, led by unimaginative throwbacks to a previous era and supported by an aging constituency, and the latter was an extension of the still occasionally interesting but highly erratic Vladimir Zhirinovsky. The Kremlin had attempted to create shadow opposition parties before most elections, but none had ever taken hold. The few legitimate opposition parties like Yabloko, with roots in the distant

Gorbachev era, or the less durable nationalist counterparts had been systematically excluded by stringent registration requirements and the
increased threshold for Duma membership or had fallen victim to their
own internal disputes.

Medvedev's political agenda soon found an institutional base outside
the presidency itself. The Institute for Contemporary Development
emerged quickly as the intellectual vanguard of the Medvedev program.
Dedicated to drawing on the views of Russia's "expert community," it was
headed by Igor Yurgens, an economist with long experience in government,
business, and academic circles. Not surprisingly, its agenda was virtually
identical to the Medvedev program set forth in "Forward, Russia." In addition, Medvedev created a somewhat more official Commission for
Modernization and Technological Development as a quasi-constitutional
body to encourage reform.

Throughout his efforts to set forth an independent economic and
political agenda, Medvedev was careful to occupy a middle ground that
reminded both supporters and critics that he understood the need for
stability. Noting that he would "disappoint the supporters of permanent
revolution," Trotsky's program for the rapid transformation of post-
revolutionary Russia, he averred "we will not rush." He cautioned against
returning to the "democratic nineties," which had "pushed Russia to the
brink of collapse."[14]

The rhetoric aside, Medvedev's four years in office, at least up to the
last few months after United Russia's surprisingly poor performance in
the December 2011 Duma elections, produced very little in terms of real
political reform. The first major change came in 2008 in the form of a
proposal to extend the presidential term to six years and the Duma term
to five years, beginning with the next election. Although the change was
billed as an effort to provide further stability, it was generally interpreted
merely as an effort to extend the control of the tandem over the executive
branch and United Russia's dominance of the legislature. The role of
regional parliaments in suggesting candidates for governor also was
broadened, but the final decision remained with the president. Attempting
to soften the impact of the new 7-percent threshold for eligibility for seats
in the Duma, Medvedev also pushed through a complicated formula that
permitted parties that received between 5 and 7 percent to get a token
number of seats. But no major reforms were initiated, although the
debate over what might be done sharpened in the run-up to the 2012
presidential election.

Judicial Reform

For a number of reasons, Medvedev made an attack on the endemic corruption of Russian society a central element of his reform agenda. "Corruption" in this context means a number of things. The petty corruption of the police throughout Russian and soviet history touches the daily lives of virtually all citizens, corroding respect for the government and the leadership. The corruption of all levels of government and authoritative institutions was deeply rooted long before the advent of democratic institutions, and it continued unabated. Getting anything done required a bribe to oil the official wheels, whether it be the government, the economy, or the church.

At a higher level, official corruption was an expected part of life. Especially as state-owned resources were sold off at bargain prices to favored oligarchs, patterns of corruption took on new political significance. Every campaign against one group of oligarchs, however successful, gave rise to the next. While a few were driven into exile and an even smaller number were imprisoned at home, the best that seemingly could be done was to try to contain, but not eliminate, the growing political power of private wealth.

There was a very good reason for that. Political power and wealth were now inexorably and very profitably linked. There was an increasing interlocking membership between the political and economic elites; important political leaders sat on the boards of key corporations, especially those that still operated as joint state-private endeavors, and virtually all players on both sides had become stakeholders in the intertwined elite. Kremlin factions that had once been identified primarily by their institutional, regional, or policy-oriented characteristics now held or were closely aligned with important economic interests.

There also was another survival of the past that Medvedev wanted to address with his reforms. During the soviet era, the courts were merely an extension of the communist party. Judges were not independent, either by law or inclination. It was called "telephone justice"; the party merely called its decisions into the courts, which applied them. Clearly there were vestiges of this during the post-communist era. Judges were still largely cast from the same mold, devoid of a legal culture that emboldened them to assert their prerogatives and working within a legal order that did little, either legally or financially, to encourage their independence.

To his credit, Medvedev tried to implement change. In 2008, a new anti-corruption bill was signed into law, and Russia's place on the global Corruption Perceptions Index improved slightly. Medvedev also created a National Anti-Corruption Council in 2008 to coordinate efforts at reform and raise public awareness of his efforts to deal with the problem, and months later a National Anti-Corruption Plan was announced that promised more severe sanctions against corrupt officials in both the private and the public sectors.[15] Despite these efforts, little real impact occurred, and the issue of continuing corruption figured prominently in the results of the 2011 Duma elections. In January 2011, well before the elections, Medvedev admitted that his efforts had failed.[16]

There were also notable moments when the judicial system returned to the worst excesses of the soviet era. By 2009, Mikhail Khodorkovsky, an oligarch whose political activities had led to an earlier conviction on corruption charges and the confiscation of Yukos, the crown jewel of his economic empire, was once again on the Kremlin's radar screen. Having served half of his initial sentence, he was now eligible for parole. Additional charges, seemingly contradicting the earlier conviction, were filed, and his second politically motivated trial began in 2009. With the matter still under deliberation, Putin spoke openly of his view that Khodorkovsky was guilty. Once again it was clear that the authorities "telephoned" the verdict to the courts. After several delays, perhaps indicating some indecision about the severity of the punishment, in December, 2009 the court sentenced Khodorkovsky to an additional 13.5 years behind bars, which it subsequently shortened to 12 years.

A host of other politically inspired convictions demonstrated the growing use of the courts to deal with opposition figures, with some of the more visible convictions acquiring cause célèbre status in the West. Typical was the case of Sergei Magnitsky, a lawyer who had been arrested when he publicly charged that government officials were siphoning funds from the Hermitage Fund, a private investment company. His death in a Russian prison sparked charges that medical treatment had been purposely withheld as a way to silence his criticism. Not surprisingly, an official inquiry cleared prison officials of any responsibility.

Even more controversial was the conviction of Pussy Riot, a singing group known for its public protests. A part of a small but increasingly active community of performers who take their message to the streets in highly visible public protests, they were convicted of "hooliganism"—the Russian equivalent of disorderly conduct—when they briefly sang their protest songs in the Christ the Savior Cathedral in Moscow.[17]

Foreign Policy

Russian foreign policy under the tandem continued virtually all the basic directions set down by Putin in his previous eight years in office. Emphasis fell on reasserting Russia's role as a major power, reaffirming its traditional sphere of influence in most but not all of the breakaway republics of the former Soviet Union, charting a new relationship with NATO that blunted efforts to extend the alliance eastward and that gave Moscow some say in the alliance's future operations, softening but not capitulating on the increasingly tense relationship with Washington, moving toward greater involvement with the global economy and contiguous regional economies, and opening new doors toward greater Russian influence and diplomatic activism in Asia, Latin America, and the Middle East. Four years later, at the end of the Putin–Medvedev tandem, the record of accomplishments would be mixed, complicated by the difficulty of defining a new and broadly accepted role for Russia as a major international actor and by the impact of Russian military action in Georgia.

As with most other issues, Medvedev and Putin worked out their respective roles. The 1993 constitution and the precedents established during the Yeltsin years and in the first two terms of Putin's rule gave the chief executive considerable powers, including the formal powers of command associated with the presidency and that office's preeminence as the chief negotiator. Medvedev's own personal style of diplomacy also suggested greater differences from his predecessor than were actually true; more open and more attuned to the sort of arguments about the importance of a knowledge-based economy and an interdependent world, he seemed to be more in sync with those in the West who were attempting to forge a new sense of what a post–cold war and post-U.S. hegemonic international order might be.

In reality, Putin was still the de facto senior partner in the tandem, even if it meant working behind the scenes on foreign policy decisions. There is no credible evidence that as president, Medvedev took any important decisions without first consulting with Putin. Even critical issues such as the decision to invade Georgia or to pursue a reset in the chilled relationship with Washington went forward with no open difference of opinion between the two halves of the tandem. Both men largely shared a consensus about the general direction of Russian foreign policy. As with all other aspects of their shared agenda, the goal of a successful foreign policy was to strengthen the Russian state, and a strong state required strong executive leadership, no matter how its component parts were arranged at the moment.

Medvedev's boldest initiative came early in the tandem. Attempting to sidestep and essentially redefine the question of NATO's future role, he called for the negotiation of a comprehensive new security treaty for Europe. Presented as a logical successor to the end of the cold war and the 1975 Helsinki Accords, it was to be open to all European nations regardless of "alliances to other blocs or other groups." Potential membership was expanded quickly to include the broader "Euro-Atlantic region," making it appear less threatening to U.S. interests. Skeptical of the proposal's intent, European leaders called for a broader discussion within the context of the Organization for Security and Co-operation in Europe (OSCE), a fifty-six-member body independent of NATO that struggled to find a role in post–cold war Europe. The OSCE debate quickly muddied the issue, and no formal proposals were put forward.

With Medvedev playing the most visible role, Russia and the United States attempted to reset the troubled relationship between Moscow and Washington. A victim of Russian actions in Georgia and the generally deteriorating U.S. perspective on the increasing authoritarianism of Moscow's domestic politics, the relationship was still important to both sides. Moscow was in the final stages of its years-long effort to join the World Trade Organization (WTO) that had stalled over reaction to its invasion of Georgia, and serious and potentially costly arms control issues such as the expiration of the Strategic Arms Reduction Treaty (START I) and the U.S. commitment to building a missile defense system in Europe remained on the agenda. Although both sides embraced the reset as a propitious moment to try to improve the level of cooperation on issues of shared interest—new presidents were in office in both capitals, both saying all the right things—neither approached the recalibration in the hope of fundamentally changing the growing rivalry between the United States and Russia. That said, the tone certainly was different, at least for a while. U.S. president Barack Obama and Medvedev met over a dozen times and developed a better relationship than George W. Bush and Putin had.

Early in 2009, Obama and Putin committed both nations to try to negotiate a successor agreement to START I, which was soon to expire. A year later, the two sides signed the new START II, limiting each side to no more than 800 deployed land- or submarine-based launchers and imposing similar limits on bombers. The treaty also limited each side to no more than 1,550 deployed warheads. Implementation had begun within a year, largely through the retirement of obsolete weapons systems. Another troubling arms control issue was taken off the table temporarily when the Obama administration announced in September 2009 that it was canceling the Bush administration's European ballistic missile defense program, which would have placed permanent installations in Poland and the Czech Republic. Now the U.S. effort would be based on the rapid deployment of mobile missile defense systems in times of rising tensions.

The tandem also continued Moscow's growing efforts to extend Russian influence on a broader global scale. Greater attention was paid to expanding contacts in Asia, in part to take advantage of economic opportunities in energy and raw materials development and in part to counter China's rising power and the Obama administration's efforts to increase the U.S. presence in the Pacific. Membership in the WTO and greater involvement with the G-8 and the G-20 seemingly confirmed Russian interest in playing a greater global economic role. The tandem also endorsed UN economic sanctions on Iran to slow its development of nuclear weapons and abstained on the critical Security Council vote authorizing intervention in Libya's civil war, although it quickly criticized the scope of military operations.

The tandem intensified policies begun during Putin's second term to build closer ties to many of the former soviet republics and to win recognition of a legitimate Russian sphere of special interests in those adjacent nations. Building on regional pacts such as the Collective Security Treaty Organization, which created a Russian-dominated and poorly defined military alliance, and the much looser Commonwealth of Independent States agreement signed when the Soviet Union broke apart, Russia attempted to expand its influence. A revised statement of Russian military doctrine issued in 2010 made it clear that the "near abroad" was now to be the highest priority in both geopolitical and economic terms. In Moldova, where a breakaway pro-Russian Trans-Dniester Republic existed, Russian military forces were still present. Relations with Ukraine, which had deteriorated after the "orange revolution," improved with the 2010 election of the pro-Russian Viktor Yanukovych, who quickly signed an agreement linking lower Russian prices for natural gas to an extension of Russia's lease of facilities for the Black Sea naval base to 2042. Moscow also applied economic leverage leading toward the consolidation of what it termed "a common economic space" and an eventual customs union.[18]

The Russian–Georgian War

The Russian–Georgian war in August 2008 confronted the tandem with a dilemma. On one hand, it provided Moscow with an opportunity to prove its ability to control events in the near abroad. But Moscow's easy victory on the battlefield cost it diplomatically; hostility to the intervention accelerated the West's growing suspicion of Russian intentions and compromised initially sincere efforts to conduct a "charm offensive" aimed at blunting efforts to expand NATO to the east and resetting Russian–U.S. relations.

The immediate conflict had its roots in the disintegration of the Soviet Union. Like the other republics, Georgia proclaimed its independence from Moscow. Sensing the weakness of the new Georgian government in Tbilisi, South Ossetia and Abkhazia, both ethnically distinct from Georgia and containing a hodgepodge of Georgian and indigenous nationalities, attempted to assert their own independence, triggering a military conflict with Georgia. The largely inconclusive clashes resulted in cease-fire agreements to be patrolled by Russian and Georgian peacekeepers. The fighting had stopped, but the underlying conflict continued.

The election of Mikheil Saakashvili to the Georgian presidency in 2003 raised the stakes for both sides. Saakashvili, a Harvard-educated and pro-Western lawyer, had risen to power in the so-called rose revolution, a Georgian variation of Ukraine's "orange revolution," which had swept reformers into power. Saakashvili quickly endorsed Georgian membership in NATO, going so far as to conduct joint military training exercises with U.S. forces, and pledged to restore South Ossetia and Abkhazia to Georgian control. Early in 2004, Georgian forces entered South Ossetia ostensibly to combat smuggling in the region. Deeply concerned by these actions and viewing U.S. support of Georgia as an attempt to foment similar "color revolutions" elsewhere, Moscow strengthened its military presence and extended diplomatic recognition to a puppet South Ossetian government that it created and to a similar regime in Abkhazia. Saakashvili's reelection in 2008 hardened positions on both sides.

On August 7, 2008, Georgia launched a large-scale invasion of South Ossetia, alleging that it was responding to attacks on the Georgian component of peacekeeping forces. Moscow responded with airstrikes and sent in armored and infantry forces. For four days, Georgian and combined Russian–South Ossetian forces fought a one-sided conflict that eventually involved Russian and Georgian naval forces and a joint Russian–Abkhazian military action against Georgian forces in Abkhazia. Georgian forces withdrew to protect Tbilisi, permitting Russians to occupy substantial territory, including Gori, Joseph Stalin's birthplace.

Stung by Russian action, Saakashvili accepted mediation by the French president Nicolas Sarkozy, and both sides signed a cease-fire agreement on

August 12. Moscow eventually withdrew its troops to predetermined areas outside of Georgia and established buffer zones around South Ossetia and Abkhazia.[19]

Medvedev and the Legislature: The 2011 Duma Elections

The December 2011 Duma elections provided a largely unanticipated slap in the face to the carefully choreographed dance of the tandem. Despite their best efforts, both honest and corrupt, United Russia suffered a stinging rebuke at the polls, losing its constitution-changing control of the body and narrowly preserving a working majority. Even this proved to be a hollow victory in the eyes of many Russians and the rest of the world; voting fraud had been so widespread and blatant that even victory seemed like defeat. United Russia had been discredited. Even more significant was the spillover effect on the presidential campaign, which was in full force at the time of the Duma balloting. Public opinion focused blame on Putin, who only weeks before had been nominated by United Russia to run once again for the presidency.

The manner by which Putin had emerged as the leading presidential candidate had done little to improve United Russia's prospects in the Duma voting. True to the scenario they had long described, Putin and Medvedev portrayed the choice as their mutual decision. Once again, they would simply swap roles, Putin returning to the presidency and Medvedev stepping down to the office of prime minister. For public consumption, the tandem had simply worked it out between themselves.

Faced with this defiant fait accompli orchestrated by the tandem, many Russian voters turned to the Duma elections as a mechanism of protest. The timing of the Duma elections could not have been better, only weeks after the tandem had announced the Putin–Medvedev swap and barely three months before the presidential election itself. Whatever political realities they faced—the polls showed that Putin would undoubtedly win, albeit with diminished support, especially from among the rapidly emerging urban middle class—voters could vent their anger and distrust by striking at a more vulnerable target, United Russia, which had always lagged behind Putin in the polls.

The voters had few alternatives. The "none of the above" option had been dropped, probably wisely, from the perspective of the leadership. The old stalwarts of the opposition—the Communists and the Liberal Democrats—were still there, but others like Yabloko had been disqualified on dubious grounds. Efforts to cobble together another officially approved center-right opposition party in the form of Right Cause had largely failed. Although the party made it on to the ballot, internal fighting and the reluctance of Mikhail Prokhorov, one of the wealthiest of the newest generation of oligarchs, to play the role assigned to him by the Kremlin's tacticians destroyed any prospects that the party might siphon off opposition votes. If the Duma elections were to be a de facto referendum on voter approval of the Putin–Medvedev years and the new arrangement, tandem II, then there was no logical focal point for opposition activity, except to vote for something other than United Russia. The success of the opposition would be measured not by how much other parties won but by how much United Russia lost.

In truth, United Russia had begun to slip in the polls. The VCIOM and Levada Center polls, both reliable indicators of public opinion, showed the party peaking at a roughly 60 percent approval rating in late 2010 and early 2011. Its approval rating fell slowly over the next year and then dipped more dramatically shortly after the tandem's announcement of the Putin-Medvedev switch. By mid-November 2011, just before the Duma elections, both polls reported the level of support at around 53 to 54 percent, still slightly above the 49.3 percent of the vote that it eventually won in the popular balloting (Table 6.1).[20]

That margin of victory still gave United Russia a majority in the Duma—238 out of 450 seats, plus whatever votes the government picked up from allied parties—but the results clearly established the 2011 election as one of the most important in the post-communist era. All the more remarkable was the fact that the drop in support for United Russia had occurred in the absence of any new serious challenger. Instead, voters

Table 6.1   2011 Russian Legislative Election

Party	Vote	Percentage	Seats
United Russia	32,379,135	49.3	238
Communist Party	12,599,507	19.2	92
Just Russia	8,695,522	13.2	64
Liberal Democratic Party	7,664,570	11.7	56

SOURCE: Central Election Commission of the Russian Federation, www.cikrf.ru/eng/, Election of the Duma of the Federal Assembly, 2011.

tended to turn to the old-line opposition parties. The Communist Party of the Russian Federation picked up thirty-five seats above its holdings in the 2007 elections, giving it ninety-two seats in the new Duma. Just Russia, a moderate social democratic party once closely aligned with United Russia, picked up an additional twenty-six seats, giving it sixty-four in the new legislature. The Liberal Democratic Party, still more an extension of Zhirinovsky than a real party, increased its holdings by sixteen seats, for fifty-six in the new Duma.[21]

No other opposition party crossed the 7 percent eligibility requirement for seats. Yabloko, the last remaining vestige of the old democratic parties of the Yeltsin era, got just over two million votes, and no seats. The Patriots of Russia got just over 600,000 votes, and no seats. And a newcomer, Right Cause, got almost 400,000 votes, and perhaps a future that no one anticipated.

Right Cause started out as one of those Kremlin-sponsored parties created to establish a loyal opposition. It was formed in November 2008 as a merger of three parties: the Union of Right Forces, Civilian Power, and the Democratic Party of Russia. None had amounted to much separately. From its inception, Right Cause sought to capture the support of a new and untested constituency, the new Russian middle class.

Initially Right Cause was so closely identified as a Kremlin-sponsored opposition party that it lacked credibility in the eyes of the voters. It won a few victories in municipal elections, but it lacked viable national leadership. That changed dramatically in May 2011, when billionaire businessman Mikhail Prokhorov announced his intention to join the leadership of the party, presumably at the invitation of the Kremlin, to lend credibility to its role as a "safe" opposition party. Months later, the political honeymoon was over when Prokhorov took the party more openly into opposition. Given the proreform stance of Prokhorov's comments, it was rumored that Right Cause was emerging as the centerpiece of an independent Medvedev bid for the presidency. That speculation ended in September 2011 when Prokhorov resigned as the party's leader, denouncing it as a "puppet" of the Kremlin. Shortly after the December Duma elections, Prokhorov announced his own candidacy for the presidency, an effort that netted him nearly 8 percent of the vote in the May 2012 balloting.[22]

The Duma Election and Voting Fraud

Virtually all previous legislative and presidential elections had engendered allegations of fraud, but the 2011 Duma elections clearly crossed some invisible line in the sand. To be sure, during the Putin years and the four-year interregnum of the tandem, the hurdles had been raised systematically, making it harder for parties to register officially, to campaign freely in light of increasing government control of the media, and to win seats in the Duma even under the best of circumstances. The deck was further stacked against the opposition through the use of government resources in favor of United Russia candidates. Although all incumbents have certain advantages, the reality of official support for approved candidates went far beyond the usual level. The machinery of government became the campaign machinery of United Russia. Voter turnout, and voting the right way, became the de facto responsibility of leadership at all levels. Regions or organizations that failed to turn out the "correct" vote faced serious penalties from the always watchful "center."

For the first time, such clear evidence of widespread corruption produced a massive backlash, at least in the major cities, where protesters took to the streets in record numbers. Their actions were a result of several factors that converged as evidence of massive voter fraud became undeniable.[23] The Duma balloting took place after the tandem had announced their intention to change places. Putin's reelection seemed inevitable, now to an extended six-year term and possibly longer since the constitution permitted him to run again in 2018. For many Russians, that was a reassuring prospect. But for others, it was the final insult that pushed them over the edge. For them, the Duma elections added insult to injury.

But there were other important factors as well. Russia had changed during the twelve years of the Putin and Medvedev presidencies. A new, better-educated, and more prosperous middle class had begun to emerge, especially in the cities. Proud of their newly acquired sophistication and wealth, many resented paternalistic treatment at the hands of the tandem. Putin and Medvedev had apparently decided the fate of the nation for the next six and perhaps twelve years *entre nous,* privately between themselves, like the tsars of old. It didn't sit well, and this new opposition movement now felt better connected and empowered to take the message to the streets with little fear of draconian reprisals.

New leaders and new technology also played an important part in this stirring public opposition. The old opposition—the leaders of the parties that had been around since the Yeltsin years—played very little role in initiating the demonstrations. To be sure, they deplored the corruption and called for new elections, and then jumped, somewhat bewildered, onto the bandwagon of public opposition that they played little role in creating. The real leadership came from a new group of activists, a new generation of opposition leaders like Alexei Navalny and Ksenia Sobchak (the daughter of Anatoly Sobchak, who brought Putin into the Leningrad reform movement), who knew how to use the Internet and opposition blogs both to define the themes of protest and to mobilize public opposition.

The 2012 Presidential Election

The presidential elections, scheduled for March 4, 2012, hardly occurred in a vacuum. Although the outcome was never really in doubt, the broader implications of how the leading candidate had been chosen and the regime's response to the protest movement created by the Duma elections made this an extremely important election. It was not just about the tandem and the short-term implications of their switching places; it was about how the regime would respond before the next Duma elections (five years in the future) and the next presidential race (six years on). That response would set the tone that would shape the nation well beyond that narrow time frame.

Remember the beginnings of tandem rule just four years earlier. Medvedev's election to the presidency and Putin's assumption of the office of prime minister created an extremely high level of uncertainty at the time. The fact that the tandem had been able to work reasonably well, both politically and administratively, and to run out the full presidential term was a surprise to many observers, even though it now seems apparent that both Putin and Medvedev had wanted it that way.

It also seemed remarkable that the two leaders had worked so well together. Despite their repeated references to a common background and commitment to the same general goals, politics is politics, and a falling out would have surprised no one. They had their differences about economic priorities and developmental strategies, and both controlled their public comments to sometimes hint at but never overly dramatize their differences. Even their mutual promise that they would work out the inevitable choice between them for the 2012 presidential election, which seemed dismissive and disingenuous at the time, turned out to be true. Whatever else may be said, the two played out a game that both had begun in 2008.

There is little reason to accept the official version that Putin and Medvedev had decided the question of who would occupy the presidency after 2012 shortly after the 2008 election. It was good political mythology, but it wasn't true. From roughly 2010 onward each had conducted a shadow campaign for the higher office, although there were no direct clashes.

For his part, Medvedev grew increasingly bold in articulating his view of meaningful economic and political reforms. His proposals ran contrary to both the spirit and the institutional stability of the vertical that had been established under Putin's rule. At the tactical level, he pressed forward with the dismissal of regional leaders, most of whom owed their jobs and personal fortunes to Putin and the system he created. He also ordered government officials to resign their seats on the boards of state corporations, seeking to break the cozy connection between corporate wealth and political power. More broadly, his vision of the future and his willingness to take action against the status quo also provided a reference point around which other reformers could coalesce, however cautiously.

There is little to suggest that Medvedev and his supporters wanted to remove Putin completely from the scene. The more likely scenario probably involved an extension of the tandem shifting more power toward the president. Medvedev would remain in the presidency (now with a six-year term) with a greater mandate to pursue a reform agenda both at home and abroad, especially in closer links to the global economy and more progress in the reset of ties with the United States. Putin would probably remain as prime minister, at least for a suitable transition but possibly longer, with de facto control over some policy areas such as internal security and a clear understanding that he would continue to play the role of mediator among factional interests. Not a perfect arrangement for either, but perhaps workable.

Not surprisingly, this outcome proved unacceptable to Putin and the more conservative and statist elements of his core constituency. In Putin's mind, the tandem had been a necessary but temporary arrangement, accepted to preserve the formal institutions of democracy while leaving in place the vertical and Putin's unique role within it. Putin would hardly be the first authoritarian modernizer to reject the notion that his vision of the future and his essential role in building it now required substantial modification. However tentatively, Medvedev's actions from 2010 onward had begun to challenge both elements.

However briefly, the quasi-public debate over Russia's future also simplified and clarified the increasingly complex game of factional politics. In the face of the Putin–Medvedev rivalry, the factions had to make a clear choice: to undo a modest but potentially disruptive reform agenda and back Medvedev for a second term or to support Putin's return to the presidency. For most of the factions—and especially for the *siloviki* and others who had benefited from the stability and prosperity of Putin's first two terms—the choice was easy.

When was the decision actually made? Probably late in the summer of 2011, shortly before the September convention of United Russia. As late as mid-April, Medvedev had told an interviewer on Chinese television that he "did not exclude" a bid for a second term. In midsummer, Putin's staff increased its public criticism of Medvedev, and Putin stepped up his public appearances and photo ops. The speculation and sparring ended on September 24 at the United Russia convention when Medvedev announced that Putin would seek reelection. Putin soon dropped the other shoe: Medvedev would reassume the post of prime minister. At least on paper, the tandem had switched places once again.[24]

Even the slightest of differences between Putin and Medvedev had raised hopes that 2012 might bring a real choice between different, if not conflicting, paths to the future. The fates of the Putin "team" and the Medvedev "team" hung in the balance, an important consideration to the inside-the-Garden-Ring players in Moscow. More broadly, even the slightest nuances between them on policy issues had important implications, not only for the fate of the economy and the nation but also for the power and wealth of those constituencies that would be affected.

There also were certain political realities that could not be wished away. From both Putin's and Medvedev's perspectives, the tandem had worked well. From Putin's point of view, it had kept him in power, if not directly in the presidency, beyond his second term. Now it presented him with the opportunity legally to return to the presidency for potentially two more six-year terms. And although Medvedev could have emerged as a serious rival in 2012, he chose not to do so. From Medvedev's perspective, the tandem had elevated him to the presidency for four years. On most things, the presidential prerogatives had been respected as the tandem worked out its *modus operandi*. Medvedev could not have forgotten that most of the briefly serving prime ministers in the Yeltsin and Putin presidencies quickly fell by the wayside—unless they found some way to move, however temporarily, into the presidency itself. It is not hard to construct an argument that both viewed the tandem as a good serviceable arrangement, both as it was constructed after the 2008 election and as it was reconstituted after the 2012 balloting.

Another unchallengeable reality was Putin's continuing popularity, if not within the growing middle class, certainly among the Russian population as a whole. For most of his term both as president and now prime minister, it had hovered somewhere in the 70-percent range. Even as the election neared, he placed in the mid-60-percent range, and the Duma election debacle lowered his approval ratings only slightly. For many Russians, he had become the symbol of stability and an acceptable level of prosperity, if not affluence. Especially outside the Garden Ring, he seemed to rise above the chattering of the political class, offering a promise of continued stability for the modest price of keeping in line those who would disrupt society. In the terms of U.S. politics, he was simultaneously the "law and order" and "chicken in every pot" candidate; both promises were very basic and down to earth, but they were better than the 1990s.

As with all politicians, Putin's public image had been manipulated to reinforce the perception of stability, strength, and responsibility. Putin was a man's man, a judo expert, a hunter, and an adventurer, some of it true but most of it inflated to play to the cameras. To women, he was offered as a paragon of responsibility, always concerned with keeping a roof over the family and food on the table. A popular song extoled his virtues; after lamenting the unfaithfulness of her former lover, a young girl begins the chorus with "I want a boyfriend like Putin" who "won't run away." Countryand-western music met Kremlin politics, and it worked.

Another reality that shaped the presidential election was the continuing organizational strength of United Russia. The party had been bloodied but not destroyed in the Duma elections. It still controlled the Duma, and, more important, its national and regional organizations were still largely intact. Probably wisely, it kept a low public profile during the presidential campaign, working primarily behind the scenes to turn out and to "guide" the vote. The advantages of incumbency were once again pushed to the limit, including both the use of government offices for campaign activities and state dominance of the media.

The unexpected scope of the protests after the Duma elections did lead Putin and Medvedev to promise reforms during the run-up to the presidential balloting in March. Although they rejected opposition claims that ballot tampering and other forms of election fraud had tipped the balance in United Russia's favor and refused to invalidate the election results, they promised more stringent monitoring of the presidential vote. Cameras were installed in all polling stations to provide constant surveillance, and election monitors were given greater access to polling stations. Registration requirements for the creation of new parties or for eligibility to place names on the ballot were reduced, implicitly acknowledging opposition claims that they had been purposely manipulated to exclude potentially troublesome candidates and parties from the ballot. In addition, the tandem promised to introduce legislation to permit the direct election of regional governors, now without any de facto veto power lodged in the hands of the president.[25]

As in the past, Putin ran with the support of United Russia. Seeking to create the appearance of a broader mandate and social base, Putin called for the creation of a broader coalition of political forces to be named the All-Russia People's Front. The Front officially dated to a May 2011 meeting convened at Putin's initiative that included representatives from United Russia and other allied parties, business organizations, trade unions, and youth, women's, and veterans' organizations. It was to be a united front in the old-fashioned sense: a coalition of diverse political forces, all endorsing Putin's return to the presidency and aimed at generating broader public support well beyond the capabilities of United Russia alone, which was dropping in the polls even before the December 2011 elections. Its job was to "invigorate" United Russia, provide new ideas, and implicitly provide Putin the opportunity to distance himself from a party in decline without surrendering the claim to widespread public support. Like most such marriages of political convenience that had been patched together before major elections in the past, it was never expected to have much sticking power. The stunning results of the Duma elections discredited its ability to play a helpful role, and it shrank into relative obscurity during the presidential campaign, which, like Yeltsin's 1996 uphill struggle to win a second term, became a highly personalized effort to establish Putin as the candidate of stability and continuity.[26]

As in previous presidential elections, the other major parties did all they could to hand the election to Putin. Even though they could smell the blood in the water from the Duma elections and see the crowds in the streets, the Communist Party and the Liberal Democratic Party put forward the same candidates and platforms that had led them to defeat in the past. The only new face was Prokhorov, who ran as an independent. For the most part, it was déjà vu all over again, not surprisingly leading to the same results.

Five officially registered candidates took the field in the presidential elections. They were Putin, nominated by United Russia and backed by another party, Patriots of Russia, and endorsed by the All-Russia People's Front; Sergei Mironov, backed by Just Russia; Zhirinovsky, nominated by the Liberal Democratic Party; Gennady Zyuganov, put forward by the Communist Party of the Russian Federation; and Prokhorov, who formerly was associated with Right Cause but ran as an independent. According to a Levada Center poll taken in September 2011, before the

Duma elections, 41 percent were pleased to see Putin listed as a candidate, 22 percent would have liked to see Medvedev also on the ballot, and 10 percent named someone else whom they wanted among the candidates; 28 percent were undecided.[27]

A number of other candidates tried to get on the ballot. Most prominent among them was Grigory Yavlinsky, who sought to run as the Yabloko candidate. His candidacy was rejected by the electoral commission because of the high number of "invalid signatures," probably falsely. Eduard Limonov, leader of the unregistered Other Russia party, also was rejected for much the same reason. Nine other potential candidates, all political lightweights or complete unknowns, were rejected.

All of the preelection polls showed Putin the likely winner, with the margin of victory ranging from 66 to 52 percent, with a slight increase in his favor over time. The other candidates were remarkably consistent in their unpopularity. Zyuganov held at between 13 to 18 percent, Zhirinovsky at 8 to 12 percent, Mironov at 5 to 7 percent, and the wildcard, Prokhorov, at 3 to nearly 9 percent. Prokhorov was the only candidate whose support level grew appreciably over the course of the campaign.[28]

For the most part, the campaign was predictable. True to his persona, Zhirinovsky was Zhirinovsky. His campaign slogan was "vote Zhirinovsky, or things will get worse," hardly a stirring call to a better future. His most prominent campaign video featured his pet donkey. Near the end, he provoked a public outcry when he called Putin's celebrity supporters, including the popular singer Alla Pugacheva, "prostitutes." She responded by naming him a "clown and a psycho." The Liberal Democratic Party's official platform, vaguely nationalistic and populist, got lost in the noise.

Zyuganov's campaign was more focused on economic and social issues, especially corruption, and on the need to form an international alliance against "imperialist circles." Considerably less than charismatic, Zyuganov never excited even the aging Communist Party faithful, much less expanded the base to a broader and more diverse constituency. Mironov was even less successful in mounting an effective campaign.

Prokhorov, the newcomer, was a very different story. He was hardly your typical presidential hopeful. Listed as the third richest man in Russia and the thirty-second richest man in the world, he was a part of the Yeltsin generation of highly successful oligarchs who, at least until now, had carefully avoided political entanglements. He initially made his fortune in the metals sector, especially nickel, and then broadened his interests to include, among other things, ownership of a U.S. basketball team, the New Jersey

Nets (now the Brooklyn Nets). Like most oligarchs, he dabbled in philan-
thropy and other charitable causes and publicly lived a lifestyle that alter-
nately awed and offended the other 99 percent of his fellow citizens. But if
nothing else, he was new and interesting, both considerable assets in the
short list of usual candidates.

In May 2011, Prokhorov announced his intention to join, at the
Kremlin's invitation, the leadership of the pro-business political party
Right Cause. Created to be another of a series of usually short-lived
"official opposition" parties, Right Cause was designed to reach out to the
growing business community, especially the small to medium entrepreneurial sector, and to the expanding and politically restive middle class.
From the Kremlin's perspective, it was to be a carefully managed opening
to the right, shoring up support from a growing constituency and perhaps providing a possible political base for Medvedev if he wished to
challenge his mentor. Whatever its intended role, the situation changed
quickly when Prokhorov balked under close scrutiny and direction from
Vladislav Surkov, Putin's long-serving political strategist. In September,
he resigned from Right Cause, denouncing it as a sham organization and
labeling Surkov as its "puppet master." In December, shortly after the
Duma elections had indicated higher than expected opposition and public
willingness to take to the streets, Prokhorov announced his independent
candidacy for the presidency.

During the campaign, Prokhorov toured the country, calling for
greater freedom for the business community, more candor and transparency in government, and a general reform agenda that promised, however
vaguely, to sweep aside the old tandem and recognize the growing maturity
and diversity of the economy and society. He clearly presented himself as
the only alternative to the old order, both the government and the stale
opposition, neither of which offered anything more than another round of
"stagnation," to borrow the pejorative term usually associated with the
multiple failures of the Brezhnev era. Provoking more interest than outright support, he attempted to shift the tone of the debate from Putin's
assurances of stability and continuity to the hope for future change.[29]

Putin conducted the campaign of an incumbent, ostensibly eschewing
"political" events so that he might discharge his responsibilities as prime
minister. Those responsibilities, of course, took him to an increasing number of "nonpolitical" events throughout Russia and garnered extensive
media coverage. Debates were out of the question, since they were distrac-
tions from the studious discharge of his duties. He made only one outdoor

public speech during the entire campaign, at a rally in the Luzhniki Stadium in Moscow. Among the 100,000 members of the audience, many admitted to reporters that their attendance had been required by their employers. While Putin stressed the usual themes of stability and continuity, he added a stronger-than-usual dose of Russian patriotism, warning against foreign interference in the nation's domestic affairs that might foment a "color revolution" similar to the allegedly externally directed "orange revolution" in Ukraine or the "rose revolution" in Georgia. He ended his speech with Vyacheslav Molotov's World War II slogan "victory shall be ours."

Election Results

The vote took place on March 4, 2012. To no one's surprise, Putin emerged as the clear first-round victor; the opposition's modest hope to force him into a run-off was denied. Putin won with 63.6 percent of the vote, far lower than his 71.9 percent in the 2004 election and lower than Medvedev's 71.2 percent in 2008 (Table 6.2). But his margin of victory was consistent with most of the preelection public opinion polls. Zyuganov came in second, with 17.2 percent of the vote, virtually the same level of support he got in 2008. Prokhorov got 7.9 percent, an encouraging figure for a candidate who had no formal organization and had entered the race late in the game. Zhirinovsky got 6.2 percent, down from 9.5 percent four years earlier; apparently the donkey wasn't helpful. At the bottom of the list, Mironov got 3.9 percent. Total voter turnout was 71.5 million, down slightly from the 73.7 million voters in 2008, despite the controversial nature of Putin's bid to return to power and the higher level of public protest.[30] Once again, Vladimir Putin was president of Russia.

Table 6.2 2012 Russian Presidential Election

Candidate	Party	Vote	Percentage
Vladimir Putin	United Russia	45,513,001	63.6
Gennady Zyuganov	Communist Party	12,288,624	17.2
Mikhail Prokhorov	Independent	5,680,558	7.9
Vladimir Zhirinovsky	Liberal Democratic Party	4,448,959	6.2
Sergei Mironov	Just Russia	2,755,642	3.9

SOURCE: Central Election Commission of the Russian Federation, www.cikrf.ru/eng/, Election of the President of the Russian Federation, 2012.

Medvedev as an Authoritarian Modernizer

It is in their conceptualization of the role of an authoritarian modernizer that Medvedev and Putin differed most. Their differences lay in nuanced interpretations of how a centralized and disciplined system should operate and of the nature of further economic and social modernization. Both men were in fundamental agreement about the need to preserve and in some way to strengthen the powers of the executive branch. It was during Medvedev's tenure that the presidential term was extended from four to six years and the Duma term from four to five. And it was his watch that witnessed the increasing national power of United Russia as a hegemonic party and the growing manipulation of the electoral process to stack the deck against the long-standing opposition. Medvedev would occasionally quibble over the need to develop a new theory of Russian democracy built around the notions of the vertical or sovereign democracy and frequently cautioned against closing out the new middle class, especially those entre-preneurial elements on which the future of both the economy and the social maturation of society would depend. But the truth remained that, at least for the four-year tenure of the tandem, these differences were real and carried important political implications.

Nowhere were these subtle differences more important than in the economy. Again, both shared a common beginning point built around the notion that modernization meant dismantling the command economies of the soviet era and replacing them with market economies that copied the profiles of the world's advanced industrial nations. But building a market economy alone was not enough. Modernization depended not only on who owned the nation's economic resources and the incentives the market would provide but also on where that economy was headed in the future. In the Russian context, that also raised fundamental and politically difficult questions about the overall profile of the economy and who would lead the way to the future.

On this fundamental question—how to move the Russian economy forward—Medvedev and Putin showed markedly different strategies. It is important not to dichotomize their points of view, but Medvedev showed a stronger tendency to emphasize the development of an advanced, techno-logically sophisticated economy willing to reduce its long-standing depend-ence on energy and raw materials exports, whereas Putin seemed more inclined to accept a slower pace of transformation and a stronger role for the state. Medvedev envisioned an economy whose further development would become heavily dependent on technological modernization, the innovative role of an emerging entrepreneurial class who would combine high technology with venture capitalism, and integration into the broader global economy. The emergence of such an economy would further promote the growth of a new Russian middle class, which would benefit from the new economic opportunities available to it and provide the stable political center. If it all played out—and it was a big *if*—it would increase the performance-based legitimacy of any president who could claim credit for successfully bridging the gap between the old and new economies. Just as Yeltsin was now accorded grudging respect for managing the tumultuous transition from communism to post-1993 democracy, any Russian leader who could manage the next stage of the economic transition not just to a market economy but also to a technologically sophisticated and globally competitive economy could legitimately claim the mantle of an authoritarian modernizer.

But what if things didn't work out that way? The short-term political risk was that any effort to substantially alter the profile of the economy could upset the balance that had produced a growing but not universally shared level of prosperity and stability. If any lesson were remembered from the late 1980s and 1990s, it was that sweeping economic reforms always made things worse before they got better. Russians had accepted a strong presidency in general and Putin in particular because they produced much desired results: stability, prosperity, and some hope for the future. Factional politics within the Garden Ring had adjusted to and in many ways stabilized a political balance that sustained those economic priorities in ways both legitimate and corrupt. The political and economic dangers were inescapable. Move too quickly to accelerate the transition to a less export-driven and technologically advanced profile, and you risk disrupting both the political and the economic foundations of the current stability. Move too slowly, and you slip further behind and settle into a downward spiral of deepening stagnation similar to the final years of communist rule.

Not surprisingly, Putin chose the side of caution over rapid transformation. To be sure, he would occasionally say all of the right things about the need to diversify and modernize the economy. But current economic and political realities won out over possible futures. In large measure, he was the architect and chief beneficiary of the status quo of the post-Yeltsin era. He had engineered and was now seen as the key arbiter in the complex system of factional politics inside the Garden Ring. No less important, he and United Russia had at least temporarily solved the problem of bridging the connection between what happened inside the Garden Ring and the broader game of electoral politics beyond the Ring in ways that brought stability, admittedly at the expense of enhanced democracy. He had brought the oligarchs into line in ways that still preserved a symbiotic relationship between private wealth and political power. Simply put, Putin had far more to lose from any venture that altered the political formula that underpinned his power, regardless of its possible long-term consequences.

Notes

1. *Rossiiskaya Gazeta,* September 14, 2009, quoted in Richard Sakwa, *Crisis of Russian Democracy,* Cambridge University Press, 2011, 349–350.
2. Sakwa, *Crisis,* 333–349; see the Institute's website at www.insor-russia.ru/en/.
3. Timothy J. Colton, "Leadership and the Politics of Modernization," in Dmitri Trenin, ed., *Russia: The Challenges of Transformation,* New York University Press, 2011, 115–144.
4. Sakwa, *Crisis,* 314.
5. Sakwa, *Crisis,* 308–313.
6. Sakwa, *Crisis,* 332–341.
7. Sakwa, *Crisis,* 318–327, 344–352.
8. Sakwa, *Crisis,* 317.
9. Sakwa, *Crisis,* 303.
10. *The Guardian,* March 3, 2009.
11. Presidential website, www.kremlin.ru, September 10, 2009.
12. See Skolkovo Institute of Science and Technology (www.skolkovotech.ru), and for the joint program with MIT, see www.mit.edu.sktech.
13. Anders Aslund, *Russia after the Global Economic Crisis,* Peterson Institute for International Economics, 2010.
14. Presidential website, www.kremlin.ru, September 2009.
15. Sakwa, *Crisis,* 327–332.
16. Robert Orttung and Anthony Latta, eds., *Russia's Battle with Crime, Corruption, and Terrorism,* 2nd ed., Routledge, 2012.
17. Graeme B. Robertson, *The Politics of Protest in Hybrid Regimes: Managing Protest in Post-Communist Russia,* Cambridge University Press, 2010.
18. Jeffrey Mankoff, *Russia's Foreign Policy: The Return of Great Power Politics,* Rowman and Littlefield, 2011; Nikolas K. Gvosdev and Christopher Marsh, *Russian Foreign Policy: Interests, Vectors, and Sectors,* SAGE/CQ Press, 2014; and Jakob Tolstrup, *Russia vs. the EU: The Competition for Influence in Post-Soviet States,* First Forum/Lynne Rienner, 2014.
19. Ronald Asmus, *A Little War That Shook the World: Georgia, Russia, and the Future of the West,* Palgrave Macmillan, 2010; Svante E. Cornell and S. Frederick Starr, eds., *The Guns of August 2008: Russia's War in Georgia,* M. E Sharpe, 2009; and Christoph Zurcher, *The Post-Soviet Wars: Ethnic Conflict and Nationhood in the Caucasus,* New York University Press, 2009.

20. Levada Center polls for March 24, 2011, April 20, 2011, May 18, 2001, June 26, 2011, July 25, 2011, October 27, 2011, November 8, 2011, November 25, 2011, at www.levada.ru/eng/; VCIOM poll for October 6, 2011, at www.wcion.com.

21. Central Election Commission of the Russian Federation, www.cikrf.ru/eng/, Election of the President of the Russian Federation, 2011; and Carnegie Endowment for International Peace, "Russian Elections: Expert Analysis," December 13, 2011, carnegieendowment.org.

22. "Billionaire Condemns Party He Led as a Kremlin 'Puppet,'" *New York Times,* September 15, 2011.

23. "5000 Protest Duma Election Results, *Moscow Times,* December 6, 2011; and "Russian Protest Mood Sweeps into Duma," *Guardian,* December 21, 2011.

24. Brian Whitmore, "The Essence of Decision," Radio Free Europe/Radio Liberty, October 18, 2011; Richard Sakwa, *Putin Redux: Power and Contradiction in Contemporary Russia,* Routledge, 2014, 102.

25. "Direct Election of Russian Governors Will Improve Governance," Reuters, U.S. Edition, April 25, 2011; Meria Selanikova and Marina Selina, "President Putin: A Constant Choice Between Carrots and Sticks," RIANOSTI, en.rian.ru, June 3, 2012; David Herszenhorn, "Russia to Ease Law on Forming Political Parties," *New York Times,* March 23, 2012; and "Medvedev Calls for Major Reforms of Russia's Political System," RT (Russian Television), rt.com/politics, December 22, 2011.

26. Vladimir Ryzhkov, "Why Putin Created the All-Russia People's Front," *Moscow Times,* May 11, 2011; and Anna Arutunyan, "Party Time for Putin's Front?" *Moscow News,* June 26, 2012.

27. Levada Center poll, at www.levada.ru/eng/, September 27, 2011.

28. VCIOM polls, at www.vciom.com, from June 2011 to March 2012; Levada Center polls, at www.levada.ru/eng/, from June 2011 to March 2012.

29. Andrew Cramer, "For Russia, a New Kind of Political Candidate: A Billionaire," *New York Times,* February 20, 2012; and Michael Schwirtz, "Mikhail D. Prokhorov To Lead a Russian Political Party," *New York Times,* May 16, 2011.

30. Central Election Commission of the Russian Federation, at www.cikrf.ru/eng/, March 5, 2012.

7

Putin II, 2012–

As the dust settled from the 2011 Duma and 2012 presidential elections, mixed signals emerged about the future course of Russian politics. On one hand, Putin's easy victory amid charges of voting fraud and the increasing repression of the regime's critics suggested a tightening of political power at the center and of more invasive controls over society. Although the term was avoided, the vertical seemed alive and well in Moscow and beyond. On the other hand, there also were indications of some degree of moderation in Putin's reassertion of controls, vigorously disputed by the regime's critics at home and abroad. Steps were taken to ease restrictions on the creation of new parties and promises were made that future elections would be monitored more carefully for voting fraud. Although greater restrictions were established on public demonstrations, local authorities, undoubtedly acting on Kremlin instructions, continued to permit some public events as safety valves for discontent. The game of factional politics inside the Garden Ring initially continued in only slightly altered form, permitting Vladimir Putin to play the role of broker and balancer. Dmitry Medvedev, once again in the number two post of prime minister, continued to call for economic and social reform, reiterating the same priorities he offered early in his presidency.[1]

The government's actions immediately after the much disputed 2011 Duma elections suggested a flexible and conciliatory response. As noted earlier, the rules that had made it virtually impossible for new political parties to form were substantially eased; by early 2012, sixty-eight new parties were in line to request formal recognition, with more to come. Local election of governors was restored, although the nominees would be "filtered" by central authorities in Moscow.

But some controls remained in place. Demonstrations after the presidential vote and subsequent inauguration turned violent, with both demonstrators and the police claiming provocation. Key dissidents such as Alexei Navalny, Sergei Udaltsov, and Ksenia Sobchak were subjected to continuing police harassment. Fines for participation in unauthorized demonstrations were greatly increased: to 9,000 rubles (nearly the yearly income for the average Russian) for mere participation; 18,000 for organizers; and 30,000 for organizations that sponsored such activities, with higher penalties for repeat offenders.

The "New" Cabinet

The formation of the first postelection cabinet and the choice of presidential advisors also gave some hints about what was to come. There is clear evidence that forming the new cabinet required considerable negotiations among the Kremlin factions. Putin and Medvedev closeted themselves to discuss the choices, and Putin did not attend a G-8 conference allegedly because of pressing tasks at home, which everyone took to mean that cabinet selection was taking longer than expected.[2]

Setting aside the individual choices for a moment, two messages emerged. The first is initial continuity at the top. A few of the most unpopular or ineffective ministers were removed, but the general pattern was one of continuity coupled with musical chairs. Medvedev's return to the office of prime minister, at first thought to be a temporary expedient, signaled a level of stability that few expected at the time. But there was no effort to reach out to opposition forces. Mikhail Prokhorov, who ran an independent campaign for the presidency, remained outside the government; he formed an independent party that he eventually handed off to his sister. Alexei Kudrin, the former finance minister dismissed by Medvedev, also remained outside government.

The second message reveals a clear strengthening of the president's power at the expense of the prime minister. Although Medvedev returned to the office, the pattern that had seen power transferred to that office under Putin was now reversed. A number of key officials who had served Putin as prime minister from 2008 to 2012 returned to the presidential staff, decamping the White House (i.e., the government offices) and relocating to the Kremlin.

At the level of individual cabinet choices, compromise seems to have ruled the day. Initial appointments reveal an effort to balance factional and institutional interests. Initially the only first deputy prime minister in

Medvedev's cabinet was Igor Shuvalov, a close Putin associate and the president's eyes and ears at the highest level. Medvedev's personal chief of staff, who held the rank of deputy prime minister, was Vladislav Surkov.[3] Once seen as the guiding spirit of Putin's power vertical and sovereign democracy, he was under attack for the botched efforts to manage the Duma and presidential elections. The appointment of Arkady Dvorkovich as deputy prime minister with primary responsibility for the economy also strengthened the reformers; close to Medvedev, he was viewed as a counterweight to those who advocated a greater economic role for the state. Dmitry Kozak, Alexander Khloponin, and Dmitry Rogozin all kept their posts as deputy prime ministers, confirming the emphasis on continuity. The power ministries—defense, both halves of what had been the KGB, and foreign affairs—remained in the hands of their previous chiefs. New appointees to less important ministries were drawn primarily from among technocrats and lower level staff within their agencies.

Putin II: Old and New Realities

On the day of his inauguration, Putin returned to the same office he had held from 2000 to 2008. Some things clearly had changed. Although victorious, he had been bloodied by the events that surrounded the 2011 Duma and 2012 presidential balloting. The always-active rumor mills talked of a new reality in which he might voluntarily choose to step down in 2018 and not seek reelection. He faced an increasingly complex world of factional interests within the Garden Ring, always watchful of whether he might underplay his hand and signal weakness or indecision or overplay his hand and threaten powerful institutional and economic interests. And there always was the question of who might come next, especially if the one-more-term-and-then-out scenario seemed possible.

But other things seemed not to have changed. Putin successfully finessed his nomination as a candidate for the presidency and Medvedev's acceptance of his demotion to the number two post. Although a visible opposition remained active, it was confined mostly to the major cities where Putin had done worse in the presidential election; outside the Garden Ring in the "real" Russia, he was still popular. To be sure, support had dipped in the polls. In June 2007, just before Putin and Medvedev announced their intention to switch offices, 81 percent of the people rated Putin favorably; just after the presidential election, his approval rating had fallen to 62 percent, and the Winter Olympics in Sochi gave him a temporary bump up of only 3 to 4 percent.[4] Only months later, with the seizure of Crimea and the support of Russian separatists in eastern Ukraine, Putin's favorability rose to all-time highs even in light of Western economic sanctions.

Within the Garden Ring, Putin continued to play the role of arbiter among an increasingly complex array of factions. Medvedev, whose days had seemed numbered because of his attempt to seek a second term, not only returned to the diminished role of prime minister—which everyone expected in the short term—but he remained in the post far longer than anyone thought likely. Although the overall circle of close advisors around the president grew smaller, the alleged and much overrated strong hand of the *soloviki* was primarily in foreign and defense policy (discussed at length later in this chapter). On other issues, and occasionally on foreign policy questions as well, Putin was careful to reflect more nuanced perspectives.

Putin also asserted a more active international role for Russia. Earlier actions in Georgia and Russian willingness to recognize and support separatist movements in Abkhazia and South Ossetia foreshadowed greater efforts to expand Moscow's sphere of influence. More broadly, the West's unwillingness to recognize that Russia had once again emerged as a major regional and perhaps global power, coupled with Moscow's criticism of American unilateralism, set the stage for diplomatic and eventual military confrontation. The theme of Russian exceptionalism reemerged, and the nation was once again increasingly portrayed as possessing a unique identity and destiny, set between but also apart from both East and West.

Economic realities also shaped Putin's return to power. For the most part, the economy had begun to recover from the 2008 global economic downturn. The GDP had decreased by 7.9 percent in 2009, but it rose by 4.5 percent in 2010, by 4.3 percent in 2011, and by 3.4 percent in 2012.[5] Still heavily dependent on energy exports, the economy also benefited from the increase in world oil prices. Russian entry into the World Trade Organization (WTO) in 2012 also paved the way for increasing trade, although progress was slow. The standard of living also increased, especially in the cities. At the same time, however, income disparities among the "haves," the "have-lesses," and "have-nots" also became more pronounced.

Maintaining the Balance within the Garden Ring

The key to Putin's first presidency, from 2000 to 2008, was his role as the balancer of factional interests inside the Garden Ring. By the beginning of his second administration, that task had become more complex. In one sense, success during the first eight years meant little more than doing a better job than his predecessor, a relatively easy task given Boris Yeltsin's lackluster performance. But now the bar was higher. The political arena was now far more complex, both in the sense of a growing number of factions competing for influence and potentially limited or diminishing resources and in the sense that a vocal opposition had emerged.[6]

One measure of the increasing complexity was rooted in the improvement of the economy after 2008. More people had more money, and although some of it went abroad (until Putin pressured Russian investors to diminish foreign holdings, albeit with limited success), much of it remained at home. In political terms, that meant there were more stakeholders anxious to influence the government to enhance and protect their interests. The increasing role of state-owned or state-influenced megacorporations like Gazprom or Rosneft brought more powerful players into the game. Informal networks, always present even during the communist era, also got increasingly into the game. Putin himself was a part of the so-called *Ozera* (Lake) group, which had formed years earlier among a group of neighbors in the Leningrad suburbs and whose members prospered as close friends and advisors to the president. The undisputed presence of widespread corruption and the off-the-books networks through which it functioned also added to the complexity of factional politics. The old Russian proverb that having one hundred friends is better than having one hundred rubles still remained true, no matter which government was printing the rubles.

Also present was the continuing task of balancing the influence of powerful individuals who have a political identity of their own. In many ways, establishing their personal standing in the pecking order may be largely symbolic. Medvedev is a good example. Although he had served Putin for years, even as the de facto second chair in the tandem, he had the temerity to launch a bid for a second term as president, drawing back at the last minute to accept a demotion to prime minister. Shortly after the election, conventional wisdom argued that his days were numbered. But more than halfway through Putin's third term as president, he is still there, subdued but still functioning. What does this mean in the context of factional politics? Perhaps it signaled that his dismissal would further embolden more conservative factions and upset the balance or that Putin was keeping his options open. Or perhaps it meant that Putin was the sort of leader who dealt generously with opponents who saw the handwriting on the wall and gracefully accepted defeat. Keeping the balance, and keeping Putin in the key role of being the balancer, required that any number of such personnel issues would have to be dealt with in the future.

Controlling the Opposition

Controlling the opposition was now a much larger issue than in Putin's first two terms in office. Putin previously had shown considerable tactical flexibility in managing the opposition. Sometimes he moved cautiously (witness his careful handling of the Yeltsin family in the beginning of his first term in 2000 and the tactical, if brief lived, concessions after the much-criticized 2011 Duma elections). At other times, he took decisive action, evidenced in his reassertion of control over the choice of the presidential nominee at the end of Medvedev's term in office. It soon became apparent that the tone of his post-2012 tenure would be marked by efforts to impose greater control on federal, regional, and local government at all levels. As described in detail later in this chapter, Putin attempted to affirm the "center's" institutional control over the state, tighten government influence over and outright ownership of important sectors of the economy, control or destroy critical elements of civil society, utilize criminal prosecution and the legal system as political weapons, and control the media. His return to power was clearly marked by coordinated and mutually reinforcing policies to establish the presidency and its current incumbent in a position of power far superior to either of his predecessors.[7]

The task of managing and controlling the opposition also has grown more complex. The possibility of a strongly articulated "left" and "right" opposition has once again has emerged. The former is potentially rooted in the political fallout of any serious economic downturn, and the latter finds support among Russian nationalists who have gotten a taste of the rediscovery of Russian national identity and its assertive role in the world. In either case, Putin or any other future president will be torn by the risks and rewards of endorsing one or the other. Putin's current shift to the right in backing a more traditional sense of national identity and a more aggressive foreign policy is clearly an expedient choice but not necessarily a permanent one.

Increasingly present is the need to anticipate and prepare to deal with opposition from "the street," the catchall term applied to anomic social protests now easier to organize and exploit in a world of social media. To be sure, the conventional control mechanisms—strict limitations on public demonstrations, harassment or confinement of dissidents and civil society, and control of the larger social media—may limit the impact of such actions. But evidence suggests that there usually is an unpredictable tipping point beyond which these demonstrations assume a life of their own, confronting the authorities with a difficult choice between concessions and outright suppression.

The Economy: Prosperity and Modernity

Putin's return to the presidency also coincided with the sharpening of two critical and interrelated debates over the Russian economy. The first deals with the usual issues that plague any nation's political leadership: Was the nation on the cusp of further prosperity or on the brink of a downturn; how did its current status and immediate future affect the well-being of a wide spectrum of stakeholders ranging from the oligarchs to the common consumer; how did the economy fit into an increasingly globalized world; and what were the implications of economic sanctions imposed in 2014 after the annexation of Crimea and support for Ukrainian separatists?

In the long run, the second debate is even more important: What is the overall economic model that will shape Russia's future, and what does it mean about the new sense of modernity that was at the heart of the nation's rejection of communism? Both elements are critical. If the interpretation of Russian history from Mikhail Gorbachev onward had any single consistent thread, it was that each leader, in his own way, rejected the original Marxist notion of modernity and sought to find a new interpretation that would lead the nation into the twenty-first century. But that debate was still open and in many ways intensifying because of Russia's desire to chart a separate course that preserved a core of homegrown modernity and a distinctive national culture. As noted earlier, the easier part of that transition had been accomplished, although not without considerable economic and political costs. And in some ways, Putin had been lucky in his first eight years in office. A general economic upturn, relative peace and prosperity for most if not all of the oligarchs, a rising standard of living, and higher oil prices all eased the transition and postponed the moment when the next round of difficult choices would have to be made.

That time was here when Putin moved back into the Kremlin.[8] The decline had already begun even before Russian action in Crimea; World Bank figures revealed that GDP growth had slowed to 1.3 percent in 2013, down from 3.4 percent in the previous year. Although oil prices remained relatively high for the first two years of Putin's second administration, they dropped dramatically from around US$100 a barrel on the WTI index to less than $60 by the fall of 2014. This drop had serious implications since 40 percent of state revenue was derived from oil sales. Economic sanctions imposed because of the seizure of Crimea and the support of pro-Russian forces in eastern Ukraine bit harder throughout 2014 (discussed at length in the section on foreign policy).[9]

Russia's increasing involvement in the global economy also presented it with difficult choices. On one hand, membership in the WTO had removed a major institutional impediment to greater trade. But the nation still remained dependent on oil and other energy exports, the long-term viability of which came increasingly into question as half-hearted efforts were made to provide Eastern Europe with non-Russian suppliers. The bright spot for Moscow was the deal quickly signed, after the sanctions took hold, to export natural gas to China. But the bad news, at least in the short run, was that Russia had to accept lower prices and the system would not be fully operational for at least a decade.

The immediate impact of sanctions aside for a moment, Russian action in Crimea and eastern Ukraine underscored a more fundamental choice that faced the nation. Foreign policy choices and economic ties to the West were clearly linked, as they had been during the cold war. Two separate but interrelated debates now emerged over the nation's future. One dealt with a possible reinterpretation of the 1990s notion of modernity, which had been largely borrowed from the successful market economies that had performed better than the plodding centrally planned economies of the Soviet Union and Eastern Europe. But now that model was open to reinterpretation, or at least to modification as Russia stepped back from its ties with the West and rediscovered an allegedly separate and superior national culture. The new economic model would be a combination of private and public sectors and a reinterpretation of how the Russian economy both engaged and protected itself from an increasingly invasive global economy. The details were vague, but the central idea was plain: We're like them (vaguely defined as the capitalist West), and yet we're different.

The second debate focused on the broader question of Russia's place in the world. Discussed more fully later in this chapter, this debate emerged in part because of the nation's increasing military power and in part because of the perception that the West, and especially the United States, regarded post-cold war Russia as a second-class power that no longer needed to be taken seriously. Even before he returned to the presidency in 2012, Putin turned to more assertive and nationalistic themes. The rediscovery of a distinct Russian identity, the modification of the notion of modernity, and a more assertive foreign policy became the new troika that would carry Russia forward toward a new non-communist and non-Western future.

While the debate continued, economic reality set in. Economic sanctions continued to take an even larger bite out of the economy, although the regime and most Russians put forth a brave face in response to the continuing economic decline. The income of average Russians declined markedly, a product of the overall business slowdown, pay reductions, diminished hours, and outright layoffs. Retail sales dropped by nearly 10 percent in 2015, and industrial output by nearly 5 percent. Hard times hit government employees as well. There were widespread staff and/or pay reductions, averaging 10 percent across the board for most government workers. Putin himself took a 10-percent pay reduction and reduced the size of his staff, and most other officials took similar symbolic action. Poverty deepened, and in late 2015, the government introduced a food stamp program modeled on the U.S. example.

Economic difficulties opened old and new political wounds. In the run-up to the 2016 budget, proposals were advanced to increase taxes on the oil industry, already hard hit by the decline in oil prices from more than US$100 to just under $50 but still the largest cash cow available to increase government revenues. Not surprisingly, oil industry executives opposed the increase, as did deputy prime minister Arkady Dvorkovich, a specialist on the economy with ties to Medvedev. The government soon backed off, saying that no decision had been taken. The final budget proposal completely reversed course, apparently with Putin's support. Taxes on oil exports were actually reduced by 9 percent.

The budget for 2016 reflected the new realities. Projections were offered only for the next year, not the usual three-year cycle, signaling both uncertainty and caution. Cuts hit hard across the board. The overall figures were calculated on the assumption of an average US$50 per barrel oil price, but prices fell to even lower levels early in 2016. The defense budget, which had risen at least 10 percent every year since 2011, was now slated for only a 0.8-percent increase, putting pressure on Russian commitments in Syria and Ukraine, its promise to increase preparedness against NATO, and its rearmament and modernization programs. Subsidies to regional governments were cut by half, increasing the likelihood that more would slip into de facto default, joining the estimated twenty regional governments that have unofficially met that end. The inevitable shortfalls at the national level will be covered by further withdrawals from the National Reserve Fund and the National Wealth Fund, rainy-day money set aside during the good years of high oil prices and now thought to be within one or two years of depletion.

Despite current and predicted hard times, Putin has held his own in the public opinion polls, signaling that his assertive policies in the Middle East and Ukraine and his reassertion of Russian nationalism have more than compensated for the nation's economic troubles, at least for now. A Levada Center poll taken late in 2015 indicated that 85 percent still trusted him to see Russia through its time of troubles, up from 55 percent in 2013.

Foreign Policy

Asserting Russia's new role in the world might be emotionally satisfying, but it would not be easy, and the collateral costs would be high. In many ways, the transition began even before Putin's return to the presidency. In his comments to a 2007 conference on security policy in Munich, Putin condemned "ideological stereotypes, double standards, and other typical aspects of cold war bloc thinking" allegedly underpinning Western policy toward Russia. He also reiterated the same message in a 2013 Concept of the Foreign Policy of the Russian Federation document.[10] Implying that the tide had already turned against the West, he averred that the trend toward a "polycentric system of international relations" should be accelerated and that the West's ability to dominate the global economy "continues to diminish," with power "shifting to the east," a vague formulation that included both Russia and China. The concept statement established the highest priorities of Russian foreign policy as the further integration of the Commonwealth of Independent States, the strengthening of the Eurasian Economic Union, and expansion of the Collective Security Treaty Organization, a loose military bloc. Relations with the European Union (EU) and the United States were placed much farther down the list. Putin's March 2014 speech to the Russian legislature on the annexation of the Crimea continued in the same vein, denouncing a "policy of containment that continues today" and asserting that "Russia is an independent participant in international affairs, and like other countries, it has its own national interests that need to be taken into account and respected."[11]

Relations with the United States deteriorated further after Putin's return to the presidency. Although limited cooperation continued on some issues where American and Russian interests coincided, the overall decline was striking even before Russian annexation of Crimea. The appointment of Michael McFaul as U.S. ambassador was taken as an affront. A prominent scholar who had advised several administrations, McFaul had written critically of the shortcomings of democratization in post-communist Russia and continued to speak openly about his concerns once posted to Moscow. Russian officials responded in kind, and a low-intensity war of words broke out as McFaul Twittered his views to all who would listen. In September 2012, Moscow requested an end to the American-sponsored USAID programs, complaining that they were interfering in the nation's domestic politics, and in January of the following year, the United States withdrew from the joint Civil Society Working Group because of increasing government interference.[12]

At other levels, however, real and symbolic cooperation continued, at least for a while. Barack Obama and Putin met in June 2013 at the G-20 conference in Los Cabos, Mexico, and jointly called for an end to the worsening Syrian civil war despite Russian support for Bashir al-Assad. Their differences aside, both nations agreed to attend an international conference on the conflict. Both nations, along with the United Kingdom, France, China, and Germany, called on Iran to suspend its uranium enrichment program. In September, Obama and Putin once again met on the sidelines of a G-20 conference in St. Petersburg to discuss the deteriorating situation in Syria and growing pressures in the West for intervention in the face of Assad's use of chemical weapons. A week later, U.S. secretary of state John Kerry and Russian foreign minister Sergei Lavrov agreed on a Russian-brokered program that would lead to Syrian destruction of its chemical weapons stockpiles.

Relations took a sharp turn for the worse in July 2013 when Russia granted asylum to Edward Snowden, a former National Security Agency employee who had stolen and subsequently leaked to the press a large number of classified documents. Angered by the action, Obama canceled a planned meeting with Putin scheduled for September 2013 in Moscow.[13]

The real downturn came with the Russian response to events in Ukraine, which backed away from an agreement with Moscow that would have closely tied its economy with that of Russia and the Eurasian Economic Union and closed the door to future collaboration with the EU and NATO. Discussed in detail in the next section, that action led to the sharpest confrontation between East and West since the end of the cold war. Russian seizure and subsequent annexation of Crimea and its clandestine and eventually open support of pro-Russian separatists in eastern Ukraine led the Obama administration to press initially reluctant European nations for increasingly harsh economic sanctions against Putin's inner circle and key sectors of the Russian economy. Moscow replied in kind, and the war of sanctions quickly spread to include big banks, big oil, and Big Macs.

Crimea and Ukraine

The turning point in Russia's relations with the West came in connection with events that unfolded in Ukraine in 2013. Russian–Ukrainian relations had a long and troubled history. The region was gradually absorbed into an expanding Russian empire from the mid-seventeenth century onward. Briefly independent after the 1917 revolution, the Ukraine was forced to join the newly formed Soviet Union in 1924. It soon emerged as the second most important union republic in the Soviet Union, favored in many ways in terms of preferential economic treatment—both Nikita Khrushchev and Leonid Brezhnev had long experience there early in their careers—but it was never fully accepted as an equal to the Russian federation. In 1954, Khrushchev transferred the Crimean peninsula from Russian to Ukrainian control, largely to win the support of the region's leaders.

Independence still left many issues unsettled between the newly constituted Russian Federation and Ukraine. Crimea was granted special autonomous status within Ukraine, and Moscow and Kiev reached and then extended an agreement permitting the Russian navy to maintain its facilities for the Black Sea fleet. Both nations squabbled over the price of Russian-supplied energy, critical to the success of the Ukrainian economy and a useful and brutally utilized tool in Russian hands. As it had always been, Ukraine was an ethnically and culturally divided nation. The western half of the nation was more ethnically Ukrainian and Catholic, more prosperous, more Europeanized, and far more prone to opt for closer economic and cultural ties with Europe and possible membership in the EU and NATO. The eastern third of the nation and the Crimean peninsula were more Russian, more orthodox, poorer, and far more interested in keeping close ties with Russia. The 2004 election brought the pro-Russian Viktor Yanukovych to power amid allocations of widespread voting fraud.

Ukrainians took to the streets in the so-called orange revolution, occupying Kiev and many other cities, especially in the western half of the nation, and ultimately forcing a second election in which the anti-Russian Viktor Yushchenko won with 52 percent of the vote.

In the 2010 presidential election, Yanukovych narrowly won in second-round balloting. He soon began negotiations with the EU that would eventually would have led to full membership and firm ties linking the economy to Western Europe, while simultaneously conducting talks with Moscow in the hope of playing one against the other. Late in 2013, Yanukovych abandoned talks with the EU and quickly accepted Moscow's offer of US$15 billion in emergency economic aid and a 33-percent discount on natural gas prices. Kiev had made its choice: It would cast its lot with Putin's hope for a Eurasian Economic Union.

The people of Kiev, and most of western Ukraine, had other ideas. Reminiscent of the orange revolution, vast crowds quickly occupied the city's Maidan Square in protest. Yanukovych clung to power, and what had begun as peaceful demonstrations turned increasingly violent as the government tried to drive protestors from the square. On February 22, 2014, protestors took control of many government buildings and most of the city. Yanukovych decamped to Kharkhiv, where he enjoyed more support. The legislature in Kiev voted to accept his abandonment as a de facto resignation, although the vote itself fell short of the three quarters needed for formal impeachment. For his part, Yanukovych insisted he was still legally president and escaped, with Moscow's assistance, across the border to Russia.[14]

Predictably the nation divided on what to make of events. The pro-European part, and most of Kiev, willingly accepted the de facto coup, quickly restoring the 2004 constitution and opting to reopen talks with the EU on economic support and eventual membership. The eastern and southern regions, including Crimea, opposed the shift and increasingly sided with Yanukovych and closer ties with Russia. Russian authorities were outraged at what they regarded as Western, and largely American, interference in what they deemed their sphere of influence and a key component of the Eurasian Economic Union.

Moscow was quick to respond by mobilizing the support of ethnic Russians in Crimea and the Donbass region. It orchestrated the activation of local Russian separatists, clandestine and eventually open military intervention, and the creation of Russian-backed "people's republics" that requested closer ties with or direct annexation by the Russian Federation. Moscow pursued but publicly denied a policy to salvage what little control it had over events in Ukraine. Only days after the fall of the Yanukovych government, unmarked military units widely regarded to be Russian special forces took control of Crimea, disarming and eventually expelling what little remained of the Ukrainian army. Soon thereafter the new pro-Russian government announced that a referendum would be held on whether to request annexation by the Russian Federation. Held on March 16, 2014, the balloting produced the expected results, and three days later the Russian legislature formally annexed Crimea.[15]

Things were not so quick or easy in eastern Ukraine. Pro-Russian residents quickly expressed their displeasure with Yanukovych's dismissal and soon took matters into their own hands, seizing government buildings in the key cities of Donetsk, Sloviansk, and later Luhansk. Russian recognition and aid were quick to come, at first limited to the encouragement of "volunteers" from Russia who streamed into the region, and eventually resulting in full-scale military assistance. Spurred on by Russian aid and diplomatic support, separatists in Donetsk and Luhansk proclaimed their independence. An already dangerous and confusing situation was complicated by the shooting down of a Malaysian Air flight on July 17, with the death of all 298 passengers.

By the late summer of 2014, the fighting had stabilized into an uneasy deadlock; Ukrainian forces were unable to recapture the core areas of opposition, and Moscow seemed willing to commit whatever forces might be necessary to maintain the unstable situation. A much-violated cease-fire was achieved on September 5, and Russian forces gradually withdrew, although it was clear that Moscow continued to supply pro-Russian forces. Throughout the fall, a series of inconclusive negotiations continued, focused in part on trying to find some political formula that would at least deescalate the conflict and in part on reaching a deal that would permit Russian gas to flow to Ukraine and beyond in the coming winter.[16]

Ukrainian parliamentary elections in October 2014 confirmed Kiev's intention to pull closer to the EU. Although no party won an outright majority, the two largest winners that eventually formed the core of a coalition government were strongly committed to a pro-EU foreign policy. Balloting was not held in those areas still controlled by pro-Russian forces. They held their own regional elections several weeks later, and to no one's surprise, pro-Russian voters carried the day. Moscow pledged to accept the results of the regional elections but was silent on how it would respond to any future requests for annexation, a prospect that it eventually rejected in the spring of 2015.[17]

The search for a political solution to the confrontation in eastern Ukraine proved difficult. The EU and the United States shared the same overall goals of reversing as much of the Russian advances as possible—although Crimea was unofficially written-off as lost—and in serving notice to Moscow that further de facto incursions into the former soviet states and Eastern Europe would be met with firmer resolve, but they differed in terms of priorities and tactics. As noted, the United States pressed for harsher economic sanctions (discussed later) and for strengthening NATO's capabilities. The EU agreed to gradually increase the sanctions, especially as it became apparent that initial penalties had provoked mocking defiance from the Kremlin. Increased military preparedness was a more difficult matter; in post-cold war Europe, most nations had cut their defense budgets and were reluctant to ante up for a new confrontation. At best, only token steps were taken, such as strengthening the NATO rapid deployment force, intensifying joint maneuvers with Eastern European allies, and promising to forward base NATO facilities closer to potential trouble zones.

In Moscow, the annexation of Crimea resulted in record high levels of public support for Putin and for virtually any policy that seemed to defy the West. His ratings in the polls rose above 80 percent. The strident tone of nationalism that had been a part of Putin's rhetoric since the 2012 presidential campaign intensified. Not surprisingly, other politicians took up the issue and demanded an even more nationalistic and confrontational foreign policy, prompting Putin to call a special meeting of legislators in August held in the Crimean resort of Yalta to caution against tipping the balance too far.[18]

Economic sanctions had at best only a limited impact on Russian actions initially. The first round in March 2014, after annexation of Crimea, limited travel of selected Russian officials (but not Putin) to the United States and the EU, although prominent Russian businessmen were added to the list shortly thereafter. The second round, which came in April 2014, increased the list of sanctioned individuals and added seventeen Russian companies closely associated with Putin's inner circle. The third round, in July during the worsening of military action in eastern Ukraine, specifically targeted two energy firms, Rosneft and Novatek, and two key banks. The list was soon expanded to ban trade with energy- and defense-related industries and to close Western capital markets to government-owned Russian banks. In September, additional industries and banks were added. Russia soon retaliated with sanctions of its own, listing U.S. and other foreign nationals banned from travel to Russia and cutting off Russian food imports from the EU and the United States. Highly visible American companies such as McDonald's were harassed, with little impact. In mid-2015, existing sanctions were renewed for six months, with additional renewals to follow as efforts to reach and then implement a more comprehensive solution stalled.

Although Russian authorities maintained a brave face in the light of growing sanctions and reminded the world that its considerable rainy-day reserves, accumulated during the economic recovery after 2008 and a period of high world oil prices, would permit it to avoid any serious pain for at least 18 months, it was soon apparent that problems would lie ahead if no political settlement were reached to end or reduce sanctions. In October 2014, the International Monetary Fund (IMF) halved its projection of Russian economic growth in 2015 to 0.5 percent, and direct foreign investment virtually disappeared. Despite efforts of the Russian central bank to shore up the ruble, it lost 20 percent of its value as uncertainty about Russia's economic future worsened.[19]

Additional costs of Russia's actions soon became apparent. The already rapidly growing defense budget was slated to increase in line with Russia's greater activism. In 2015, it stood at 3.4 percent of GDP, close to the U.S. level of 3.6 percent of GDP, although the total gross expenditure was far lower because of the smaller Russian economy (US$81 billion, as opposed to $582 billion). Moscow's new commitment to absorbing Crimea also proved costly. Anxious to demonstrate that annexation was economically good for the region and to tie the local economy to that of the new motherland, authorities committed large sums to infrastructure and other improvements, sometimes canceling planned investments in other regions.

Moscow sought to reduce the impact of sanctions by expanding trade with other nations. Most significant was the US$400 billion agreement with China to send Russian natural gas eastward. On the bright side, Moscow now had an alternative market for its critically important energy exports in the face of European efforts to find alternative suppliers in the West, and Beijing was willing to advance funds for the construction of the needed pipelines and pumping facilities. The good news was temporary at best; the spreading global economic downturn in 2015 and beyond led to postponement or cancellation of many of these projects. Russian reverse sanctions also affected the European economy. Putin banned food imports from the EU, and other aspects of what had been a US$400 billion a year exchange flagged. Sanctions hit hardest at Germany, whose economic growth had begun to sputter even before the Crimean and Ukrainian crises.[20]

In September 2014, the Minsk I agreement attempted to broker a military disengagement and political settlement. It provided for a cease-fire in eastern Ukraine, withdrawal of all forces to established boundaries, amendments to the Ukrainian constitution to provide a poorly defined degree of autonomy for the rebel-held areas of eastern Ukraine and new local elections, and the restoration of Kiev's control over the border, including the critically important demarcation line with Russia. Not surprisingly, it proved difficult to implement many of these arrangements. Conflict slowly scaled down but never completely ended, stoked by Moscow's interest in keeping a hand in the game, Kiev's interest in using the conflict as a rallying point for the unstable coalition that emerged from the post-Maidan election and its refusal to amend the constitution to provide for greater autonomy in the east and the unwillingness of both Ukrainian and Russian separatist forces to lay down their arms at Kiev's and Moscow's command. Economic sanctions were renewed on both sides. Moscow and the West hardened their positions in light of their reading of the other side's intentions. The West strengthened NATO, professing increased fear of a Russian military threat against territories of the former Soviet Union; Moscow averred that the action proved Western hostility toward Russia. Both sides spoke of a new cold war, each blaming the other for the chill.

Minsk II, penned in February 2015, picked up where Minsk I left off. Many of the old issues had to be revisited. Once again, a withdrawal of military forces and heavy weapons was agreed to, this time with more complete but not perfect implementation on both sides. Amendments to the Ukrainian constitution granting autonomy to rebel areas and new local elections were promised, but little was accomplished on the ground. Moscow was eager to achieve some resolution to the remaining issues, in part to end the sanctions and in part to remove an important obstacle to the broader diplomatic role it wished to play in Syria and elsewhere. While increasingly suspicious of Russia's intentions toward the other nations of Eastern Europe, the West seemed willing to accept some diplomatic compromise that would move what everyone regarded to be a fait accompli to a back burner. Some hint of a possible compromise emerged early in 2016 when U.S. assistant secretary of state Victoria Nuland met privately with Vladislav Surkov, a Kremlin troubleshooter close to Putin. Surkov's assertion that the two had been "brainstorming" for a solution seemed hopeful, as did the announcement that Prime Minister Medvedev and not foreign minister Lavrov would head the Russian delegation to the upcoming annual security conference in Munich, a venue at which Moscow had launched initiatives in the past. Hopes were abandoned, at least temporarily, when Medvedev took a hard line at the meeting, indicating either that his presence was intended to underscore uniformity within the Kremlin or that a sincere trial balloon had been shot down by opponents. In any event, the deadlock continued, and a Minsk III conference could not be ruled out.

Russian Foreign Policy and the World

While Russian foreign policy was dominated by its deteriorating relations with the United States and events in Ukraine, the hardening tone of Moscow's diplomacy also touched its relations with other nations. Russia intensified its efforts to be and, perhaps more important, to be *thought* to be a global power. Increasingly vocal criticism of a "unipolar" or "hegemonic" world—clear slaps at American power and interventionism—met receptive ears in other parts of the world. Moscow also increasingly added the argument that perhaps Western political, cultural, and economic models might not be as universally applicable as once believed. If Russia could assert its own unique path into the modern world, why could not others, especially if these unique and distinct paths pulled them away from the West? Moscow began to use its own version of "soft power"—a term that entered into the discourse of Russian diplomats and scholars—as a counterpoint to the West's alleged cultural, economic, and political superiority.

In Latin America, Russian diplomatic initiatives focused on traditional allies like Cuba, Nicaragua, and Venezuela, which shared Moscow's anti-American views. Brazil and Peru also received renewed attention, more for economic than diplomatic reasons. Russian relations with African nations were far less clearly motivated. Medvedev had visited South Africa, the region's major economic power, but little came of it in terms of trade or closer diplomatic ties. Moscow's haphazard ties with the continent seemed motivated more by attempts to counter China's increasing economic and diplomatic presence. New overtures toward India and Vietnam were intended both to shore up relations with old allies and to counter China's expanding role.

In the Middle East, the fallout of the Arab Spring challenged Russia's traditional role. The U.S. presence in Afghanistan and Iraq closed out Russian influence. The failed democratic revolution in Egypt left the pro-Western military once again in power, although Cairo's relations with the United States had been badly bruised. Western intervention in Libya toppled Muammar Gaddafi, leaving Moscow once again to argue against growing Western power in the region. Turkey increasingly took its own course that put it at odds with both U.S. and NATO policy but did nothing to bring it any closer to Moscow. When revolution turned to bloody civil war in Syria, Russia cast its lot with its only remaining friend in the region, Bashir al-Assad. Ties between the two nations were close, and the Russian navy maintained a small repair and refueling station at Tartus. Diplomatically, Russia sided with Syria in the face of increasing condemnation of Assad's brutal pursuit of the rebels, and used its veto in the Security Council to block UN action. Moscow scored a diplomatic victory in brokering an agreement for the destruction of Assad's chemical weapons stockpile and is involved in so-far unsuccessful efforts to find a way to end the conflict.[21]

Moscow's interest in playing a greater role in the Middle East was motivated by more than just concern for its long-standing ties to Syria. In the face of continuing deadlocked attempts to broker a peace with Ukraine that would end economic sanctions, Moscow hoped eventually to earn grudging approval from the West by creating the military and diplomatic preconditions for a negotiated settlement in Syria, although the short-term impact would be to escalate the hostilities. A dramatic reassertion of its global role also would deflect attention at home from the worsening economy. Putin had begun to increase military shipments to the Assad government as early as 2012, which he expanded in the summer of 2015. Moscow enlarged its existing naval base at Tartus and created a large airbase at Latakia capable of handling both Russian fighters and Antonov cargo aircraft.

Moscow initially maintained the transparent fiction that its actions were intended to fight ISIS-related and other terrorist elements, although its actions targeted primarily non-ISIS opposition forces that had been at war with Assad's regime since the failure of the Arab Spring. Russian involvement increased markedly after a formal request for aid from the regime at the end of September 2015.

Talks began between U.S. and Russian diplomats to reduce the chances of accidental but potentially dangerous encounters between U.S. and Russian aircraft operating in the skies over Syria and soon involved other nations with varying levels of involvement in the conflict. In the broader context, long-standing UN-sponsored talks in Geneva continued to discuss the possibility of a cease-fire and an eventual political settlement. Diplomatically, the major sticking point was the future status of the Assad government after hostilities ended, with the dictator insisting that he must continue to play a role in any postwar government. Moscow initially seemed to support his assertion but gradually backed away from its once-firm commitment. Although Moscow's public support of Assad remained firm, it made no secret in private contacts with Western diplomats that the matter was negotiable. In late 2015, the head of Russian military intelligence, Igor Sergun, secretly delivered a message from Putin saying that Assad should be prepared to step aside; frustrated with its vehement rejection, Moscow publicly revealed the communication in January 2016, noting that granting Assad asylum would be "easy" but that it was "premature" to discuss the matter now.

The Three Arenas of Russian Politics

As noted earlier, post-communist Russian politics plays out in three different but interconnected arenas. The first lies within the Garden Ring and comprises the insiders' world of competing factions. The second lies outside the Garden Ring, composed of the broader realities of Russian society, in part transformed by the events beginning with Gorbachev's first attempts to reform the old soviet order and in part shaped by the continuing realities of Russian history and culture that dictate the evolution of democracy in the Russian Federation after 1991. The third lies in the mechanisms that connect the two arenas: parties, civil society, and the media.

Inside the Garden Ring: Factional Politics in Putin II

Although the post-2012 world of factional politics has grown more complex, two realities remain. The first is the shifting nature of factional composition and alliances. Factions form and re-form along lines of institutional identity, philosophical or policy orientations, individual leaders, and short- or long-term advantage. Although the game is now more complex because of the increasing number of institutional players and stakeholders and because of the possible emergence of divisive zero-sum confrontations in hard times, the overall goal remains the same: to work out an acceptable division of power and resources without permitting any fundamental change in the essential nature of the inside-the-Garden-Ring game itself.

The second reality concerns the ways in which accommodations are reached. In the absence of a self-correcting mechanism in which all major players place mutual and self-limiting accommodation above the maximization of factional gain, the role of a balancer is essential to the survival of the system and the long-term interest of all players. Stated more simply, someone or something needs to keep the balance of power within acceptable boundaries. In the old communist system from the 1950s onward, that role fell to the general secretary, with Khrushchev eventually losing control of the game and Brezhnev playing it masterfully. Since 1993, it has fallen to the president. Yeltsin sometimes succeeded and more often failed, and Putin has placed the mastery of the game at the center of Russian political life.

But the game is changing constantly. The factional identities and alliances described in earlier chapters have morphed into new alignments, not completely different but not exactly the same. Richard Sakwa, whose writings over the past two decades have offered the best picture of factional politics, now speaks of the emergence of "two broad constellations."[22] The first group, collectively named the "liberals," is composed of the surviving and regrouping elements of the old pre-2008 balance. Returning to the presidency in 2012, Putin increasingly distanced himself from this element and drew closer to an inner core of advisors usually referred to as the *siloviki*, former associates with current or past careers in the KGB or its post-soviet successors, the military, and internal security forces. Other factions whose roles had defined the first Putin administration such as the democratic statists (closely identified with Putin) or the liberals (associated with Medvedev) lost ground but were not completely defeated. The survival of key individuals such as Medvedev, whose quick dismissal was predicted by many who saw him as an easy and symbolic example of Putin's reassertion of control, or the dismissal and quick return to an important position of Surkov, who was blamed for the debacle of the 2011 Duma elections, confirm the importance of maintaining a visible and symbolic balance of factional interests.

Sakwa labels the second group the "traditionalists," composed of newly created nationalist groups, the more extreme pre-2012 nationalists who had been kept on the sidelines, elements of the still internally divided *siloviki*, and the economic statists who advocate greater state ownership and control of the economy. Already drawing close to the *siloviki* inner core,

Putin soon became even more closely identified with greater control over the economy, an increasingly traditional and nationalist interpretation of Russia's cultural identity, and an increasingly aggressive reassertion of Russia's role in the world.

Other more complex delineations of Kremlin factions exist, each offering its own insight into the details of the confrontation. Konstantin Gaaze, a Russian commentator writing in *Vedomosti* in March 2012 described three major factions centered around institutional and/or philosophical points of reference.[23] First is the "liberal technical" faction, centered on Deputy Prime Minister Shuvalov and backed by the Ministries of Finance and Economic Development. They are the "post-Medvedev modernizers" and technocrats who favor privatization and market-oriented reforms instead of greater government control. They are philosophically close to the former finance minister Kudrin, ousted by Medvedev and widely seen as a possible future prime minister should Putin decide to move to the political and economic center. The second faction is labeled the "statist group," which opposes further privatization and favors expanded state ownership and control. Their views are close to Putin's current economic priorities and are echoed by Sergei Ivanov, Putin's chief of staff. Third is the "anti-Western" faction, combining those who reject Western economic and social models and advocate a return to the state capitalist model, greater emphasis on defense-related industries, and a more assertive foreign policy. Their most prominent advocates are Dmitry Rogozin, the deputy prime minister with primary responsibility for the defense sectors, and Sergei Shoigu, the defense minister with close ties to Putin. Putin's role in this threefold factional universe remains that of balancer among contending groups.

The most complex delineation of Russian political factions has been offered by Evgeny Minchenko, whose analysis is based on interviews with over sixty members of the political and business elites shortly after the 2011 Duma and 2012 presidential elections.[24] In institutional terms, the increasing role of the executive office of the president is seen as key to the expansion of Putin's control. Rapidly growing to over 1,600 specialists and advisors dealing with all aspects of policy, it now is capable of competing with the formal ministries, most of which are ostensibly under Medvedev's control as prime minister. Many of its top officials held cabinet-level posts while Putin served as prime minister and transferred to the presidential staff after the 2012 election. Adding to the growing power of the presidency has been the creation of special presidential commissions in key areas such as energy or defense, a move defended as necessary because of the interagency significance of broad policy issues and the growing fragmentation of the earlier alignment of Kremlin factions.

Minchenko avers that the highest echelons of the leadership are analogous to the structure and function of the former soviet-era Politburo, which by the end of the Brezhnev era had become a microcosm of the soviet establishment. He argues that "Russian power is a conglomerate of clans and groups that compete with one another over resources." But unlike the Politburo, they never meet as a policy-making body, and the members' formal position in government or the business community is not the sole determinant of their real power. Four "circles" exist, each broadly dealing with foreign and defense policy and internal security, domestic politics, technical and administrative issues, and the business community. Within this structure, there is no single hierarchical chain of command. Minchenko terms the often-cited power vertical as "just a propaganda cliché." Within this arrangement, Putin's role is that of an "arbiter and moderator, but a powerful arbiter who has the last word (at least for the time being) in conflict situations."

Shortly after the presidential election, the "full members"—the old term for the true inner circle—included Medvedev, once again prime minister but significantly reduced in power and whose continued presence was necessary to counterbalance more conservative and nationalist forces and to offer reassurance to the modernizers and private-sector interests that they would not be shut out despite the general movement toward increasing the role of the state; Ivanov, a member of the *siloviki* faction and Putin's chief of staff; Igor Sechin, also with strong ties to the *siloviki* and transferred from government service to head Rosneft, a major energy producer; Sergei Chemezov, initially the dominant figure in the military industrial complex, although he quickly lost ground to the rapidly advancing Rogozin and Shoigu; and Gennady Timchenko and Yuri Kovalchuk, businessmen connected with the energy sector and with ties back to the Ozera group, Putin's initial circle of business partners in Leningrad, seen as a possible foil to Sechin and Rosneft. Also within the inner circle is Sergei Sobyanin, current mayor of Moscow with important ties to the Urals, and a potential prime minister. Last within the inner circle is Vyacheslav Volodin, seen as Putin's chief political advisor tasked with securing the president's control over political affairs both inside and outside the Garden Ring and correcting what were widely seen as the errors of his predecessor, Surkov, whose abrupt but short-lived dismissal in 2013 was revised only months later in his return to a lower-level position on the presidential staff.

Lower echelons, termed "candidate members of the Politburo" by Minchenko, are divided into functionally specific groups. The "technical bloc" contains experts in the economy, foreign affairs (foreign minister Lavrov), the media (presidential press secretary Dmitry Peskov), and regional issues and the "near abroad," that is, the former soviet republics. The "political bloc" is divided into its "liberal" wing (Kudrin, former finance minister; Anatoly Chubais, former advisor to Gorbachev and Yeltsin; and Alexander Voloshin) and its "conservative" wing (Patriarch Kirill and including tolerated opposition leaders such as Prokhorov, who unsuccessfully challenged Putin in 2012, and Vladimir Zhirinovsky, erratic leader of the Liberal Democratic Party; Gennady Zyuganov, head of the Communist Party; and Sergei Mironov, head of Just Russia). The "business bloc" is composed of Putin's associates from the Ozera group and prominent second- or third-generation oligarchs such as Vladimir Potanin and Oleg Deripaska. The last group is the "security bloc," largely made up of *siloviki,* military, and police elements, although the group itself is far from unified in terms of career patterns and institutional roles.

Minchenko describes the entire arrangement as an "unstable equilibrium," affected by shifting institutional alignments, the fate of individual players, and the changing policy agenda. The details of the late 2012 balance that emerged from his interviews undoubtedly has changed in light of Putin's growing assertiveness and the increasing importance of Moscow's actions in Crimea, Ukraine, vis-à-vis the West, and the growing threat of an economic downturn. But the overall factional game most likely remains essentially the same, now increasingly complex as the factions proliferate and the stakes of the game increase.

A year after the Russian annexation of Crimea, Minchenko issued a revised version of his assessment. His earlier interpretation described the distribution of power in terms of "a bipolar coordinate system with two poles of elite attraction (Igor Sechin, the leader of the siloviki government hardliners, and Dmitry Medvedev, the leader of the system liberals)." He continues, "due to significant weakening of the liberal authorities, it is more appropriate to use a sectoral chart."

That "sectoral chart" revises and expands his earlier notion of the "circles" of policy and authority.[25] Now included in this more complex portrayal are sectors labeled (1) domestic politics (Ivanov, head of the presidential executive office; Volodin, first deputy head of the presidential executive office; Sergei Naryshkin, speaker of the Duma; Valentina Matvienko, speaker of the Federation Council; Sobyanin, mayor of Moscow; Ramzan Kadyrov, president of Chechnya; and Rustam Minnikhanov, head of Tatarstan); (2) social policy, including ideology and religion (primarily Medvedev, prime minister, with diminished authority over this less-than-critical policy arena, and lower-level government officials); (3) finance (Shuvalov, deputy prime minister; Elvira Nabiullina, head of the central bank; German Gref, head of Sberbank; Chubais, head of Rusnano, and others); (4) infrastructure projects (Timchenko, head of the Gunvor group, which reputedly administers the private wealth of many within the inner circle, including Putin; Kovalchuk, largest shareholder in Rossiia Bank; Arkady Rotenberg, SMP Bank; Vladimir Yakunin, head of Russian Railways until his resignation in 2016); (5) energy and metallurgy (Sechin, Rosneft; Viktor Zubkov and Arkady Miller, Gazprom; Vagit Alekparov, Olig Derepaska, Viktor Vekselbert, Roman Abramovich, Alisher Usmanov, and Vladimir Potanin, all oligarchs with holdings in energy and metallurgy); (6) foreign policy (Lavrov, foreign minister; Yuri Ushakov, top foreign policy advisor; Surkov, foreign policy advisor; Sechin, Rosneft); (7) defense policy (Shoigu, defense minister; Rogozin, deputy prime minister in charge of military and defense industries; Ivanov, head of the presidential executive office); and (8) internal security and courts (Alexander Bortnikov, head of the Federal Security Service; Yuri Chaika, procurator general; Alexander Bastrykin, head of the Investigative Committee; Nikolai Patrushev, secretary to the Security Council; and others). Several individuals hold membership in a number of related sectors, giving them greater influence and usually signaling a close association with Putin.

In addition to his role as mediator, Putin exercises close supervision over the sectors dealing with energy, foreign and defense policy, and law enforcement. On these key issues there is considerable evidence that the circle of advisors is limited to a core of Putin's closest associates linked to current or past *siloviki* and business interests. In contrast, Medvedev's portfolio is now limited to the less important sector dealing with social policy. His acceptance of that seeming demotion probably explains his continued survival as prime minister, coupled with the likelihood that Putin finds it tactically wise to keep some vestiges of the reformers in place as a symbolic counterweight to the now-ascendant hardliners.

Putin also seems to have expanded his efforts to develop a de facto system of checks and balances by creating competing pairings within important sectors. Within the economic sector, Sechin and Timchenko are viewed as competitors, as are an even larger group of oligarchs. Within law enforcement, Bastrykin and Chaika are paired, as are Patrushev and Bortnkov. Similar competitive pairings are present in most other sectors.

A Note on the *Siloviki*

As a reference to a specific faction within Kremlin politics, the term *siloviki* often is helpful in our analysis. Broadly regarded as including a wide assortment of party and government officials dealing with domestic and international security issues, it historically finds its institutional roots in the soviet-era KGB (which then dealt with domestic and international security and intelligence matters, the former in its downtown office on Lubyanka Square and the latter in its modern office building on the outskirts of the city), the military and its own military intelligence agency (known as the GRU), the civilian police operating through the Ministry of Internal Affairs, the intelligence branch of the foreign ministry, and a host of more specialized agencies, some operating openly, some clandestinely. Hardcore *siloviki* undoubtedly prefer the narrower interpretation linked to the mystique of the KGB, while others in related activities prefer the broader umbrella.[26]

That said, the all-inclusive term still remains useful in identifying a mindset rather than a specific institutionalized locus of power. Whatever their institutional differences, the *siloviki,* broadly defined, see themselves as "the sword and the shield" of whatever Russia has called itself over the past century. Precisely what that means at any given moment has been controversial. And merely internalizing that special role cannot obliterate all other elements of one's institutional and personal identity. But it does suggest a common mindset that embodies a sense of historical national identity and destiny, a strong sense of patriotism frequently extending to exceptionalism, a demand for respect in the international community, a preference for order and discipline, and an intolerance of dissent and pluralism at home.

A commonly held but differently nuanced mindset tells us only a part of the story. In the day-to-day world inside the Garden Ring, a plethora of other factors figure into the identities, preferences, and alliances of the *siloviki.* Certainly institutional identity plays a role, both in shaping its own particular version of the common mindset and in stoking conflicts among diverse players over critically important issues such as budgets, jurisdictional disputes, and the agency's place in the institutional pecking order. Generational issues or the presence of cohort groups figure in as well, especially in times of rapid change, and always present are the networks of friendships and tactical alliances that permeate any bureaucracy.

At the core of the *siloviki* has always been the former Committee for State Security, or KGB, tracing its roots back to the Cheka created by Felix Dzerzhinsky immediately after the Bolshevik seizure of power. Yuri Andropov, a future Communist Party general secretary after Brezhnev's death, served as its director from 1969 to 1982 and is widely credited with professionalizing its ranks and diversifying its recruitment of a broader spectrum of the nation. After the fall of communism, the KGB was split into two primary jurisdictions, the Federal Security Service (FSB in Russian), which deals with domestic affairs, and the Foreign Intelligence Service, which focuses on international affairs and clandestine operations abroad. Still kindred spirits, both have witnessed rivalries between themselves and with other elements of the *siloviki,* sometimes so severe and open that Russian commentators began to refer openly to the "*siloviki* wars" while Yeltsin was in office.

The military establishment, also a key element of the broader notion of the *siloviki,* also is beset by its own factional enemies and internal divisions. Although Putin was careful to maintain civilian control at the top of the chain of command, his most recent appointments as minister of defense were hardly to the uniformed military's liking. One was Anatoly Serdyukov, whose past accomplishments included a successful career in the furniture industry and a stint as the director of the internal revenue service. As a successful bean counter, he was tasked with cutting through the fog of corruption in the military, which he did until he was himself brought up on similar charges. His replacement was Shoigu, another civilian who had proved himself an adept manager of the federal emergency response ministry and governor of the Moscow province (not the city itself).

The national police force, formally under the control of the Ministry of the Interior, also fits within a looser definition of *siloviki.* The target of largely unsuccessful reforms during Medvedev's presidency, it has lost ground to the newly created Investigative Committee, aggressively headed by Bastrykin, a graduate of the St. Petersburg University law school and reputedly close to Putin. Usually compared with the U.S. FBI, it has focused on the suppression of political opposition and some high-profile corruption cases. Its creation in 2011 was seen as providing a counterweight to the

FSB and the Ministry of the Interior. An earlier effort in 2002 to counter-balance the KGB and the Ministry of the Interior through the creation of a Federal Drug Control Service was far less successful; it ended up on the losing side of the *siloviki* wars and has slipped into relative obscurity. The most recent addition is the National Guard, headed by Viktor Zolotov, a close associate of Putin, and seemingly tasked with a quick response to any civil or political unrest. Created in 2016, it is seen as a sort of praetorian guard to be used against widespread uprisings or the much-feared "color revolutions."

Outside the Garden Ring: Politics in the Rest of the Russian Federation

There is, and always has been, another Russia—the one outside Moscow's Garden Ring. Controlling it and mobilizing its resources have always been a dilemma for central authorities. In the soviet era, the presence of a ubiquitous Communist Party and the omnipotence of an invasive and repressive state gave Moscow the control it needed. In the post-communist period, the task became more complicated but not less important. Two elements are involved. The first is the conventional problem of control, and the answer eventually given after the chaotic years of the Yeltsin era was very traditional and predictable: The state would reassert some, but not all, of its powers over the regions, the political process, the economy, and the individual citizens themselves. For those within the Garden Ring, it was an act of empowerment—or re-empowerment—that at least partially restored the center's influence. For those outside the Garden Ring, it was a mixed blessing, celebrated in part because it restored the sense of order that had slipped away after 1985 and eventually lamented in part because it diminished or at least redefined their role as citizens in a fledgling democracy.

The second element of the new relationship is about connection, not control. Even in an imperfect democracy, the two needed somehow to "connect"—to talk to one another and establish a common political vocabulary, to create political institutions such as parties and a civil society that somehow would link the two, to jointly participate in an electoral process that could be manipulated but not ignored, and to create a new class of stakeholders who had a vested interest in the success and stability of the new order.

Dealing with the first task—establishing control beyond the Garden Ring—involved both the resurrection of conventional mechanisms that strengthened the government's influence over political and economic life and the creation of a new "political formula" that redefined and justified the new order of things. The first was about the nuts and bolts of an increasingly authoritarian government—tightening control over the electoral process, political parties, the media, the courts, civil society, and the selective repression of individual opponents. The second was more ambitious and in the long run probably more important. It involved the creation of a new political formula that was meant to define and justify a broader political reality. Like Lenin's "new economic policy," Stalin's "socialism in one county," or Brezhnev's "developed socialism," it was meant to define and inspire in ways that justified the creation of an increasingly repressive and nationalist regime and that reinterpreted the sense of modernity it promised to deliver.

The second part of the task—creating a new class of stakeholders—can be risky business for those who want to lead a nation. Having a stake in something is a double-edged sword. You identify with it and grant those who lead it some degree of latitude to fulfill its promise. But you also expect something from it—in this case, the order, prosperity, respect, and pride associated with the visionary promise, all within the boundaries of a loosely defined democracy that still gives you some role in determining the outcome. It doesn't have to fulfill all that it promised, at least in the short run, but it needs to fulfill enough of its promises so that you continue to identify with it. And it doesn't need to be perfectly democratic, especially for those with whom you disagree, but it better not shut you out or marginalize those whom you support.

The Authoritarian Modernizer Revisited

A central theme in our analysis of post-communist Russia has been the transformative role of authoritarian modernizers who rejected the Leninist model and sought to substitute their own post-communist interpretation of modernity. As with many nations undertaking such transformations, the meaning of *modern* changed over time. Whatever their differences, Gorbachev and Yeltsin shared roughly similar visions of a future built around the notions of democracy, the creation of a market economy, and the integration of Russia economically and culturally into an increasingly globalized world. Putin has substantially altered but not completely rejected that vision of the future, creating an alternative, idiosyncratic, and more distinctively Russian version of modernity that lies at the core of his political formula since his return to the presidency in 2012. There is nothing particularly unique in this change of focus. On their way to a future they initially borrowed from others, many nations rediscover desirable and perhaps inescapable elements of their past. This is especially true as leadership passes from the hands of those who first rejected that past into the hands of a second or third generation of leaders who must cope with the disorder of half-transformed institutions and societies. Authoritarian modernizers morph into modernizing nationalists, with the notions of "authoritarian," "modern," and "nationalist" transformed by the needs of the leadership (and perhaps a single dominant leader), the nature of the society now caught between a redefined future and a rediscovered past, and the nation's place in the world.

The nature of that redefinition in post-2012 Russia is predictable and brutal. The predictable elements should surprise no one with a perspective on Russian history—the return of more authoritarian leadership couched within the survival of altered but still formally democratic institutions; the increasing role of a single dominant leader who has defined a new political formula and created a modern version of a cult of the personality; the rediscovery of a sense of Russian identity, combining European and Asian elements into a new sense of Eurasianism, cultural superiority, manifest destiny, and exceptionalism; the return to a more traditional economic model that maintains its reliance on energy exports and accepts an increasing role of government influence and control, albeit still far short of a return to public ownership and central planning; and a more assertive role for Russia on the international stage, short of a new cold war but aggressive within what it regards as a legitimate Russian sphere of influence. The brutal elements also should come as no surprise—increasing manipulation of what remains of the democratic process; the suppression of dissent; increasing control over the media and civil society; the growing rejection of diversity and pluralism, spurred on by the leadership but also deeply rooted in traditional Russian culture; a sense of victimization at the hands of the West, as a consequence of both the breakup of the Soviet Union and Western economic and cultural penetration of Russian society; and the increasing assertiveness and militarization of foreign policy.

Although the emergence of the post-2012 political formula and the redefinition of modernity have broad implications for all aspects of Russian politics, they are particularly important for our understanding of the regime's impact on what happens outside the Garden Ring. In many ways, Putin is attempting to change the nature of the way in which the two spheres interact. The formal democratic institutions will remain intact and continue to have the final say in the choice of future presidents and legislatures, but the game has changed. The new political formula that reasserts traditional priorities in foreign and domestic policy effectively reaches out to a broad and more sympathetic constituency beyond the Garden Ring. Whatever its undeniable faults and excesses, Putin's persona, coupled with the role of being a modernizing nationalist, strikes a responsive chord in much of the population. Already material stakeholders in the growing prosperity of Putin's first two terms in office, they are increasingly symbolic and emotional stakeholders in the new but still recognizable Russia that he now promises. But there are risks. Economic failures can erode citizen identification with a regime that had, at least for a while, improved the standard of living and implicitly promised continuing good times. Less tangible emotional and symbolic stakes in a renewed and respected Russian state also can erode without continuing proof of the nation's successes both at home and abroad, perhaps tempting the leadership to engage in ever more extreme efforts to assert the uniqueness of the Russian experience or to venture into more dangerous confrontations with the West and the former soviet states.

The Legal System and the Courts

As noted earlier, a major element of the post-2012 political formula was the growing power of the state. Although that idea had always been a part of the etatism (statism) of the power vertical and a strong presidency, it was institutionalized more invasively as Putin returned to power. The mechanisms that connected those inside and those outside the Garden Ring—political parties, the electoral process at the local and regional levels, civil society, and the media—were increasingly brought under government control. For the most part, the regime has pursued an orchestrated program of tightened controls sometimes followed by token concessions in the face of domestic or international opposition—a sort of stick-and-carrot approach, with the stick always larger and the carrot always smaller at the end of the day.

Changes in the legal system are a good illustration. Never strong even in the most hopeful days of democratic reforms, the courts and the legal system had been somewhat improved, especially during Medvedev's brief tenure. Even before 2012, they had once again begun to fall under the sway of "telephone justice" in which the authorities dictated who would be prosecuted and found guilty, usually as a warning to others. Mikhail Khodorkhovsky, critics such as Alexei Navalny and Sergei Udaltsov, and groups like Pussy Riot had all been victims of Putin's initial efforts to establish boundaries. But things got worse after 2012, at least for some. Longtime critics like Navalny and Udaltsov were more harshly treated and indicted on what were widely regarded as trumped-up charges, although the former was granted a brief respite to run a highly visible but always doomed campaign to become mayor of Moscow. At times, the authorities also showed their version of leniency. Khodorkhovsky was released from prison and permitted to leave the country in December 2013, and the members of Pussy Riot were also released, albeit under close surveillance. But in 2014, Vladimir Yevtushenkov, another oligarch, was placed under investigation, a move widely interpreted as a warning to others. In late February 2015, Boris Nemtsov, another prominent critic, was assassinated near the Kremlin, with Putin credited with ordering the killing or at the least having created an atmosphere in which reactionary forces acted without his formal instruction.[27]

Institutional changes in the legal system also strengthened the government's hand. The Supreme Arbitration Court, a survival from the soviet era that dealt with business-related and contract disputes, was abolished. Widely held as fair and even-handed, it saw its functions transferred to an enlarged Supreme Court more easily controlled by the authorities. Medvedev's efforts to professionalize the police and the legal profession also languished, and earlier reforms have failed to make significant changes.[28] The creation of a powerful Investigative Committee—a sort of Russian FBI—shifted important elements of prosecutorial power from the Procuracy to an aggressive body that now takes the lead in politically sensitive actions against political opponents and those accused of economic crimes, a catch-all category that often includes real or potential opponents as well as corrupt officials.[29] More ominously, military units once under the control of the Ministry of the Interior are now reconstituted as a new National Guard, under the command of Viktor Zolotov, the former head of Putin's private security team and a long-term associate from St. Petersburg.[30]

More draconian control of opposition activity also has marked the second Putin administration. Concerned that the demonstrations that followed the Duma elections in late 2011 signaled the possibility of a spontaneous public uprising similar to that of the Ukrainian orange revolution or the Georgian rose revolution, the regime tightened controls over public gatherings. Fines for individual participation were raised in the summer of 2012, and higher fines were levied against individuals or groups that organized such actions or repeat offenders. For the most part, the new laws harkened back to soviet-era charges of "hooliganism" or the destruction of public property. Nongovernmental organizations (NGOs) that received foreign funding were required to register as foreign agents; many simply chose to go out of business, and those that fought the new regulations or actually complied in the hope of continuing to operate faced increasing harassment by the government and patriotic organizations.

At first, some of the regime's critics tried to fight back, forming an Opposition Coordination Council shortly after Putin's return to power. Never an action-oriented group in its own right, it sought to bring disparate opposition groups and prominent individuals into better contact with one another. Even these modest efforts failed, and the council dissolved in October 2013.[31]

The upsurge of Russian patriotism made it even harder for dissidents to get their point across. Much of the dissident community saw the handwriting on the wall and fell silent. The government kept up the pressure against key figures such as Navalny or Uldaltsov, NGOs with foreign ties, and—as a relatively new target—cultural figures in the literary or artistic community and other members of the intelligentsia and academic community who thus far had walked the tightrope between acceptable commentary and opposition. Now the always-fuzzy line was shifting to the right, and it was harder to keep one's balance.[32]

Connecting Those Inside and Outside the Garden Ring

Politics on both sides of the Garden Ring are connected. In viable democracies, that connection is a two-way street that permits power and influence to flow in both directions. The institutional forms may vary, but they almost always include a viable party system, supported by widely accepted electoral systems that permit free and openly contested elections; a civil society in which NGOs and associations organize and broker various interests and serve as a bridge between private and public life; a reasonably free and pluralistic media, although some elements may be identified with

partisan interests; and, perhaps as a final resort, the possibility of spontaneous social action in opposition to widely disputed election results or
government policy. To be sure, no democracy is perfect. The playing field
never is completely level. That said, it is still possible to assess the rough
balance of these elements. Clearly from the Gorbachev era onward, that
balance initially shifted from the so-called transmission belts of total
Communist Party dominance to a more pluralistic and open system. Even
in Putin's first two terms as president, from 2000 to 2008, that openness
survived at least partially in the face of a strengthened state and the power
vertical. Putin's return to the presidency in 2012 has witnessed a reversal
of that relationship.

Political Parties

Continuing a policy dating from the early days of democratic reform, Putin
has continued to distance himself from formal party alignments. From
2008 to 2012, he formally served as the head of United Russia while holding
the office of prime minister. In the run-up to the 2012 presidential race, in
May 2011, he presided over the creation of the All-Russia Popular Front,
officially a nonparty coalition of existing parties and social organizations
that backed his policies and would emerge as the centerpiece of his bid for
reelection in 2012, especially after United Russia's losses in the 2011 Duma
elections. It has continued to meet periodically after his return to office to
endorse his policies and create an aura of broad public support and has
opened a small number of regional offices outside Moscow. It has not,
however, made any effort to nominate candidates of its own for regional or
local elections or to endorse the candidates of other more conventional
parties. It will most likely continue in this diminished role until the run-up
to the 2018 presidential elections, possibly reemerging as a broad pro-Putin
coalition if he chooses to run or shifting to his chosen successor if he
endorses a replacement.[33]

Despite its losses in the 2011 legislative election, United Russia, now
formally headed by Medvedev, has edged closer to being a real party in
power at all but the presidential level. In the December 2011 elections, it
won 238 of the 450 seats in the Duma, down 77 seats from its previous
high. In practical terms, it has been able to garner enough votes from the
other parties to keep a working majority on most issues. It also has
remained in de facto control over the Federation Council, where its

dominance over regional government and legislatures shapes the choice of council members. Its continuing dominance at the regional and local levels remains unchallenged. In the October 2012 regional elections, its candidates won all five governorships at stake and dominated all six regional legislatures up for election. It also did well in most municipal council and mayoralty elections.[34] Two years later, in 2014, its wins were even more impressive. Thirty of the eighty-five regions held gubernatorial elections, including the newly acquired Crimea; United Russia's candidates won in twenty-eight venues, with an independent claiming victory in the Kirov region and a Communist Party candidate winning in Orlov. In the Moscow city council elections, thirty-eight of the forty-five seats went to United Russia, with the Communists claiming five, and the Liberal Democratic Party and the nationalist Rodina party getting one each. Turnout was extremely low, rarely exceeding 40 percent in the regional elections and dropping to 21 percent in Moscow, once the hotbed of anti-Putin sentiment.[35] The real secret to United Russia's strength came not from its growing popularity with the voters but rather from the increasingly blatant manipulation of the nominating process to preemptively exclude serious opposition candidates, who were disqualified for petty clerical errors in their paperwork or through indictment or conviction on trumped-up charges. Although United Russia continues to remain largely outside the factional game of politics inside the Garden Ring, it now plays the single most important role in projecting Moscow's control over what happens in the rest of Russia.

In addition to tighter control over the nominating process, recent changes in electoral procedures have further stacked the deck against the opposition. In 2013, the law on elections to the Duma returned to the earlier format in which 50 percent of the seats will be chosen in single-member districts and 50 percent by proportional representation. The new arrangements increase the likelihood that United Russia would win in single-member-district balloting and that smaller parties would be less likely to gain meaningful representation through proportional representation within the second bloc. The restoration of the popular election of governors was compromised by a new provision that permitted regional legislatures to forego elections and appoint governors from a list of candidates approved by the president; the measure is seen as a hedge against the future possibility that central authorities might lose their de facto control over the nominating process.[36] A year later, similar legislation ended direct election of mayors in most of the major cities.

Under the new provisions, mayors would be selected (and potentially removed) by the members of the city legislatures, themselves selected by the regional legislatures.[37]

Only a small number of other parties are permitted to function at the national level in the gray area between occasional partners and tolerated opposition. Aside from United Russia, only three parties met the cutoff for seats in the initial balloting for the 2011 Duma elections: the Communist Party, with ninety-two seats; Just Russia, with sixty-four; and the Liberal Democratic Party, with fifty-six. Even setting aside the manipulation of elections procedures, none would be likely to win widespread support if Putin or United Russia should stumble. The Communist Party might take advantage of deteriorating economic conditions, but it continues to be led by an unimaginative aging cadre of leaders with limited public appeal. The Liberal Democrats remain as a much-diminished protest party, and Zhirinovsky's erratic leadership sidelines them as an effective opposition. Just Russia, initially created as an opening to moderates and reformers, has limited elite and public appeal. New to the stage, Rogozin's Rodina (Fatherland) party could potentially appeal to conservative and nationalist elements.

From a broader perspective, the number of political parties has fallen precipitously since a brief loosening of registration requirements immediately after the disputed 2011 Duma election. In 2013, the Ministry of Justice, which supervises registration, listed 150 officially accepted parties; by August 2014, the number had fallen to 76, only 63 of which took part in the September regional and local elections. The majority of those excluded fell victim to the politically motivated manipulation of rules that governed record keeping or petition issues.[38]

The 2015 regional elections clearly demonstrated the impact of the regime's efforts to stack the deck in its favor. Preelection filters disqualified many potential opposition candidates. Election officials thwarted the efforts of Navalny's Party of Progress and smaller opposition parties to place candidates on the ballot. PARNAS, another opposition party, was permitted a token victory in getting on the ballot in Kostroma, reversing an earlier ban, but it fell below the 5 percent requirement for participation in the regional legislature. Voting, which took place on September 13, gave United Russia easy victories in the vast majority of elections. It won twenty-one regional governorships, dominated in over 1,300 city races, and ended the day in charge of eleven regional and twenty-five city legislatures.

Civil Society

The creation of an autonomous and politically active civil society has never been an important part of Russian democratization. Gorbachev encouraged the creation of limited nonparty organizations that became the nascent core of a future civil society. But even under the best conditions, most usually confined themselves to economic or social activities, becoming the core of business and professional groups that for the most part avoided confrontation with the authorities. Some, however, took up political issues, leading to the creation of some of the early parties or single-issue groups like *Pamyat* (Memory), which sought to remind the nation of the victims of the purges. Some of the bolder groups established connections with foreign organizations, usually with the benign intent of reaching a broader audience or learning the nuts and bolts of creating a democracy.

That began to change as Putin sought to restore the power of the state. From his perspective, an active civil society presented two potential threats. The first was that a vigorous civil society challenged the concept of etatism that lay at the core of the power vertical. As time went on, an even greater threat allegedly emerged: Western democracies were using such organizations to shape the evolution of Russian democracy, and they and their domestic allies had been at the core of the color revolutions that brought down governments in Ukraine and Georgia.

The real crackdown came shortly after Putin returned to power in 2012, although such groups were harassed even before. In July 2012, a new law required all NGOs that received foreign funding to register as foreign agents, an ominous designation harkening back to the Stalin era. Groups that did not register could be heavily fined or closed down. Registration requirements were made more stringent even for those NGOs that operated without foreign funding, and many were forced to shut down.[39]

The regime also has made limited efforts to create elements within civil society that support the government. These go well beyond the ad hoc pro-government demonstrations that are offered as counterpoints to opposition actions. During Putin's first two terms in office, United Russia formed a youth group named *Nashi* (Ours). Small and always politely vocal in its support, it never really caught on with the younger generation it claimed to represent. During the more hotly contested 2012 presidential election, Putin openly welcomed the support of blue-collar workers loosely organized as a sort of Joe-the-plumber response to growing opposition from middle-class white-collar urbanites and the intelligentsia.

From 2012 onward, the regime shifted to a more subtle long-term strategy focusing on building support among youth, particularly those who have gained little from earlier economic and political reforms. Targeted at largely urban youth, a new group called *Set* (Network) attempts to use the Internet and social media to reach young people who ignore more traditional media. The message is simple: You're not alone, and it's okay to support the government and the president, to be proud of your country, and to be critical of those who oppose the government. An even more insidious program has been termed Putin's "class of 2014." Shortly after the 2012 election, the regime began to recruit a large cadre of young people in their twenties and thirties from poor families in the far-flung provinces, vetting them for loyalty to Putin and bringing them to Moscow to fill low- to middle-level posts in government. Historians quickly compared it to Stalin's creation of the loyal and long-serving "generation of 1939."[40]

Control of the Media

Increasingly invasive controls have been established over all facets of the media. Although formal censorship by the government always looms over the heads of journalists and commentators, harsh controls also come from self-censorship and the ownership of the dominant media. Virtually nothing remains of the cacophonous and open media of the early days of glasnost. Control over the major television channels and the print media by oligarchs occasionally critical of the regime has diminished; the remaining major outlets are in the hands of a new generation of owners more friendly to—or perhaps just more afraid of—the government. The government itself controls a substantial portion of the media, and other elements are held by government-friendly corporations like Gazprom. Self-censorship also undoubtedly plays an important role in defining what reaches the public.

Late in 2013, the government reorganized the media to bring them more closely under control. The main news agency, RIA, which had preserved a degree of independence, was abolished. Its replacement is Russia Today, a government-controlled and highly centralized news agency reaching into all of the broadcast and print media. Named as its director was Dmitry Kiselev, a conservative nationalist with ties to Putin. It soon became apparent that the new official voice of the Kremlin was to function more as a sounding board for government policy than as an independent news agency.[41]

Opposition media were dealt with harshly. Harassed by the government over petty administrative details, they found it difficult to function on a day-to-day basis. Supplies of newsprint or other necessities simply dried up, or technical issues became unresolvable. Reporters were sometimes harassed or beaten, and everyone remembered the 2006 murder of Anna Politkovskaya, a prominent reporter killed because of her aggressive coverage of the war in Chechnya. *Dozhd* (Rain), an opposition television station with a wide following, was virtually silenced early in 2014 when the government put pressure on the major cable networks to pull it from their offerings.

The Internet and other social media also have come under increasing control. Laws passed in 2014 permit the government to shut down websites and compel blogs with over 3,000 subscribers to disclose their ownership and be legally responsible for the accuracy of their content. *Vkontakte* (In Contact), Russia's largest social network, roughly equivalent to Facebook, has come under heavy pressure, and its creator, Pavel Durov, has voluntarily left the country.[42]

The Leadership Cult as a Connection

Russian history is not alone in its dependence on the persona of a dominant leader in shaping a particular era. Russian tsars were "great" or "terrible" or perhaps just "little fathers" to their people, just as post-1917 leaders were revolutionaries like Lenin, autocratic nation builders like Stalin, well-meaning but harebrained reformers like Khrushchev, corporate managers like Brezhnev, vacillating and pedantic reformers like Gorbachev, bold but erratic democrats like Yeltsin, or—and now it gets more difficult to choose the words—authoritarian reformers like Putin. Whatever the label, there always was ambiguity and contradiction.

The fall of communist rule changed the modalities but not the continuing reality of highly personalized leadership. In truth, much of the new political order has directly or indirectly facilitated continued reliance on dominant executive leadership. But there is another side to that coin. Personalization of leadership also implies personalization of responsibility. In parliamentary systems, prime ministers can shuffle cabinets to deflect blame; in presidential systems with a separation of power between the executive and legislative branches, presidents can hope to point the finger at a "do-nothing congress"; and in mixed presidential-parliamentary systems like the Russian Federation, presidents can name new prime ministers to put a fresh face on their administration. But to some degree, Harry Truman's dictum almost always applies there as well: The buck stops at the apex of the executive chain of command. That places an exceptional burden on whoever holds that office, and that burden is enhanced to the degree that leadership is highly personalized. In institutional terms, there is little to mediate or mitigate the direct assessment of presidential performance other than the ability to shape the persona of the leader in ever-changing ways to win public support. Even the manipulation of the electoral process in itself is probably insufficient to guarantee the continued rule of a president who has lost a public mandate, save only in instances in which single-party control is created or the regime feels able to defy widespread and potentially violent public rejection in a sort of Moscow Spring. That could happen, of course, creating several different future authoritarian scenarios (discussed in Chapter 8). But even if it were to occur, sweeping Putin aside either through the loss of a presidential election or through a Moscow Spring-style uprising that led to his resignation, his successor would still need to establish a strong personal sense of connection with the voters, at least in the short term.

Putin as an Authoritarian Modernizer

The assessment of Putin as an authoritarian modernizer brings us full circle back to the original premise of this study—that much of Russian history, and certainly the evolution of authoritarian leadership and the contemporary presidency, are related to the recurring presence of authoritarian modernizers. But that evaluation must begin with several caveats. First, the definitions of both *authoritarian* and *modern* are moving targets; they mean different things at different times and to different leaders, and sometimes they change within the tenure of a single long-term leader. Both are highly situational, defined and redefined by the political realities of the moment, the means at hand to create authoritarian or modernizing institutions, and the international milieu within which they exist.

There is a second caveat that is perhaps even more important. Those who begin as authoritarian modernizers almost always fail to fulfill their original promises about the new and improved nation they hope to create. Perhaps the original vision was hopelessly utopian; perhaps the leaders themselves lacked the skill to implement their program, or internal opposition forced them to make concessions; perhaps the people themselves resisted the changes needed to fully implement the original vision; or per-haps international pressure forced adjustments. Whatever the reason(s), the shortfall forced a painful choice. What is to be done (to borrow from Lenin)? Compromising the hope for a transformational revolution, or eas-ing off efforts to force the pace of change are possibilities. Lenin did just that with the New Economic Policy, but he clearly labeled it as temporary, a "breathing space." But with the "breathing space" for the nation as a whole also came the tightening of institutional controls over the Communist Party and the deepening of the party's domination of society. From 1921 onward, *modern* was postponed but not abandoned under Lenin. A decade later, it was redefined by Stalin into the notions of a centrally planned econ-omy and "socialism in one country." A significant part of that redefinition involved the resurrection of traditional elements of Russian identity and national aspirations under new labels. The new mix was a hybrid of tradi-tional and revolutionary elements, each altered in ways that facilitated the synthesis and made them mutually reinforcing. The unique features of the "new soviet man" preserved the sense of exceptionalism deeply rooted in Russian culture; "socialism in one country" was a new version of Moscow as the third Rome; the pervasive and controlling role of the Communist Party harkened back to the stern but benevolent paternalism of the tsar; and the power of the soviet state reaffirmed Russia's place among the nations of the world. The new was now old, at least in part, and the old was now new.

That brings us to a third caveat. At that critical turning point, author-itarian modernizers frequently turn their attention to the consolidation of their hold on power. To be sure, all successful revolutionaries face this moment: Now that we've got power, how do we hang on to it? But for authoritarian modernizers, this moment of reinterpretation presents unique intellectual and political dilemmas. At the doctrinal level, the rein-terpretation of what the revolution was all about and the fusion of these interpretations with elements of the traditional culture call into question the very legitimacy of the new order. We—the authoritarian modernizers—overthrew the old order and began to force the pace of change because we knew what was best; it had to be done for the sake of the future. But now we're beginning to question that certainty, at first only tactically (as with the New Economic Policy) but eventually more fundamentally. And we're resurrecting, on our terms, certain elements of the traditional culture and authoritarian institutions that were slated for destruction. Black and white fade to gray, and gray is ambiguous.

The political dilemma naturally follows. If our vision were flawed, or even just partially flawed, why are we still in power? And even more important, how do we stay in power, assuming that we are unwilling to confess our errors and retire from public life? Part of the answer flows from the continuing assumption that even an amended vision of the future must be willed into existence; someone must lead, and we're still the key to building a better, if amended, future. Part also stems from the argument that the further transformation of society will be more complex and lengthy than first imagined. We, the modernizers, will need even greater authority to fulfill that extended mandate. That greater power may be institutionalized in many ways: through the *nomenklatura* system that made the Communist Party the controlling core of all other social institutions, through the strengthening of the role of a single leader, or through the strengthening of the state apparatus, known variously as the "dictatorship of the proletariat," the "all-people's state," or the "power vertical." Whatever it was called, it was more than just a cynical mechanism to hang on to power, although that survival instinct was an important, and sometimes seemingly the most important, component.

And it certainly wasn't new. After Stalin, other Russian leaders undertook similar reinterpretations. After his fashion, Khrushchev offered a confusing array of reforms that would have changed the orientation, if not the structure, of the economy; offered "peaceful coexistence" and modified Russia's international role; and, most important, tried to transform the party and its interface with society. Brezhnev promised "developed socialism," which copied many of the elements of Western postindustrial society, including a high-tech and knowledge-based economy and a new managerial role for the party. And as we have noted, Gorbachev began as a modest reformer, intent on fixing the system through the creation of a modern and market-oriented economy and a Europeanized redefinition of the nation and its people.

Any assessment of Putin as an authoritarian modernizer should begin with a recognition of the complexity reflected in this earlier experience. The current reality is a nuanced combination of the soviet and early post-communist experience, conditioned by the continuing reinterpretation of an initially vague model of modernity, the reassertion of elements of traditional Russian and soviet culture, and the political opportunism of post-communist leaders responding to changing circumstances and their own will to power.

In most ways, Putin has not yet significantly departed from the general prototype of authoritarian modernizers. He initially embraced, and then significant altered, the concepts of modernity that underpinned Gorbachev's first efforts to transform the Soviet Union. Admittedly and perhaps purposely vague from the start, the ideas about economic and political change, cultural redefinition, and Russia's place in the modern world invited prolonged conflict over what they meant in the real world. In the thirty years since these reforms began in the late 1980s, much has changed beyond the breakup of the Soviet Union. Most important, none of the changes that began with Gorbachev's reforms has played out to a universally acknowledged and accepted conclusion. All are still works in progress, and most are still deeply contested issues about how Russia is to be governed, the nature of a modernity it wishes to embrace, and its place in Europe and the world.

Putin, like most of his contemporaries, initially embraced the early democratic reforms that began under Gorbachev in the late 1980s. But while the acceptance of democracy as a new and experimental form of government helped to sweep away the old order, it was clear that Gorbachev's creation of the Congress of People's Deputies and the presidency were informed by tactical as well as philosophical goals. It was obvious these democratic reforms were intended to strengthen Gorbachev's hand and weaken opposition to his proposed changes, and it was clear these new institutions were hedged with provisions that transferred key powers to the new presidency (not yet popularly elected) and to the Supreme Soviet, the indirectly elected upper house of the popularly elected Congress of People's Deputies. Democracy was good, but institutionally it had its limits consistent with the tactical needs of the moment. Moreover, Putin's first-hand experience with the democratic process in Leningrad soured as his patron, Anatoly Sobchak, fell victim to political intrigues. Putin experienced the realities of nascent post-communist democracy on a broader scale when he transferred to Moscow. While his new and initially distant patron, Yeltsin, had earned high marks for defending Gorbachev's democratic reforms against the August 1991 coup, his administration quickly slipped into institutional gridlock as the Russian legislature blocked his every move and as power shifted from the central government to regional authorities. Yeltsin's solution was dramatic and instructive: Dissolve the recalcitrant legislature, draft a new constitution, and establish a strong presidency, at least on paper. Despite the reforms, the central government remained weak, and Yeltsin vacillated between moments of forceful engagement and absenteeism. As Putin served in increasingly important posts within that new institutional structure from 1993 to December 31, 1999, it became increasingly apparent that institutional reform alone would not restore central authority or end factional conflict within the political elite.

From his election to the presidency in 2000 to the end of his second term in 2008, Putin strengthened the power of central authorities and emerged as a broker of factional conflicts. Both measures unquestionably increased his own personal power as president, as did the growing personality cult. But to interpret the emergence of the power vertical simply as a personal power grab would be misleading; like Gorbachev's creation of the Congress of People's Deputies and the presidency and Yeltsin's 1993 constitutional reforms, it also was a purposeful change of both institutional arrangements and political processes intended to reanimate and redirect the transformation of Russian society begun in the late 1980s. It was a new political formula—a transformational agenda linked to the political realities of the moment—and it would be Putin's way of putting his own stamp on Russia's future.

Like all earlier political agenda, it changed over time. Much remained ambiguous and controversial, at least at first. In many ways, the new agenda resurrected many aspects of the past rooted in the export-driven economy and an important role for state-owned or state-directed industries, the emergence (and, in some cases, the reemergence) of powerful vested interests, and the rediscovery of traditional Russian cultural identity and exceptionalism. But side by side with them also stood many elements of the original reform agenda, a bit battered by the chaos of the Gorbachev and Yeltsin years, but nonetheless present to remind the nation of what it meant to be a democracy, a modern and diversified economy, and a part of a global community.

Throughout Putin's first two terms, from 2000 to 2008, and through the Putin–Medvedev tandem from 2008 to 2012, the balance tipped in favor of the vertical and the enhancement of the presidency and the central government in Moscow. The regime tightened controls across the board. Traditional opponents like the Communist Party or the Liberal Democratic Party were brought into quiet working arrangements with Putin and United Russia; less compliant opponents were marginalized, harassed, imprisoned, or killed; the media and social networks were brought under control; and organized demonstrations or spontaneous "flash mobs" were limited. But the regime also was careful to avoid or finesse serious political or constitutional crises. Putin followed the letter if not the spirit of the 1993 constitution in stepping down from the presidency in 2008, and the 2011 Duma elections, which saw clear voting fraud in favor of United Russia was followed by relatively clean balloting in the 2012 presidential election that returned Putin to the top office. In similar fashion, Putin found at least a temporary balance among the many political and economic factions within the Garden Ring, positioning him as more than just first-among-equals but less than an absolute autocrat. Just as important, the new political formula incorporated and reinterpreted elements of traditional Russian culture that served the new arrangement. Russian nationalism became a major theme of social and political unity, and the reinforcing notions of cultural and political exceptionalism and victimization at the hands of the West grew stronger. A sense of national destiny reemerged, justifying efforts to reclaim elements of the former Russian and soviet empires such as the Crimea and to strengthen the nation's defenses against potential enemies.

Notes

1. Richard Sakwa, Putin Redux: *Power and Contradiction in Contemporary Russia*, Routledge, 2014, 134–189.

2. Sakwa, *Putin Redux*, 154–157; "Return of the Clans," Radio Free Europe/Radio Liberty (hereafter RFE/RL), March 14, 2012; "Factions Jockey for Cabinet Posts," *Moscow Times*, May 14, 2012; "Putin Rewards Former Minister with Advisor Post," RIA Novosti, May 22, 2012.

3. Sakwa, *Putin Redux*, 138–139; "Surkov's Last Stand," RFE/RL, May 15, 2013; and "Russia's Putin Looks Isolated in New Kremlin Term," Reuters, May 10, 2013.

4. RIA Novosti, May 15, 2014; VCIOM, March 6, 2014.

5. James Nichol, *Russian Political, Economic, and Security Issues and U.S. Interests*, Congressional Research Service, August 8, 2013.

6. Sakwa, *Putin Redux*, 148–152; "Return of the Clans"; and Nick Ottens, "Russia's Putin Sidelines Liberals in Conservatives' Favor," *Atlantic Sentinel*, May 11, 2013.

7. Sakwa, *Putin Redux*, 159–181; and "What the Alexei Navalny Case Says about Life in Putin's Russia," *The Atlantic*, April 22, 2013.

8. Nichol, *Russian Political*, 30–34; Andrew Kramer, "Competing Visions for Russia's Economic Future," *New York Times*, May 22, 2014; "Russia's Economy: Tipping the Scale," *The Economist*, May 3, 2014; "Even without Sanctions Russia's Economy Is Looking Sicker Than Ever," Bloomberg Newsweek, April 25, 2014; and "Russia Economic Report," World Bank no. 31, March 2014.

9. "IMF Sees Russia Close to Recession as Ukraine Sanctions Bite," Business News, January 7, 2014; "Investment Bankers Prepare for Long Russian Winter," *Moscow Times*, September 30, 2014; "IMF Halves Russian Forecast," Reuters, October 1, 2014; "Russians Lose Faith in Banks as Ruble Falls and Sanctions Bite," *Moscow Times*, October 15, 2014; "Russia Boosts Currency Defense Firepower as Ruble Hits Fresh Lows," *Moscow Times*, October 15, 2014; Kenneth Rapoza, "Russian Oil Major Rosneft Seeks Government Relief," *Forbes*, October 22, 2014; "Putin Invincible to Economic Decline," *Moscow Times*, October 15, 2014; "Ukraine Crisis: Russia and Sanctions,"

BBC, December 19, 2014; "Crimea Sucks Funds from Infrastructure Mega-projects in Russia's Regions," *Moscow Times*, May 13, 2014; "Russia's GASPROM Asks Government for Aid," *Moscow Times*, March 6, 2015; "How Putin Managed to Dodge the Blame for Russia's Recession," *Moscow Times*, February 2, 2015; and "Despite Economic Woes, 85 Percent of Russians Still Support Putin," *Moscow Times*, January 29, 2015.

10. Ministry of Foreign Affairs website, February 12, 2013.

11. "Address by President of the Russian Federation," March 18, 2014, http://en.kremlin.ru/events/president/news/20603.

12. Kathy Lally, "McFaul Leaves Moscow and Two Dramatic Years in Relations between U.S. and Russia," *Washington Post*, February 26, 2014; and "Recalling McFaul: Four Views on Outgoing Ambassador to Russia," RFE/RL, March 27, 2014.

13. Steven Lee Myers and Andrew E. Kramer, "Defiant Russian Court Grants Snowden Year's Asylum," *New York Times*, August 1, 2013; and Alec Luhn and Mark Tran, "Snowden Given Permission to Stay Three More Years," *The Guardian*, August 7, 2014.

14. Klaus Bachmann and Igor Lubashenko, eds., *The Maidan Uprising, Separatism, and Foreign Intervention: Ukraine's Complex Transition*, Peter Lang, 2014; Andrew Wilson, *The Ukrainian Crisis: What It Means to the West*, Yale University Press, 2014; Gideon Rose, *Crisis in Ukraine*, Council on Foreign Relations, 2014; Rajan Menon and Eugene B. Rumer, *Conflict in Ukraine*, MIT Press, 2015; and Richard Sakwa, *Frontline Ukraine: Crisis in the Borderlands*, Tauris, 2015.

15. Brian Jenkins, *Crisis in Crimea: An Historical Lead Up to the Conflict between Russia and Ukraine*, CreateSpace, 2014; and *Crimea: Anatomy of a Crisis*, Transaction, 2015.

16. "Russian Military Developments and Implications," Committee on Foreign Affairs, U.S. House of Representatives, March 28, 2015; Agnieszka Pikulicka-Wilczeweska and Richard Sakwa, *Ukraine and Russia*, E-International Relations, March 13, 2015; and "U.S. Foreign Policy toward Ukraine," Committee on Foreign Affairs, U.S. House of Representatives, May 22, 2014.

17. Steven Pifer, "Ukraine's Parliamentary Elections: What Happened? What's Next?" Brookings Institution, October 27, 2014; "Ukraine's Election: Good Voters, Not Such Good Guys," *Economist*, November 1, 2014; and David M. Herszenhorn, "Ukraine President Claims Big Win for Pro-West Parties," *New York Times*, October 26, 2014.

18. *Moscow Times*, August 14, 2014.

19. Reuters, October 1, 2014.

20. Patrice Hill, "Russia's Sanctions Risk Lasting Damage to Europe's Shaky Economy," *Washington Times*, September 15, 2014; and Kenneth Rapoza, "Russia's Latest Retaliation against Sanctions Puts American Multinationals in Crosshairs," www.Forbes.com, September 25, 2014.

21. Nicholas K. Gvosdev and Christopher Marsh, *Russian Foreign Policy: Interests, Vectors, and Sectors*, SAGE/CQ Press, 2014, 335–401.

22. Sakwa, *Putin Redux*, 196.

23. RFE/RL, March 24, 2012.

24. Evgeny Minchenko, "Vladimir Putin's Big Government and the Politburo 2.0," Minchenko Consulting Communications Group, www.Minchenko.ru.

25. Evgeny Minchenko, revised version of "Putin's Big Government and the Politburo 2.0," www.globalinterests.org/2015/04/02-politburo-2-0-can-putin's-inner-circle-survive-the-crisis?

26. Amy Knight, *The KGB: Police and Politics in the Soviet Union*, Unwin Hyman, 1990; Christopher Andrew and Vasili Metrokhin, *The Metrokhin Archives*, Penguin, 2006; Yevgenia Arbats and Catherine Fitzpatrick, *The State within a State: The KGB and Its Hold on Russia- Past, Present, and Future*, Farrah Straus and Giroux, 1994; Fiona Hill and Clifford G. Gaddy, "How the 1980s Explain Vladimir Putin," *The Atlantic*, February, 2013; Fiona Hill and Clifford G. Gaddy, *Mr. Putin: Operative in the Kremlin*, 2nd ed., Brookings, 2013; "Silovikiland and Its Discontents," RFE/RL, October 26, 2011; "Resetting the Siloviki," RFE/RL, October 21, 2011; "Putin's Praetorian Guard," Institute of Modern Russia, www.imrussia,org, October 10, 2013; and "Russia's Economic Crisis Forces Secret Service FSB to Downsize," *Moscow Times*, February 11, 2015.

27. Nichol, *Russian Political*, 17–20; "Navalny Is Released from Jail," *New York Times*, March 6, 2015; "Navalny Is a Thorn in Putin's Side," Reuters, December 31, 2014; "Russian Police Raid Home of Navalny's Associate over Alleged Painting Theft," *Moscow Times*, February 6, 2015; "The Contradictory Accounts of Boris Nemtsov's Murder," *Moscow Times*, March 13 2015; and "Decoding the Political Game behind Nemtsov's Murder Arrests," *Moscow Times*, March 9, 2015.

28. "Putin's Legal Vertical: Kremlin Seeks to Consolidate the Court System," RFE/RL, October 9, 2013.

29. "Russia: Powerful New Investigative Body Begins Work," RFE/RL, May 14, 2014; and "Putin's Political Police," RFE/RL, October 10, 2012.

30. "Putin's Praetorian Guard."

31. "Q&A: Russia's New Opposition Council," BBC, October 23, 2012; and "Anti-Putin Opposition Elected in Russian On-line Poll," www.kso-russia.org.

32. "Targeting the Intelligentsia," *Moscow Times*, September 1, 2014.

33. "Russia Popular Front Conference," December 5, 2013, http://en.kremlin.ru/events/president/news/19787.

34. "Russian Elections Building an Elite of Lackeys," *Moscow Times*, September 11, 2014.

35. "Russian Regional Election Day Showcases Kremlin Grip," *Moscow Times*, September 14, 2014.

36. Leonid Peisakhin, "Russia's Local Elections: A Sign of Things to Come," *Washington Post*, October 1, 2014.

37. "Duma Bill Ending Mayoral Elections Passes First Reading," *Moscow Times*, April 16, 2014; and "Vladivostok Gets Rid of Direct Mayoral Elections," *Moscow Times*, February 19, 2015.

38. "Russian Crackdown on Political Parties Sees Number Cut in Half," *Moscow Times*, August 29, 2014; "Moscow's 'Most Diverse' Election Offers No Real Choice," *Moscow Times*, August 14, 2014.

39. "Russia's Beleaguered Human Rights Defenders Vow Resilience," *Moscow Times*, September 9, 2014; and "Veteran Human Rights Group Abandons Most Operations in Russia," *Moscow Times*, September 29, 2014.

40. "Putin's Class of 2014," RFE/RL, October 17, 2014.

41. "Putin Dissolves State News Agency, Tightens Grip on Russian Media," Reuters, December 9, 2013; and Steven Lee Myers, "Without Notice Putin Dissolves News Agency," *New York Times*, December 9, 2013; "Russia Sees Harsh Crackdown on Independent Media," Associated Press, December 21, 2014.

42. Neil MacFarquhar, "Russia Quietly Tightens Reins on Web with Bloggers Law," *New York Times*, May 6, 2014.

8

The Future(s)
of Russian Politics

The plural is intentional. As this chapter is being written, Vladimir
Putin is well into his third term as president. By all conventional wisdom,
he has taken a significant turn toward a more authoritarian political order.
The presidency as an institution has grown stronger as greater formal and
informal powers accrue to the office. As a leader, Putin has become an even
more dominant presence, surrounded by an inner core of advisors
and a personality cult; his job approval ratings are at their highest point.
The Duma and the Federation Council are under his control. With the
exception of United Russia, all other political parties are in retreat, openly
collaborating with the government, or quietly biding their time. Civil
society is under greater control, with some of the groups that advocated
democracy or human rights closed down. The media are more tightly
controlled. The economy is under greater government ownership or supervision, and an economic downturn and foreign sanctions have not produced
widespread discontent. Political opponents are cowed into silence, driven
abroad, arrested on trumped-up charges, and—just to be sure everyone
gets the point—occasionally murdered on the streets of Moscow.

Is this the way it's going to be? Or maybe worse? Or maybe better? The
honest answer is that no one really knows the exact trajectory of Russia's
future. Just as no one could have predicted in 1985 where Mikhail
Gorbachev's initially modest reforms would take the nation, today's political realities may or may not be a template for the future. That said, we
would be wise to avoid speculation that oversimplified the possible futures
into two dichotomous paths: Russia will become either more or less democratic. Reality is never that simple, and measuring the nation's progress

toward whatever future lies before it in such black-and-white terms con-
ceals the nuances of the complex game of Russian politics. A more sophisticated understanding requires us to examine the many forces that will
shape that future.

The Future of the Russian Presidency(ies)

Again, the plural is intentional. Although the title of this book refers to the
Russian presidency, there have in fact been several very different iterations
of that office since Gorbachev first created it. Understanding the potential
future(s) that Russia may pursue requires us to expand on the notion of how
the office of the president may evolve. It has always been a moving target.
Gorbachev's presidency of the Soviet Union was at best a transitional office,
created as a potential counterweight to an antireform establishment and
from the outset compromised by an assertive legislature, its status as an
indirectly elected executive office, and Gorbachev's increasing vacillation in
the face of hard decisions. Even from the beginning, Gorbachev's leadership
was flawed; he was always better at discrediting the past and launching
well-meaning but poorly orchestrated reform than he was at managing the
process of change.

In many ways, Boris Yeltsin suffered the same fate. A brilliant strategist
who mobilized public support to stage an unexpected comeback and to
create and win a popularly elected presidency for the Russian republic, he
soon found that that office was less powerful than he had hoped. To be
sure, he had a clear public mandate. But he also faced growing hostility
from the soviet-era Congress of People's Deputies, from a host of political
rivals who resented his rise to power, and from an increasingly disillu-
sioned public that saw things go from bad to worse. His 1993 coup that
dissolved the legislature and created a seemingly more powerful presidency
only partially clarified the question of who led Russia. Legislative elections
in 1993 and 1995 produced strong but usually poorly coordinated opposition to Yeltsin's reforms. Not surprisingly, Yeltsin did what he did best:
sometimes sallying forth against his enemies to win important but usually
temporary victories, and sometimes retreating to within an ever smaller
circle of advisors and compromising on issues like the selection of prime
ministers acceptable to both the White House and the Kremlin. When he
was good, he was very, very good—the 1993 coup and the 1996 presidential
campaign were good examples—but when he was bad, or just disengaged,

which got worse with time, the potential strength of the office meant little in the hands of a weak leader.

All of that seemed to change with Vladimir Putin's election in 2000. Political reality dictated that he move slowly at first, especially in dealing with the Yeltsin family, the oligarchs, and factions within the leadership. One by one he brought them into line. The family was marginalized; the oligarchs were taught the new rules of the game, with appropriate rewards for those who got the message and sanctions for those who did not; and the factions soon learned that Putin was useful as a mediator of intraelite conflicts. The vertical soon emerged, bringing power back to Moscow, the "center" of the federation, and to the presidency, the increasingly undisputed apex of political power.

The 2008 presidential election prompted conflicting conclusions about the power of the office itself. There was no doubt that the vertical was still firmly in place, supported by the power of United Russia, the first presidential party that seemed to have some sticking power beyond a single election. Putin had won easy victories in 2000 and 2004, and was riding a wave of popularity that easily would have returned him to office. All he had to do was let his minions in the Duma amend the constitution to permit a third consecutive term. But he didn't. Instead, he chose Dmitry Medvedev as his successor, with the understanding that Putin would serve in the tandem as prime minister. What happened over the next four years reveals much about the inherent nature of the presidency. There was little doubt that in the new arrangement the prime minister would be more powerful than the president, constitutional details aside. Although Medvedev and Putin developed a working relationship that acknowledged the constitutionally mandated differences in their separate offices, it always was clear that Putin was first among equals. The important point is that power was not inherent in the office itself; it depended on who was in it, especially if the generally acknowledged leader held a different post. The *presidency* (read: formal office) and the *president* (read: the real leader) were not the same thing. Real executive power lies somewhere in the flexible amalgam of the office and its incumbent. More enticingly, it was inherently a flexible relationship, subject to political if not institutional redefinition virtually at the will of those who occupied the top echelons of political life. The point is that any present assessment of the office of president, and any attempt to understand how it will evolve over time must accept this continuing ambiguity. Is power inherent in the office? Yes, to some degree. Does it attach to the persona of a recognized leader who happens to be in that office? Yes, to some degree.

Or could it attach to the persona of a recognized leader who stands apart from the office of the presidency? Yes, to some degree. A weak leader like Yeltsin could not rule effectively even with a strong presidency, and a strong leader like Putin could rule from a second-tier position in the formal hierarchy.

In one sense, the 2012 presidential election seemed to return things to "normal," if normal is defined primarily in institutional terms. Real power flowed back to the office of the president, even before Putin took action to strengthen the office even further. Both the office and the personality cult that surrounded Putin grew, each reinforcing the other. But if the evolution of the presidency since Gorbachev's time has taught us anything, it is that each leader has redefined the boundaries of the office, emboldened by his own drive for power and the opportunities before him, and circumscribed by his own sense of political realism and the nature of the institutional and political milieu within which he operates.

If this assessment is true, it has several implications for our projections of the possible futures for both the presidency and the nation. The first implication dictates caution on our part as we approach these predictions: The presidency has been and will probably remain a moving target. As the different scenarios suggested in this chapter imply, there are many possibilities given the demonstrated flexibility of the institutional setting and vagaries of Kremlin politics. Some scenarios seem more likely than others—today's best bet foresees increasing power to the president at the expense of the reality if not the form of democratic rule—but there are other possible outcomes. Factional politics could rein in a president's power, or a Moscow Spring could completely change the game. Or a strong-willed or challenged president could press for full-throated authoritarian rule.

The second implication is that any assessment of the future must begin with a clear understanding of the starting point—where we are now as a benchmark for our analysis. Any answer to that question will be intellectually and politically controversial. Analysts have generated a whole new cottage industry of "transitionology"—that is, the way in which nations undertake the transition from communist rule to whatever comes next. As are most such intellectual undertakings, it is filled with intense debates about what happens, how it happens, who wins or loses, and how the credit or blame should be apportioned. It is not our purpose to engage in or to attempt to resolve this debate. But that debate does give us a convenient starting point in the descriptions of "electoral" or "competitive" authoritarianism.

Both notions are about transitional moments somewhere between the attempt to build democracy—the electoral or competitive features of the system—and the possibility that the system may regress into authoritarianism, either by returning to something very much like the old order or by evolving into a new form of authoritarian rule. Our point of departure for assessing the future of Russia and its presidency is the assumption that the nation is now at that critical watershed moment.

What are *electoral authoritarianism* and *competitive authoritarianism?*[1] Both are eclectic and overlapping descriptions of states and societies presumably in transition from authoritarian rule toward some form of democracy and pluralism. They are characterized by inherent and unstable contradictions, embodying elements of authoritarianism (strong presidencies, sometimes termed "hyperpresidentialism"; a single dominant political party or movement; and a far-from-level playing field in which incumbents enjoy overwhelming advantage) as well as elements of real democracy (an organized, if disadvantaged, opposition; other viable political parties; a functioning civil society; and an electoral process in which the opposition can still reflect popular discontent and hope to win at least a share of political power if not total victory). As Levitsky and Way put it, "[e]lections still matter, and they matter a lot, even in the context of electoral manipulation."[2] Under the right conditions, they can change the course of events.

The troublesome truth is that such hybrid systems are inherently unstable, with a host of forces tugging them toward either greater democracy or authoritarianism. Levitsky and Way argue that three elements weigh heavily in shaping their evolution: (1) linkage with the West (greater linkage promotes democratization), (2) the organizational power and adaptability of the hybrid state (greater power increases the likelihood of authoritarianism, especially in terms of the dominance of the executive branch over the legislature and the coercive power of the state, and greater adaptability enables the state to maneuver in the face of challenges), and (3) Western leverage over the hybrid government (leverage refers to the ability to reward or punish evolution in either direction).[3]

This point of view certainly helps us to understand and categorize the Gorbachev, Yeltsin, and Putin eras. Under Gorbachev, the balance tipped in favor of democratization, which eventually led to the breakup of the Soviet Union, despite his efforts to limit the pace and impact of political and economic reforms. Under Yeltsin, the balance began to tip toward electoral or competitive authoritarianism. From 1993 to 2000, a strong presidency (admittedly then in the hands of a weak and inconsistent president) coexisted with a functioning and usually combative legislature, all underpinned by a competitive party system and a growing civil society. To be sure, it was often messy and frequently gridlocked, but such was the inherent nature of competitive authoritarianism. During Putin's first two terms from 2000 to 2008 and the Medvedev interregnum from 2008 to 2012, the balance shifted toward greater presidential power, an expansion of the influence of the central government, and increasing controls over the media and civil society. Putin's third term, beginning in 2012, is usually regarded as the tipping point when the elusive boundary between competitive and full-fledged authoritarianism was crossed, resulting in a cascade of mutually supportive measures that have fundamentally changed the nature of the system.

While focusing on the degradation of electoral or competitive authoritarianism into genuine authoritarianism tells us much about the course of Russian politics, it shows us only a part of the picture. One of the central ideas behind our analysis is that there are several different but overlapping arenas of Russian political life that deal with factional divisions at the top (the "inside-the-Garden-Ring" arena), the broader question of electoral politics at the national and regional levels (the "outside-the-Garden-Ring" arena), and the connections that link the two arenas. Changes in each of these arenas influence all others, suggesting that if we want to understand the possible future(s)—again, the plural is purposeful—we must assess how changes in any one arena will potentially affect all others.

What Will Drive Change?

If our point of departure is correct—that contemporary Russia may be broadly characterized as an electoral or competitive authoritarian state since the end of communist rule, and that it now is rapidly approaching or may already have crossed the threshold into full-fledged authoritarianism—what possible futures lay ahead? No single answer emerges. A clearer path toward understanding these possible outcomes lies in focusing on the factors that will shape the future. What drives change? Just as the present reality has been shaped by the sometimes purposeful and sometimes serendipitous interaction of many causes, the future will be shaped by potential changes across a variety of factors. These include (1) changes in the nature of factional politics; (2) changes in the nature of electoral politics at the national, regional, and local levels; and (3) the potential for spontaneous public action that upsets the carefully choreographed interaction of the first two arenas: a Moscow Spring, a color revolution, or any other outpouring of widespread public discontent.

Changes in the Nature of Factional Politics

One of the most important realities of Russian politics has been the increasing significance of factional politics, what we earlier termed the inside-the-Garden-Ring arena and the role of the president as a balancer of competing factional interests. Since Putin's elevation to the presidency in 2000, both the choice of national policy and the stability of the regime have depended on accommodations worked out within this inner circle. Although the overall logic of the arrangement is clear and simple—the major factions have a mutual interest in compromises that simultaneously satisfy their core interests and preserve the stability of the system—there are always factors that complicate the game. As noted, the sheer number of factions has grown over the years, prompting some analysts to speak of an inner core (the full members of what Minchenko terms "Politburo 2.0") and a larger and presumably less powerful outer ring (the candidate members of Politburo 2.0. The greater the number of factions or subfactions, the greater the potential for intraelite struggle, especially in a world of diminishing economic and social resources. And the greater the number of factional players, the greater the potential number of shifting coalitions and alliances. The game is different from the perspective of the president, for whom an important part of leadership lies in bringing together workable but probably shifting alliances that simultaneously address major policy issues and preserve overall stability. But like any chief executive in this sort of institutional setting, presidents are anxious to expand their own authority and flexibility and loath to accept the limitations imposed by competing factions who agree that, whatever their other differences, it is wise to limit the president's power.[4] Within these overall constraints, several possible scenarios exist that could fundamentally transform the nature of factional politics. They are described in the sections that follow.

The president loses the ability to balance factional interests or demonstrably favors one over others. In simple terms, the president is no longer seen as a "neutral" figure or is perceived as no longer capable of brokering agreement. In reality, any president will have his own policy preferences and political base, either of which may lead him to favor—or to be thought to favor, which is just as bad—one faction or coalition over another. The growing complexity of the task also raises the possibility that the president will find it increasingly difficult to cobble together long-term balances. An economic downturn or other scarcities may reduce the number of "carrots" with which to entice factions to continue to play the game, and a president whose capabilities seem to be waning will hold fewer "sticks" with which to deter or punish defectors. Overwhelming policy failures also may erode the president's ability to attract factions into a balanced coalition, especially if the president and leading factions attempt to shift blame to one another. The timing of such destabilization also would be important. If it occurred in the run-up to a presidential election in which the incumbent were a candidate, the search for a new mediator would be complicated by the need to find someone capable of winning the trust of major factions as well as able to win the upcoming election. The constitutional sleight of hand in 2008 that led to Medvedev's election to the presidency and the selection of Putin as prime minister illustrates that such dilemmas may produce jury-rigged solutions if no obvious successor emerges capable of accomplishing both tasks. If the challenge to the president's role as de facto mediator occurs early or midterm, the likely solution will confront a different dilemma. Even if it is possible to agree on a new mediator, how do you institutionalize the arrangement? Several possibilities exist. The president could remain as a figurehead under the de facto leadership of a newly appointed prime minister acceptable to the factions; in this arrangement, real political leadership would come from the seemingly subordinate post, as with the Medvedev–Putin tandem from 2008 to 2012. This would avoid the necessity for an immediate presidential election if the chief executive were forced from office, thus keeping the game as much within the Garden Ring as possible and avoiding the unpredictable involvement of other presidential hopefuls. Once in place, the prime minister as de facto leader would be well positioned for the next regularly scheduled election, perhaps even rising to the top post in a well-orchestrated late-term resignation by the president, as happened at the end of Yeltsin's second term. To be sure, a president under threat of such manipulation by disgruntled factions might turn the threat of resignation against his opponents; such action would automatically elevate the current prime minister to the presidency and require a quick presidential election, a reality that the factions might want to avoid unless their choice as a new mediator also was a likely shoo-in for the office.

One faction or a coalition of factions attempts to upset the balance, capturing or marginalizing the president. The difference from the first scenario is that a faction or coalition of factions takes the initiative to upset the existing balance. Such action would be seen as a coup d'état within the Garden Ring, leading to one faction or a coalition of factions dominating the world of intraelite politics and controlling, sidelining, or ultimately replacing an incumbent president.

It would not be easy. The expanding world of factional politics would make it increasingly difficult to put together a large enough coalition to be assured of victory, even if only the top-level players (what Minchenko calls the full members of Politburo 2.0) were involved. Even at this level, Putin has institutionally subdivided the major factions to pit agencies and individual leaders against one another in an informal system of check and balances. Political reality dictates that some factions would be more important than others, at least at first. The multiple institutional homes of the *siloviki* would have to be included and be in reasonably close agreement about what would be done and who would pick up the pieces. Support from at least an important segment of the oligarchs and those who lead major sectors of the economy also would be required. There also would need to be agreement about the new institutional arrangements: What would happen to the president if he accepted the new order of things, and what if he resisted? What about the prime minister? Who would be the new president or prime minister, if both were required? Who would be a part of the inner core of the new arrangement, since an end to the president's balancing act necessarily implies a new world of winners and losers? What sticks and/or carrots could be used to cow or win support from others? How would it be presented to the public, and how would the new leadership handle the possible public responses? And most difficult of all, how could it all be done in secret and escape the notice of the president and his entourage?

A daunting task, doable or at least attemptable under the right conditions, but probably only to be undertaken as a desperation measure. The closest comparison would be the attempted coup against Gorbachev in August 1991 to prevent the signing of a new Union Treaty. The effort was similar in many ways to the preceding scenario. Gorbachev was given the option of signing off on the changes and keeping his post or going peacefully into retirement "for reasons of health." Although the circle of those involved in the coup represented a much smaller clique of what remained of the soviet establishment—essentially the security forces and the military—they initially thought that other elements of the party and government would back them once they had taken control of events. Defeat came at the hands of the nation's first unlabeled "color revolution" led by but not created by Yeltsin, and because the military refused to fire on the crowds.

Under the present circumstances, Putin's resources both to detect and to react to such a scenario are undeniably overwhelming. Operating from within an inner circle of supporters with ties to all important segments of the political and economic factions, he is well positioned to learn about and react to any threat by preemptive coercion, cooptation of real or potential opponents, or playing of various factions and subfactions against one another. The increasing complexity of the game also works to his advantage. There is more to watch and potentially fear, but also more to manipulate in a complex game that inherently favors whoever is at the top of the pyramid. No less important has been Putin's skillful manipulation of domestic and foreign policy to win broad public support largely independent of the vagaries of the factional games. Stoking popular support for social conservatism, national pride, and Russian exceptionalism, as well as offering seeming victories in Crimea and Ukraine, Putin has banked a deep well of popular support that would be difficult to overcome. To be sure, that support could evaporate quickly if a real grassroots rebellion resulted from future policy failures, especially in the economy, or from the perception that his regime had stolen an election. But that is a scenario to be considered later in this chapter.

Putin himself precipitates a crisis by attempting to escape the collective restraints imposed by the need to balance factional interests. Soviet leaders from 1953 onward faced their own version of this dilemma: How do you maximize your own power and still work within the framework of "collective leadership?" Nikita Khrushchev launched a frontal assault through de-Stalinization, efforts to get the aging generation of Stalin-era leaders to modernize, and programs that would have forced the retirement of the old guard. His largely unsuccessful persistence cost him his job. Leonid Brezhnev tried the carrot rather than the stick, promising stability and "respect for cadres" while summoning them to better things through developed socialism and the "scientific management of society." In the end, he fared no better.

The desire for any leader—party general secretary or president—to challenge the limits is inherent in the arrangement. Leaders are expected to lead, to accomplish something. They come to office with some form of mandate. Both compel them to make their mark, it is hoped by the skillful manipulation of the overlapping worlds both inside and outside the Garden Ring. But sometimes that is not enough. The issue is too important, at least to them; the opposition seems too quarrelsome and unreasonable; or perhaps it is just time to teach someone a lesson about where power lies. If they are wise, they pick their battles carefully.

Both Gorbachev and Yeltsin found themselves at such moments. For Gorbachev, it came as a series of interrelated crisis beginning with glasnost, perestroika, democratization, and the creation of a presidency of the Soviet Union and ending with the attempted coup aimed at scotching the passage of a new Union Treaty. For Yeltsin, the crisis came in 1993 with his dismissal of the Congress of People's Deputies and submission of a new constitution for popular ratification. Most observers argued that both were on the side of the angels in what they did, but from the perspective of the old guard they were upsetting an established order that somehow held them in check.

Under the present arrangement, in which the need for factional consensus potentially places limitations on what any Russian president can realistically do, it is not difficult to imagine a scenario in which Putin or any successor might want to revise these de facto check and balances. Putin's creation of an inner core of advisors after the 2012 elections only partially qualifies as such an effort. Although the inner core, dominated but not exclusively limited to the *siloviki* and Putin's closest advisors, has greater authority over foreign and defense policy and internal security, it still operates within the context of a growing spectrum of factions, themselves inhabiting a multitiered universe of political actors, each with its own institutional interests, policy preferences, and ambitious leaders eager to make their mark.

In contemporary Russian politics, what would an attempt to escape the de facto limitations of collective leadership look like, and how would it work? One approach would be to further strengthen the office of the presidency itself, moving it even more into the realm of "hyperpresidentialism." In institutional terms, much has already been done: The presidential term has been extended to six years, presidential control of or influence over regional and local elections has been expanded, and the power of the presidential staff and executive office has grown. Although United Russia no longer singlehandedly commands a constitution-changing majority within the legislature, Putin probably would have little difficulty in securing amendments, including an end to the two-consecutive-term limit on presidential incumbency. Putin could also occasionally return to the use of public referenda on important policy issues; such referenda were successfully used by Gorbachev and Yeltsin. The 1993 constitution still permits their use under certain circumstances, and it is likely that a popular president facing opposition within the Garden Ring could overcome whatever legal objections might be raised. Although such referenda could be easily manipulated by Putin or any future president to reinvigorate his mandate, they also carry inherent risk. They would inevitably be seen as a de facto vote of confidence on any incumbent bold enough to use them.

Moving beyond possible changes to the presidency itself, Putin could further strengthen his hand in other ways. Although he has maintained a respectable distance from United Russia, which Medvedev heads, he did not dissolve the broader popular front coalition, the All-Russia People's Front, which backed his return to the presidency in 2012. Although that coalition is likely being held in reserve for the 2018 election, it could be reanimated as an ongoing organizational base. As noted in Chapter 7, some evidence indicates that Putin has attempted to reach out to potentially disaffected youth through social media and selective recruitment into a new "generation of 2014."

Putin also could attempt to reduce factional control over his actions by a more draconian use of the sticks and carrots at his disposal. This is not to suggest anything as drastic as a purge or wholesale replacement of major factional leaders at the top of the chain of command. But selective dismissal or scapegoating have always been effective ways to control opponents. Few will fall victim, but many will learn the lesson. Less draconian measures also are possible. An extension of the current effort to build de facto checks and balances by playing various institutions or factions against one another could be expanded, or politically inspired dismissals or promotions at the lower tiers—the candidate members or lower in Minchenko's scheme—can become the preemptive skirmishes of a larger battle. Minchenko suggests a strong likelihood that the ranks of the candidate members probably will be culled from time to time in an effort to keep the playing field manageable as long as overall factional balance can be maintained.

Putin also holds an impressive number of carrots, even in a time of economic hardship and foreign sanctions. Some are political and symbolic; the growing power of the presidency also extends the reach of presidential patronage, either through the de jure power of direct appointment or through the de facto realm of political influence. The close and admittedly corrupt relationship between government and the private sector also extends Putin's influence deeply into society. Even in a time of economic troubles, there will be winners and losers; someone will get government contracts, some city or region will get the new factory or public works project, and some sector of the economy will win out over another.

That said, there are limitations to a president's ability to strengthen his hand. At first glance, it seems reasonable to argue that the increasing powers of the presidency, as well as Putin's earlier experiences in the KGB, would suggest that the ultimate "stick" lies in the application of coercion against recalcitrant factions that could not be won over or frightened into compliance. That is not the same thing as applying such coercion to elements outside the inner circle of the existing factions, to political opponents who sought to mobilize popular support, or to a spontaneous color revolution. Turning overt coercion inward would create a very different reality, the sort of crossing of the Rubicon that occurred when Stalin instructed the secret police of his day to ferret out opposition within the Communist Party itself. That is a threshold that even the most frustrated and hamstrung president would ponder carefully. As noted earlier, the *siloviki* are far from monolithic; they are divided—purposefully, as a way to divide and limit their power—into a number of independent agencies and missions, each pitted against the others in terms of political loyalties, institutional jurisdictions, and missions. No one faction and no single person— not even the president—controls all. Opening the door to anything resembling the competitive use of such coercion could revive and intensify the *siloviki* wars of the 1990s. That is an uncertain playing field onto which all elements of the conflicted game of Kremlin politics would be reluctant to venture.

Changes in the Nature of Electoral
Politics at the National, Regional, and Local Levels

Although in the short run changes in the nature of factional politics will be the most likely cause of larger changes in the nature of Russian politics, elections are still important, if not quite in the same way they were in the Yeltsin era. Even if post-2012 politics is approaching or just over the tipping point separating electoral authoritarianism from full-fledged authoritarianism, the electoral process will remain, at least for a while, an important battleground in challenging or confirming the power of those who hold office. To be sure, most of the mechanisms for increasing repression seem to be in place, at least since the 2012 presidential election. Presidential authority has been strengthened, coupled with the growing impact of a personality cult and a genuinely high approval rating of Putin's performance in office. Although bloodied in the 2011 Duma elections, United Russia remains in control of national political life, with a bit of help from what is left of the other major parties that tactically find it wise to cooperate, at least until the next election cycle. At least on paper, the party's influence also extends into regional and local politics, although its popularity is based more on its association with Putin's current successes and its status as the latest in a long series of "parties of power." Controls over political life have been strengthened. The media are no longer free to criticize the government, and opposition from an aggressive civil society has been silenced. More important, controls over the electoral process itself have been tightened; the regime manipulates the registration of opposition groups and parties, willfully denies candidacy to real or potential opponents through complex and unevenly applied registration requirements, gerrymanders voting districts to divide potential opposition strongholds, and at the end of the day still counts votes and announces the results. Powerful tools these, ones that can be used as blunt weapons of repression or more deftly to coopt or divide opponents. If the past is any guide, they will probably be used in both ways.

Periodic but isolated electoral losses by United Russia, especially in Moscow and St. Petersburg or troubled areas. Not even the best oiled political machine wins every time. Especially at the regional or municipal level, local issues may trump even the best laid plans. Malfeasance in office or corruption are still endemic and in many ways getting worse. Sometimes Moscow acts preemptively, dismissing local officials before a popular rebellion at the polls. While local losses usually mean little in terms of the overall scheme of things, they are always touted as bellwethers by opponents anxious to portray any visible cracks in the façade as tokens of more widespread weakness.

In Moscow and St. Petersburg, public opposition will continue to be strong and vocal, and occasionally may rise to significant levels in other major cities. Putin always has enjoyed high approval ratings, but the "street" has never been his forte, even when officially sponsored "spontaneous demonstrations" have turned out to counter usually much larger and genuinely spontaneous opposition rallies. To some degree, limited opposition rallies have been and probably will continue to be tolerated as safety valves. But the "street" must still figure prominently in the regime's thinking.

Local politics in the major cities such as Moscow and St. Petersburg also can be manipulated to make a point. In September 2013, the Kremlin was uncharacteristically permissive in letting Alexei Navalny, a leading critic of the regime, run against the incumbent Sergei Sobyanin, Putin's handpicked successor to Yuri Luzhkov. Although the deck was stacked against Navalny, he eventually won a surprising 27 percent of the popular vote in a reasonably fair election. The implied message to Navalny and other critics was clear: You had your chance and you lost, even in Moscow, the hotbed of the opposition. But where there are sticks, there are also carrots. Moscow is currently in the initial stages of drafting an extensive public works campaign to transform the city into one of the world's major urban complexes. Economic and political opportunities will abound, with most going to those who know how to and are willing to play the game.

Serious opposition within or loss of control of the Duma. This remains a possibility even with the regime's increasing controls on the electoral process and opposition in general after 2012. All of the Dumas elected on Yeltsin's watch or in Putin's first term contained serious and frequently gridlock-producing divisions generated by odd-couple alliances (the tacit "red-brown" alliance of communists and nationalists), the ill-fated efforts to create officially approved "opposition" parties, and the internal divisions within the "party of power" at the moment. While United Russia labored to present a united front to the rest of the nation, the inside-the-Garden-Ring factional battles over its creation and choice of candidates and policies was always more complex and contentious than the façade of unity. The 2011 Duma elections revealed the potential weakness of any political machine accused of stealing an election. Although it maintained majority control of the lower house, United Russia lost its larger constitution-amending majority. At the regional and local levels, the jump-on-the-bandwagon effect and the power of patronage have extended United Russia's reach far beyond Moscow. But continued support for these reasons is always tenuous at best; locally elected politicians can jump off a faltering bandwagon as quickly as they jumped on.

What could possibly rattle United Russia's seeming dominance of Russian politics? In the short run, the regime is unlikely to loosen its control over the electoral process, although after the public reaction to the 2011 Duma elections it will tread more cautiously, except in those cases in which it wants to make an example of a particular candidate or group. It is even likely that it will tolerate an occasional wildcard candidacy, someone like Navalny who is unlikely to succeed but can be presented as an example of the openness of the system. Officially sponsored opposition parties or candidates cannot be ruled out, although they will likely be kept on a short leash.

Serious challenges are more likely to arise either from perceived policy failures or from further instances of the alleged theft of an election. Policy failures would have to be of major proportions—significant foreign policy reversals or an economic crisis that cut deeply into the standard of living of the average Russian more than the narrow circle of oligarchs—and not easily scapegoated on the hostility of the outside world or the normal economic cycle. They also would have to be exploitable by the regime's political opponents in ways that clearly attached blame to Putin and United Russia. Although these outcomes are possible, they are probably unlikely in circumstances in which the authorities control the media, the formation of potential opposition groups, and the gateways to being nominated and mounting a credible campaign for public office.

Far more likely is the possibility of strong opposition based on the perception that the regime has falsified the results of a legislative or presidential election. The 2011 Duma elections produced such an outcome, bringing heretofore unprecedented numbers of demonstrators into the streets in the major cities and forcing the regime to loosen controls and more carefully monitor the presidential balloting in March 2012. Soon thereafter, the regime tightened controls over all aspects of the electoral cycle, making it easier to strike preemptively at its potential opponents and deny them the opportunity to get on the ballot. Draconian and probably more effective, these measures also deny the opposition the moment of drama after the votes are (mis)counted to allege fraud. But in reality, allegations of electoral misconduct and voter fraud or manipulation will continue to be justifiably advanced after every election, and their impact on the political process will depend on both how they are perceived and whether the opposition can find a way to capitalize on them.

The regrettable truth is that "normal" manipulation will continue to exist but produce little likelihood of becoming a real political issue except within a small community of domestic and international critics, neither of which can do much about it. But there is a chance that it may at times provoke a greater response, perhaps because it was particularly blatant or widespread in a particular election, or perhaps because the overall level of public acceptance of the regime has dropped. In those instances, there may be blood in the water, creating the opportunity to exploit the issue, especially near the end of a presidential term if the incumbent is unlikely to seek reelection.

The opposition could exploit that window of opportunity in two ways, even though overall advantage still rests with the regime. First, it would probably embolden others to challenge the regime at all levels in upcoming elections. Any success would encourage further challenges—and realistically, probably further efforts at imposing greater central control. At the national level, an emboldened opposition could try to secure official recognition for new political parties or form de facto informal political alliances based on the still imperfectly controlled social media. In April 2015, nine of the most prominent opposition parties agreed to form an alliance for the 2016 Duma elections, promising to offer a common platform and a joint list of candidates to the voters, although cracks have already begun to appear. If successful, it could create a third force within the Duma to challenge the de facto cooperation of United Russia with the more traditional opposition parties like the Communist Party and the Liberal Democratic Party. The new opposition bloc spans a diversity of views across the political spectrum from left to right and contains several presidential hopefuls such as Alexei Navalny and Mikhail Khodorkovsky, creating significant hurdles in finding a common political identity apart from their shared opposition to Putin.

More significant would be the possibility that the officially accepted opposition parties in the Duma would rethink their willingness to operate as de facto junior partners with United Russia. To be sure, established parties like the Communist Party or the Liberal Democrats probably would need to find new leaders and issues, but a perception of the regime's vulnerability might tempt them to such action. Within the Duma, tacit cooperation could turn to increasingly vocal criticism, both to test the limits of United Russia's willingness to accommodate them and to gain the ear of future voters. Odd-couple coalitions are possible and perhaps tactically wise, even if they do not approach the level of blocking coalitions as they did in the Yeltsin years. In exceptional circumstances, such coalitions might attempt to block or hamstring legislation or threaten no-confidence votes against the prime minister. Although the president still has the upper hand, such efforts would complicate the day-to-day business of government and, more important, signal yet greater strength in the hands of a gathering opposition.

Despite the presence of blood in the water, Putin or any future president still has the upper hand, even with the thinnest majorities in the Duma. Under challenge from even a minority in the legislature, the president could further strengthen the growing role of the executive office and the central government in Moscow. The center can always ratchet up the powers of the vertical, unless of course regional authorities also sense weakness, in which case they will be tempted to try to reclaim as much power as possible at their level. Outright coercion and repression also can be stepped up at the president's command; the tools are there to be used at the leadership's discretion, if they determine that the benefits exceed the costs.

The calculation of benefits and costs will be critical in shaping Putin's or any future president's response. It is easy to construct a scenario in which increased central control and outright repression will be the response of choice, especially if initially limited opposition seems to be gathering in size and intensity or events are spilling into the streets, suggesting that a color revolution may be at hand. But quick action of this sort probably would depend on fairly broad agreement among the major factions. Although it could be initiated by the inner circle and the *siloviki*, moving without broader factional agreement could weaken the president's hand in the long run. An equally viable initial response to growing opposition could begin with a series of tactical concessions and accommodations designed to divide the opposition and coopt some of its elements, even if only temporarily. Yeltsin did just this in the second round of the 1996 presidential election, and Putin employed a similar strategy after the 2011 Duma elections. To be sure, the carrot eventually was replaced by the stick, and sometimes an even bigger stick. But the tactical flexibility shown by the leadership permitted them to weather the crisis with minimal political and social disruption.

A presidential election with a serious challenge to an incumbent seeking reelection or open competition over the selection of a new president. Even in a system characterized as electoral authoritarianism, an incumbent seeking reelection might face serious challenge or there may be a competitive field of candidates in the choice of a new first-term president. Such scenarios would most likely arise when policy failures undercut an incumbent's bid for reelection, when a relative outsider—or someone who portrays himself as an outsider—enjoys widespread public support despite the advantages accruing to the incumbent, or when the major factions are divided on the issue of presidential succession. A presidential election under any of these circumstances would be especially volatile if it were to follow a shift in power in the most recent legislative elections. Serious slippage of a dominant party like United Russia or the rise to power of another party headed by a presidential hopeful or a coalition of opposition parties would reshape the political calculations of all parties and potential candidates in the next race for the presidency.

Public confidence in a leader is always tenuous, even in the presence of the overwhelming advantages held by an incumbent. Yeltsin's popularity ebbed and flowed over the course of his presidency, although he found ways to rise to the occasion when things seemed at their darkest. Although more stable over time, Putin's popularity has slipped at times, especially on economic issues. At such moments, he has recouped his losses by deftly shifting the focus of public concern to other issues—usually foreign policy successes or a host of real or imagined enemies—but the success of such sleight of hand cannot always be guaranteed.

The greatest challenge would probably come from a popular wildcard opponent whose strength lies not in an existing party, a stable and effective organizational base, or a track record of established leadership. The more likely challenger would be someone who has crafted a public identity that stands apart from the inner core of the regime: a business leader and public activist (Mikhail Prokhorov, an oligarch who eventually ran as an independent in 2012), a victim of repression or regime harassment (Mikhail Khodorkovsky, a former oligarch whose dabbling in politics in the first Putin term resulted in his imprisonment on trumped-up charges, or a prominent dissident like Alexei Navalny, who has an independent political identity and core following), or a current or past member of the regime who is making a bid for the presidency (Alexei Kudrin, the former finance minister now at odds with Putin's economic policy; Dmitry Medvedev, the former president during the tandem and now the much-diminished prime minister in Putin's third term; Dmitry Rogozin, a leader of a small right-wing party in the Duma and current deputy prime minister with special responsibility for defense policy and the military industrial complex; or Sergei Shoigu, the current defense minister who led the emergency response ministry, served as governor of the Moscow province [not the city itself], and has attempted to rebrand himself as Russian Orthodox despite his Buddhist heritage as a Tuvan). The mayors of Moscow and St. Petersburg, both federal cities with special status, also could be in the running. Moscow's former mayor, Yuri Luzhkov, was a perennial possible candidate until he was dismissed by Medvedev, and the current mayor, Sergei Sobyanin, regularly shows up on the lists of possible future candidates. Prominent regional leaders might also be on the list, although it would be difficult to turn local success into a national platform. New leadership of a revitalized Communist Party might also be in the running, especially if the party could shift concerns from foreign policy to the economy and the distribution of wealth in Russian society.

Potential candidates anxious to join in this expanded race would face two critical decisions. The first would be the selection of the issues with which to appeal to the voters. Although "anybody but Putin" or "throw out the regime of crooks and thieves" would win widespread support, specific issues such as the economy, social inequity and justice, social policy, and a host of deeply emotional foreign policy issues also would find a place. The second choice addresses leadership style and "branding," a catch-all phrase for crafting the candidate's public persona. Each candidate must craft that image for many different constituencies. The possibilities are many: "adjusted continuity," or Putin lite, preserving the core of strong leadership and factional balance but modifying the implementation and loosening controls; "greater democratization," drawing back from the brink of full-fledged authoritarianism to something more pluralistic but less chaotic than the Yeltsin years; "a regime of technocrats," suggesting but never fully delivering on the idea of a transparently managed and depoliticized political order; "social justice," focusing on leveling the economic and political playing fields and making amends for the treatment of dissidents and minorities; "a strong leader and a strong nation," prioritizing a greater role for an authoritarian president, expanding the role of the state, increasing social and intellectual controls, and stressing an assertive foreign policy and the notion of Russian exceptionalism. All are possible options, and choices would have to be made.

All candidates would face an uphill battle against even the most tarnished incumbent or an anointed successor who still enjoyed widespread support among the major factions and was helped by the election-winning powers of the presidential office. The prospects for a competitive race would improve in an open election of a new first-term president and rise even higher if the outgoing incumbent did not name a chosen successor or if there were major divisions among the factions, even in the face of a presidential endorsement. Greater emphasis also would shift to the broader arena of grassroots support and the mobilization of opposition-leaning voters through social media and public actions. To be sure, relative advantage still accrues to those closest to the existing but now divided establishment, especially if the prospect of the election of an outsider causes them to circle the wagons. But in the real world, this is as close as Russian politics is likely to get to a genuine grassroots transfer of power through the voting booth. This scenario is not yet a color revolution, at least if that term means the advent of large-scale and frequently violent demonstrations that are beyond the existing electoral process. It could easily become a color revolution if the divided establishment overreacts and is perceived to have stolen an election that it could not otherwise win at the polls—a scenario we consider at length later in this chapter.

A lack of consensus among the major factions would also complicate an open presidential race in which there was no incumbent running for reelection, no presidentially supported successor, or disagreement over backing the incumbent's choice. A last-term president would be under considerable pressure to favor one or another of the factions, or to find a candidate acceptable to all. He would be likely to choose a number of prime ministers in his last years in office, as did both Yeltsin and Putin, leaving him some choice and well positioned to bargain about his own post-incumbency status. From the perspective of the inside-the-Garden-Ring factions, prolonged and publicly visible disagreement about the choice of a candidate and the strength of support from the major factions should be avoided at any cost. For the factions, a better outcome lies in the resolution of intrafactional disputes before the run-up to the election and agreement on a candidate meeting the dual criteria of widespread factional backing and the ability to win public support at the polls. Efforts were made to find such a replacement candidate in the run-up to the 2008 presidential election, but to no avail. No potential frontrunner emerged to replace Putin as a factional mediator and widely popular candidate, prompting initial consideration of amending the constitution to permit Putin a third successive term and then producing the agreement on cobbling together the tandem with Medvedev.

Such disagreement almost certainly will emerge again, most likely at the end of Putin's third or fourth term, or less likely in the aftermath of an unanticipated resignation or death while in office. If it occurred as a part of the normal election cycle—that is, in the run-up to the 2018 or 2024 elections—the battle for position would begin long in advance among the factions, fought out both behind closed doors and in the broader public arena as potential candidates tested the waters. Wildcard candidates—lesser players within the Garden Ring, regional leaders, or true outsiders such as business-men or dissidents—would have to operate more openly, forcing others to acknowledge their public appeal. A snap election in the wake of a resigna-tion or death in office would more likely generate a short-term compromise among the factions unless an acknowledged frontrunner already existed. De facto or de jure power sharing would be the likely outcome, as with the tandem, and there would be much uncertainty about how long the arrange-ment would last.

An incumbent president seeking reelection or an anointed successor loses in the first round to an opponent who wins a clear majority. How would the loss by an incumbent or a chosen successor play out if a challenger captured the presidency with a majority of the votes in the first round. A number of scenarios are possible. Much would depend on whether the loser were an incumbent seeking reelection or a chosen suc-cessor. The former scenario would be viewed as a serious challenge to the regime and would be more likely to elicit a rapid and forceful response. Important also would be the assessment of why the incumbent or the anointed successor lost. If it were concluded that the winner had a broader and more lasting base of public support than anticipated, factional support might begin to slip away from the incumbent and, more likely, from an anointed successor to whom the incumbent had not been able to transfer voter support. Even more serious would be an assessment that the incum-bent or successor simply had run a bad campaign; now perceived as dam-aged goods, the first-round loser would be seen as having lost much of his ability to challenge the results or to govern as a strong president if he should somehow survive. It would also be difficult or impossible for a lame-duck incumbent to balance factional interests and to maintain sup-port at the regional or local level, where former supporters would begin to distance themselves from a damaged leader whose coattails no longer improved their standing.

To be sure, the incumbent or the chosen successor could simply accept the defeat, a scenario far more likely if the potential risks of defying the results and staging a presidential coup were unacceptably high and if the winning candidate were willing to negotiate an exit strategy that would facilitate his departure from public life. If he chose to defy the results, a defeated incumbent would have to assess the likelihood of sustained and widespread public protests, the level of support from important factions, and the prospects that key elements in the military and police would respond to his orders to suppress public resistance. Whatever the nature of the president's initial action—a recount of the ballots, invalidation of the results by the election commission, or action in the government-controlled courts—the confrontation would soon end up in the streets. For his part, the new president-elect would have to engage in the same calculus. Would there be significant and prolonged public opposition to a presidential coup? Would such public opposition convince the incumbent to accept defeat, or would it drive him into a corner and provoke defiance? Would major Kremlin factions remain committed to the incumbent or seek accommodation with the new leadership? How would the security forces react in such a confrontation? What concessions would the president-elect have to make to the incumbent to ease his departure, and would those accommodations be accepted by his own supporters? Despite a clear victory at the polls by the challenger, the transition would not likely be a by-the-book transfer of power. The limited precedents that exist—from Gorbachev to Yeltsin, from Yeltsin to Putin, and from Putin to Medvedev and back again—suggest that any transition will be complicated and politically charged.

A first-round loss by an anointed successor probably would be less likely to produce the sort of violent confrontation that would result from the defeat of an incumbent. Placing the blame for the loss would be critical. Blame could primarily attach to the candidate himself, exculpating the outgoing president who chose him and the major factions that supported him. In this scenario, any serious consideration of defying the election results would have to be weighed against the prospects of trying to deal with a potential popular uprising and govern the nation for the next six years under the leadership of an untested newcomer. If blame were to attach to the outgoing president or the factions, a nasty game of recriminations and finger-pointing would probably make it more difficult to create a united front supporting the nullification of the election results and a willingness to accept the risks involved. For his part, the president's chosen successor would be unlikely to have the power to defy the election results on his own, especially if the outgoing president and the major factions were unwilling to risk their own future by backing a damaged candidate. A more likely scenario would result in the president's tacit acceptance of the results, probably combined with an acceptable exit agreement, and at least some of the factions distancing themselves from their earlier choice and opening talks with the president-elect. In the end, a tolerable fait accompli would be better than an uncertain confrontation that neither side could be sure of winning.

The first round of presidential balloting is inconclusive, forcing a run-off between the top two candidates. This situation arose in the 1996 presidential election in which Yeltsin received 35.8 percent of first-round votes, Gennady Zyuganov, the Communist Party candidate got 32.5 percent, and Alexander Lebed, head of the nationalist Congress of Russian Communities party and, more important, a former military commander who had taken up the cause of Russians living in the near abroad, got 14.7 percent. In a deal the outlines of which had been struck even before the election, Lebed asked his supporters to back Yeltsin in the second round, receiving in return assurances of an important post dealing with foreign and military policy. In the second round of voting, Yeltsin won with 54.4 percent. After brief service as the secretary of the Security Council and national security advisor to the president, Lebed was quickly marginalized, eventually reinventing himself as elected governor of Krasnoyarsk province from 1998 to 2002.

Any future replay of these events would depend on the immediate circumstances. An incumbent seeking reelection and forced into a runoff would face a serious blow to his leadership, even if he were to win in the second round. A second-round runoff in a closely contested open presidential race would be less disruptive, especially if the outgoing president had not designated or strongly supported a chosen successor or there were no clear consensus among the factions. It is likely that runoffs would occur more frequently in open elections, given the clear advantages enjoyed by any incumbent. But fighting an uphill battle against an incumbent might tempt the different elements of the opposition to put aside their frequently intractable differences and form a common front, denying the president a first-round victory and hoping to have some influence in the negotiations that followed between the first and second rounds. In most of these scenarios, an incumbent who had been bloodied in the first round would still probably have the upper hand in the bargaining over what comes next, especially if that incumbent had received a larger plurality than his second-round opponent. Only if the two remaining candidates had been fairly close in the first round, and there existed a substantial percentage of now-uncommitted votes, would both of the second-round candidates be on a fairly even playing field.

Ultimately cobbling together a majority victory in the second round would depend on the leading candidates' ability to hold their first-round supporters together, to entice defections from voters who had supported the other candidate still in the run-off, and to win endorsements from at least some of the also-ran candidates who had fallen by the wayside. The composition of the final winning coalition would be determined by the negotiations among parties and candidates after the first round and by the way in which the final choice was framed for the voters. At one level, these negotiations would involve usual issues such as commitments to policy choices, naming a cabinet, and perhaps even the selection of the prime minister. Several elements would be a part of these political calculations: the number of potential votes that an also-ran could deliver, and the likelihood that the voters would follow his or her lead in shifting support; whether the also-rans were personally demanding appointments in the government; whether the also-rans had an ongoing and institutionalized base (a loyal constituency or, more important, a political party with seats in the Duma) or were merely wildcard candidates with no political base; and the broader implications of such agreements or appointments in the world of factional politics. All participants in these negotiations would be acutely aware of the instability of any such agreements.

Outright theft of a presidential election. One of the most serious challenges to the stability of the system would emerge as a consequence of the outright theft of a presidential election that returned an incumbent to power or placed his chosen successor in office. To be sure, more than just the "normal" irregularities would be needed. But blatant and unchallengeable voting fraud would be a flashpoint that would leave both the regime and its opponents on the banks of the Rubicon.

Several scenarios are possible. After a brief period of relatively isolated demonstrations and ineffectual challenges in the courts, the outcry could simply die down and things would go on much as before. Opposition activities would be most extensive in Moscow and St. Petersburg and perhaps in some of the other major cities, but grassroots Russia would side with the regime, and especially with a popular leader like Putin. A major determinant of the eventual outcome would be how much opposition spread throughout the nation and whether it solidified and mobilized particularly important constituencies such as the growing middle class or youth. Also important would be the response of the major factions. A public showing of unity behind the incumbent or the newly elected president would signal that even a disputed election was unable to alter the game inside the Garden Ring. If the regime were selective in its suppression of public demonstrations and seemingly addressed some of the concerns of those in the streets, it would likely weather the storm. And each time it would get easier, creating a growing acceptance that electoral fraud was the new normal of Russian political life.

Disunity among the major factions could substantially alter the picture. Such disagreement in the reelection of an incumbent would probably signal that factional disputes before the election had not been settled; while the incumbent publicly remained the establishment's candidate, deep divisions remained and could resurface. A disputed open election would be even more tenuous. Many different scenarios could emerge. The first would involve a new round of negotiations between a weakened incumbent and the factions that had opposed or were lukewarm in their support of his chosen successor. Leverage would accrue to the lame-duck incumbent because of his key role in dealing with ongoing protests to prevent a larger upheaval that might fundamentally change the nature of the game. Leverage also would accrue to the factions because of the obvious weakness of the lame-duck president's position. The outcome probably would be a redefinition of the postelection balance of forces within the Garden Ring and a newfound willingness of all elements to support repression of the opposition.

Another scenario is possible. A challenged incumbent might choose this moment to escalate the level of repression against the opposition in the streets and simultaneously move to acquire greater power over increasing factional disunity. The second half of that scenario—a president trying to acquire greater power over the factions—was considered earlier under conditions not linked to a disputed election. Under the new circumstances, the president's hand would likely be even stronger unless attempts to suppress street dissent backfired and caused a full-fledged color revolution in more than just Moscow and St. Petersburg. The outcome in these circumstances would be uncertain—a scenario considered in the next section as a color revolution or Moscow Spring.

Politics Moves to the Street:
A Color Revolution or Moscow Spring

Despite the best efforts to manage challenges, things might get out of hand and create the possibility of a spontaneous uprising, usually referred to as a color revolution after events in Georgia in 2003, Ukraine in 2004, and Kyrgyzstan in 2005, or a Moscow Spring after similar uprisings in the Middle East from 2011 onward. Such uprisings are potential game-changers, bringing new players into the streets and potentially revising the playbook of politics as usual. To the regime in power, they are new and frightening challenges to the arrangements that have been cobbled together over the years, to be feared, blamed on foreign inspiration and manipulation, and prepared for almost as a new form of political warfare.

What Is a Color Revolution?

Above all else, a color revolution is a potential tripwire event. Whatever else it may be about, it is quintessentially about changing the way the political game is played in favor of the opposition that has given up on politics as usual and has gone to the streets. In its contemporary usage, the term goes back to the 1986 "yellow revolution" in the Philippines or the "velvet revolution" in Czechoslovakia in 1989. A color was an easy symbol to unite the opposition. Since 1986, similar uprisings have taken a color as their symbol (orange in Ukraine in 2004; blue in Kuwait in 2005; saffron in Myanmar in 2007; green in Iran in 2009), or a flower (a carnation in Portugal in 1974; a rose in Georgia in 2003; a tulip in Kyrgyzstan in 2005; a lotus in Egypt in 2011), or an object that symbolized the opposition (a bulldozer in Yugoslavia in 2000; a cedar in Lebanon in 2005; blue jeans in Belarus in 2006; a grape in Moldova in 2009). Most of these "revolutions" never caught hold and sputtered out. Some brought striking change in the short run, which later evaporated. Some were brutally repressed. Few brought lasting change.

Whatever their outcome, they all shared certain similarities in terms of why they occurred, how the opposition played its hand once protest spilled into the streets, how events took on a life of their own and evolved into something more complex than the initial confrontation, and how the regime responded. Understanding these elements will help us assess how such a "revolution" might influence the future of Russian politics.

Virtually all of these uprisings began with a tripwire event that unleashed pent-up frustration. Sometimes it was the perception of a stolen election: The regime had gone too far this time, beyond manipulating the advantages of incumbency and garden-variety vote tampering to blatant election fraud that could not be accepted. Sometimes it was about government corruption or malfeasance: A government of "crooks and thieves" had to be driven from office. Sometimes it was about a specific government decision that provoked protests: For example, in November 2013, Ukrainian president Viktor Yanukovych chose closer economic cooperation with Russia and rejected closer association with the European Union, prompting his critics to demonstrate in Maidan Square. Whatever the event, it was a spark, to borrow Lenin's term, that kindled a larger fire.

The spark also led to a social revolution that drew many different elements of society into the streets. Some elements were common to most uprisings. In the beginning, students frequently were the most numerous and vocal supporters, and for a time it seemed that the protest was almost a generation-defining event. But then others joined in, depending on the event that triggered the initial demonstrations. If it were about a stolen election, the leaders of the opposition were also there from the beginning, urging their supporters into the streets. If it were about economic issues, those who had not prospered and other marginal social elements were there too. Sometimes issues of national identity played in, bringing others into the mix. Initially the demonstrators seemed to be in basic agreement about what they wanted: a new election, an honest government, a fair deal. Things got more complicated if the rebellion took root and seemed to have some prospect of success. Then competing leaders and goals emerged, and the agenda grew larger and usually more radical. Similar demonstrations sometimes began in other cities, and the rebels reached out for support and advice from abroad, especially from other countries whose color revolutions had been successful.

The response of the government also shaped the trajectory of the uprisings. If the regime responded quickly and decisively, and especially if it presented a united front against the demonstrations, the events usually took one of two turns. Either the uprising was subdued quickly or both sides dug in for a long and usually violent confrontation. Other color revolutions followed a different trajectory because the leadership initially responded indecisively or was internally divided. Either situation usually intensified the rebellion, at least at first. The government was weaker than anticipated, and there was blood in the water. Internal divisions within the regime sometimes intensified, sometimes because the factions now played the blame game and sometimes because certain factions considered whether siding with the regime's critics might be a better long-term strategy. Open defections by important leaders were rare but game-changing events, as were instances in which the security forces tacitly or openly sided with the rebels and refused to fire on their fellow citizens.

The outcomes of these color revolutions were as diversified as the uprisings themselves. Some were brutally suppressed, and controls were tightened to prevent similar events in the future. Some won initial victories—a disputed election was nullified and a new vote taken, or a hated leader was driven from power—only to see the situation gradually return to politics as usual or a decisive counterrevolution. Some enjoyed mixed results, as the regime survived by offering limited concessions and then returned to more selective but successful repression.

The outcomes aside, the color revolutions also produced two very different learning curves. For the regime's critics, the lesson was that there was a new way to bring pressure on a repressive government and perhaps topple it from power. A new playbook had to be learned, to be used selectively and with caution—but used when the time was right. For repressive or just unpopular regimes, the lesson was that a new threat loomed, to be studied, prepared for, and blamed on internal subversion or foreign interference. But most of all, the threat was to be taken seriously.

A Russian Color Revolution?

The sheer number of attempted color revolutions over the past two decades suggests that we consider this as a possible mechanism of change. It is obviously a matter of serious concern within the Kremlin. Putin has promised "preventative work" to head off such revolutions, and both foreign minister Sergei Lavrov and defense minister Sergei Shoigu have referred to them as a new kind of warfare. The central government has begun to counsel regional governors on how to respond if such demonstrations break out in their bailiwicks. No overall plan of response has been officially set forward, but Moscow's preparations as well as its criticism of Kiev's unsuccessful response to the early Maidan Square demonstrations suggest that it is thinking in terms of a combination of preemptive actions against opposition groups and individual leaders, quick and forceful suppression of the initial demonstrations, limitations on the ability of opposition forces to come to the demonstration sites or start similar demonstrations in other parts of the country, and efforts to rebrand opposition actions as unpatriotic or the result of foreign inspiration and manipulation. Once the original demonstrations have been brought under control, it is likely that the authorities initially would offer limited or symbolic concessions in an effort to divide the opposition or buy off general public support, especially if economic issues were central to the original protests, followed by efforts to fine-tune their response to any future rebellion.[5]

The most likely spark for such a color revolution would be a disputed national election such as the 2011 Duma balloting in which widespread and blatant fraud brought demonstrators into the streets, primarily in Moscow and St. Petersburg. Both the government and opposition leaders were caught unawares at first, and both responded cautiously. The Kremlin limited and controlled demonstrations, arresting the leadership and others who directly challenged the rules that had been laid down, but not resorting to widespread violence. For their part, opposition leaders also avoided a head-on clash, keeping the demonstrations focused on voting fraud and broader issues of corruption but never urging a full-scale uprising against the government. Shortly after the demonstrations subsided, the government promised more transparency in the upcoming presidential election but also tightened the laws governing future demonstrations. It also intensified its control over opposition groups, the media, and civil society.

Future election disputes could easily bring the opposition into the streets again. The most serious scenario would involve a disputed presidential election. Public challenge to the reelection of an incumbent president would be the most volatile scenario, especially if an opposition candidate had done well enough in the first round to force a runoff, only to lose by an unexpectedly large margin in the second round. Open presidential elections probably would be less likely to produce such disputed outcomes, unless the outgoing president had designated a successor who had done unexpectedly well in the balloting or a runoff were marked by widespread voting fraud. In either event, the outcome of such an open challenge would turn on the government's ability to contain the demonstrations in the major cities and to win the support of Russia's "silent majority" throughout the rest of the nation. Overreaction to the first stages of the demonstrations could have a catalytic effect, bringing others into the streets, but indecisive reaction could signal weakness or division, potentially having the same effect. Worst of all from the regime's perspective would be surprising resilience on the part of the demonstrators, with initial repression clearly failing, and larger and more diverse elements spilling into the streets, finding leaders from among their own numbers.

The preservation of unity among the major factions inside the Garden Ring would also be vitally important to maintaining control, even if different elements had backed separate candidates in an open presidential election. If the demonstrations were seen as an open challenge to the stability of the system, the factions would probably be inclined to circle the wagons and back the disputed winner, even while trying to bargain for greater factional power within a weakened government now open to challenge. If one or more factions thought they could turn the street demonstrations to their favor, the political game could substantially expand, temporarily blurring the distinction between the inside-the-Garden-Ring and outside-the-Garden-Ring players until the winners and losers had been sorted out. Defections and public opposition from the regime's tacit allies in the Duma also would raise the stakes, especially if parties going over to the opposition had done well in the most recent election or had had strong leaders who might emerge as a potential replacement for the winner of the disputed election. At least for a while, this new and expanded game would present the greatest threat to the overall stability of the de facto accommodations of Russian political life since Putin's rise to the presidency in 2000. With factional and street politics now linked in new and unstable ways, other issues would quickly be put on the agenda. What started essentially as protests over a disputed election would become an expanding conflict over a wider range of issues. Economic issues would probably top the list, followed by corruption, culture and life style, human rights, national identity, ethnic issues, foreign policy, and other issues, and all would somehow be linked to factional competition. The outcomes would be uncertain, the strategies harder to choose, and the stakes unquestionably higher.

Any break in the regime's ability to repress the initial demonstrations would be a clear sign of weakness and possible disunity at the top. Even the best trained and indoctrinated police and military units sometimes break under pressure, openly siding with the opposition or quietly melting away when confronted with orders to fire on their fellow citizens. Yeltsin owed his political survival in the attempted coup in August 1991 to the unwillingness of elite troops to take him into custody. Similarly, his efforts to keep control in Moscow at the time of his 1993 coup against the Congress of People's Deputies were hampered by the reluctance of top officers to back the president without direct orders that would exculpate them of personal responsibility should things go badly.

One final thing would be needed for a color revolution to succeed—an exit strategy acceptable to both sides. To be sure, no unpopular leader enters into such a confrontation publicly admitting that he knows he could lose and already has his bags packed just in case. And no rebellion begins with an admission that it will do any less than punish the old order to the fullest extent possible. But most successful rebellions end with far fewer black-and-white conclusions.

Assuming that neither side can win a decisive victory and that both sides agree that a negotiated transition is better than prolonged strife or even a civil war, several elements would be needed to facilitate a mutually acceptable accommodation. First would be a decision on the fate of the deposed leader. Several scenarios are possible. He could simply slip into exile, presumably with the open or tacit agreement of a host country, and with sufficient wealth already abroad in off-shore accounts to ease the way. Some understandings would need to be in place concerning the size of an entourage that might accompany him, with amnesty or promises not to seek indictments in place for those who remained in the country. Agreement about efforts to attempt to extradite the exiled leader also would be a part of the deal. The ousted leader might remain in his home country, with appropriate assurances for his own status and that of his entourage. Gorbachev's resignation from the presidency in December 1991 followed hard bargaining, some of it directly between Gorbachev and Yeltsin, about the ex-president's future role in private life. Yeltsin's early retirement carried with it the promise of a presidential pardon by Putin and the political reality that the Yeltsin family would remain an important but no longer dominant political presence during a suitable transition period. It is likely that any negotiated solution to a Russian color revolution would include such arrangements.

A negotiated end to a color revolution also would contain some agreement about the composition of the new government. In many ways this would be a far more complex task, with any short-term agreement likely to dissolve as the winners compete to pick up the pieces. Some clarity would emerge if the rebellion had been about a disputed election; new balloting would take place and produce a clear winner (unless, of course, allegations of voting fraud once again emerged). Events would be less clear if a presidential departure were linked to some other issue. At least in the short run, the Russian constitution would elevate the prime minister to the presidency (unless he joined the president in exile), with the requirement that a new election be held quickly. That election would be the first test of how long the coalition that staged the rebellion would hold together in the new political world. Broader issues of constitutional change also would emerge quickly, especially over reducing the power of the presidency per se, the role of the Duma, and the repeal of the old regime's repressive laws on registering new political parties, voting, the media, civil society, and the like.

It would not be easy or simple. Whatever order and stability that existed under the former regime would disappear, at least in the short run. To the extent that political life became more open, competitive, and transparent—all likely to be the professed goals of those who deposed the previous leader—it would also become more divisive, cacophonous, and volatile. All revolutions inevitably produce these periods of transformation, but not all manage to successfully create a stable and democratic political order as the new normal begins to emerge.

Notes

1. Steven Levitsky and Lucian A. Way, *Competitive Authoritarianism: Hybrid Regimes after the Cold War*, Cambridge University Press, 2010; and Andress Schedler, ed., *Electoral Authoritarianism: The Dynamics of Unfree Competition*, Lynne Reinner, 2006.

2. "Introduction," Levitsky and Way, *Competitive Authoritarianism,* 12.

3. Levitsky and Way, *Competitive Authoritarianism,* 183-200.

4. Evgeny Minchenko, revised version of "Putin's Big Government and the Politburo 2.0," www.globalinterests.org/2015/04/02-politburo-2.0-can-putin's-inner-circle-survive-the-crisis?

5. *Moscow Times,* March 4, 2015; Radio Free Europe/Radio Liberty report, September 11, 2013; *Moscow Times,* June 21, 2015.

Index

CQ Press, an imprint of SAGE, is the leading publisher of books, periodicals, and electronic products on American government and international affairs. CQ Press consistently ranks among the top commercial publishers in terms of quality, as evidenced by the numerous awards its products have won over the years. CQ Press owes its existence to Nelson Poynter, former publisher of the *St. Petersburg Times,* and his wife Henrietta, with whom he founded Congressional Quarterly in 1945. Poynter established CQ with the mission of promoting democracy through education and in 1975 founded the Modern Media Institute, renamed The Poynter Institute for Media Studies after his death. The Poynter Institute (*www.poynter.org*) is a nonprofit organization dedicated to training journalists and media leaders.

In 2008, CQ Press was acquired by SAGE, a leading international publisher of journals, books, and electronic media for academic, educational, and professional markets. Since 1965, SAGE has helped inform and educate a global community of scholars, practitioners, researchers, and students spanning a wide range of subject areas, including business, humanities, social sciences, and science, technology, and medicine. A privately owned corporation, SAGE has offices in Los Angeles, London, New Delhi, and Singapore, in addition to the Washington DC office of CQ Press.